RACE AGAINST TIME

Human Relations and Politics in Kenya before Independence

Richard Frost

RACE AGAINST TIME

Human Relations and Politics in Kenya before Independence

Rex Collings: London
Transafrica Book Distributors: Nairobi

First Published in 1978 by Rex Collings Ltd., 69 Marylebone High Street, London, England and Transafrica Book Distributors, Kenwood House, Kimathi Street, P.O. Box 49421, Nairobi.

ISBN 0860 360 814

ERRATA

p. 38, l. 4 *for* not all *read* not at all

p. 51, l. 27 *for* as *read* was

p. 94, l. 20 *for* Chairman *read* Chairmen

p. 103, l. 22 *for* Sir Mitchell *read* Sir Philip Mitchell

p. 124, l. 7 *for* aplpreciation *read* appreciation

p. 124, l. 8 *for* feeing *read* feeling

p. 131, l. 11 *for* throughout, Kenya *read* throughout Kenya

p. 158, l. 27 *for* is *read* in

p. 183, l. 22 *for* at all *read* to all

p. 183, l. 32 *for* erea *read* area

p. 203, l. 30 *for* consitutional *read* constitutional

p. 253, l. 24 *for* Mennon *read* Mennen

p. xvii, note 2; p. 42 note 62 *for* C. Give Haimes *read* C. Grove Haines

Printed and bound in Kenya by Kenya Litho Ltd., Changamwe Road, P.O. Box 40775, Nairobi, Kenya.

To my wife

To my wife

Contents

ix

7 THE CIVIL SERVICE AND THE POLICE

8 THE INFLUENCE OF CHURCHES, SCHOOLS AND VARIOUS ORGANISATIONS

9 THE NINETEEN-FIFTIES: A DECADE OF PROGRESS

11 THE FINAL YEARS

ABBREVIATIONS

H.C.D.	=	House of Commons Debates
L.C.D.	=	Legislative Council Debates
E.A.S.	=	*East African Standard*
K.W.N.	=	*Kenya Weekly News*
E.A. & R.	=	*East Africa and Rhodesia*

PREFACE

In 1947 I started the work of the British Council in East Africa.
Eight years later I was posted to England, first to Cambridge and
then to Oxford. In 1963 I was posted back to Kenya a few months
before Independence. The Kenya to which I returned in 1963 was
astonishingly different from the Kenya to which I first went in
1947. African progress in many fields had been great. In education
and the professions, in government service and in business Africans
had advanced in a measure which few would have dared to prophesy
in the years immediately after the War. A remarkable change had
occurred also in the European community. The racial extremism,
which had been so prevalent in earlier days, had to a great extent
been replaced by a liberalism which was willing to see through the
divisive barrier of colour and to put humanity above race. A few
years later, after my retirement from the British Council, I decided
to write a book on the subject of politics and human relations in
Kenya during the years between the end of the War and Independence. To ensure the discipline of scholarship and avoid the danger
of writing unconfirmed generalisations and argument not supported
by fact it seemed wise to work for a higher degree at Oxford. This
book is based on the thesis which I submitted for the Degree of
Doctor of Philosophy in 1973.

My first Supervisor was the late George Bennett. His death in
1969 deprived us all of one of the ablest of historians of East Africa
and me personally of a friend and supervisor, whose advice helped
me greatly in the initial stage of my research. I owe him much. I
was fortunate when Professor Kenneth Kirkwood, the Rhodes
Professor of Race Relations at Oxford, agreed to be my supervisor
in his stead. He was very generous of his time, and his criticism,
based on wide knowledge and experience and always accompanied
by encouragement, was of the utmost value. I am happy to have
this opportunity of expressing my gratitude to him.

Rhodes House, Oxford, has a wealth of material on Kenya,
but research in the National Archives in Nairobi and discussions
with people in Kenya were also necessary. I am extremely grateful
to the Trustees of the Leverhulme Trust Fund for the generous
grant which they gave me to finance a visit to Kenya from November
1969 to April 1970. The need for a British Council Representative
to be politically 'unaligned' had enabled me in the past to make

friends among people of all kinds with all manner of political views. All, in Kenya and in England, have been willing to discuss my subject in the many interviews which I have had.

Access to restricted papers was of inestimable value. In Oxford I have had privileged access to Sir Philip Mitchell's Diaries and the twenty-four boxes of files deposited by Sir Michael Blundell, who asked that I should have complete acess to them. Lt. Commander J. P. B. Miller's files in Rhodes House have been available to me at his request. In Kenya Sir Wilfred Havelock, formerly Minister for Health and Local Government, and Mr. Kendall Ward, formerly Executive Officer of the Elector's Union, both exempted me from restriction when they deposited their papers in the National Archives in Nairobi. I was lent papers by Colonel Sir Arthur Young in England and by the late Mr. S. V. Cooke in Kenya, Mrs. Joyce Raw, the Chief *Hansard* Editor and a former leading member of the Capricorn Africa Society, Mr. George Tyson, a leading business-man and former Mayor of Nairobi, and Mr. Richard Hughes, formerly President of the Kenya Branch of the Capricorn Africa Society. I have also some original papers in my own possession. I thank all those who helped me by allowing me access to their papers or giving time for discussion. I am grateful to them and to my wife who did so much typing for me throughout.

Richard Frost
March 1976

INTRODUCTION

"However important policy and policy-making may be, human relations are still more important in successful government and development".[1] Such was the conclusion reached by Sir Andrew Cohen after long service as head of the African Department of the Colonial Office, Governor of Uganda and British Representative on the Trusteeship Council of the United Nations. His judgement did not question the significance of economic factors or the effects of nationalism and political ambitions. It did not minimise the need for sound policies and calculated plans, the importance of the regulation of labour relations, the study of overseas investment and local trade, of the growth of trade unionism and the use of agricultural and industrial possibilities. He was well aware of the many sides of colonial administration, but his experience had led him to the conclusion that the most carefully calculated policies and the most expert plans for development might fail unless the people whom they would effect had confidence in each other and mutual goodwill.

In Kenya at the end of the Second World War the small European community was in a position of great political power, the Indian artisans and traders had a monopoly of crafts businesses and small retail trade, and among the Africans the effects of wartime experiences, of simple technical training and, in a small degree, of secondary education were making themselves felt. Self-government for the colonies was the expressed aim of British policy and, because Britain as trustee for the indigenous people of the colonies would wish to educate them along the lines which she herself knew, it would be parliamentary self-government on the Westminster model. Autocratic action by the Administration against the vote of the unofficial representatives would be no way of educating a colony for independence, but thinking in Kenya was always along racial lines and the majority of the unofficial Members of the Legislative Council were Europeans elected by European voters. As the Members depended on their electorates, co-operative and progressive policies, which might be desired by the Colonial Office and the Secretary of State, could only be implemented if the European electorate were to some extent willing to accept them and support their Elected Members in voting for them or if the Government ignored the votes of the unofficial Members and imposed its will by force rather than by agreement. The latter course would have impeded progress in parliamentary democracy and so the need was for conscious efforts to liberalise the European voters.

Power had given the Europeans on the whole a master-race mentality. All too often arrogance and rudeness characterised their dealings with Africans and Asians; they resented any intrusion into their social exclusiveness; and colour bar and discrimination were fostered to maintain European privilege. There were exceptions, more than was sometimes realised, Europeans who recognised the advance being made by the Africans and who had a true sense of trusteeship and, however dimly, an appreciation of the progressive nature of the plural society. It was on such European men and women and on increasing their number that the future of co-operative race relations depended.

The word "liberalism", as used in this book, meant the ability to accept without resentment the fact that education, technical training and experience would produce an increasing number of capable Africans, that at some future time there would be more well educated Africans than Europeans, and that the principles of democratic government would then place the preponderance of power in African hands. It meant acceptance of the idea that colour bar and discrimination must be replaced by cultural and social criteria and that in the end a non-racial structure would replace the communally organised framework of life in Kenya. It meant the possession of adaptable and moveable minds in contrast to the mental immobility of die-hards whose main aim was to retain the *status quo*.

Because the key to future inter-racial co-operation was so largely in the hands of the Europeans, it seemed necessary, in an introductory chapter dealing with the position of the racial communities at the beginning of the period under review, to give what might otherwise be regarded as undue length to a survey of the earlier development and current composition of the European community. At the beginning of the period the great majority of Europeans thought along the same racial lines, but the new realities and problems of the post-War period soon began to cause divisions in European opinion and the efforts made to liberalise European thought made a growing impact as the period wore on.

The political history of Kenya in the years between the end of the War and the attainment of Independence has received much attention from historians, but the growth of goodwill and desire for inter-racial co-operation has been largely overlooked. In the nineteen fifties British Members of Parliament, American scholars, journalists and even the Secretary of State seem to have been unaware of the growth of liberalism among the Europeans. Although the political history can be accepted as fact, it cannot altogether be explained without knowledge of the split which occurred in the European ranks and of the victory of liberalism over the die-hard and un-realistic outlook of what became the minority.

The value of the leadership which the Europeans could give was widely recognised by Africans, but it had to be leadership, not domination. Good relations required an awareness by Europeans of African educational progress and a willingness to meet the new elite face to face. It was not easy for Europeans to meet them without taint of curiosity or patronisation and opportunities arising from participation in common interests had to be provided. Often too some third party with friends among all communities could act as a catalyst in inter-racial relations. During the nineteen fifties the moderate, co-operative centre grew at the expense of the extremes of African nationalism and European die-hard attempts to hold on to social isolation and political power. After retiring from his long career as a colonial administrator, Sir Philip Mitchell expressed the same opinion as that which Sir Andrew Cohen reached some years later when he said, ". . . it must surely be seen that the great, the overwhelmingly great, problem overshadowing all else, is the human problem".[2]

1. Sir Andrew Cohen: *British Policy in Changing Africa*, p. 64.
2. Sir Philip Mitchell: "Africa and the West in Historical Perspective", *Africa To-day*, ed. C. Give Haimes, p. 24.

1

THE RACIAL STRUCTURE

The Official Racial Categories

On the 12th December, 1944, Sir Philip Mitchell became Governor of Kenya. On the 12th December, 1963, Kenya became an independent nation. The nineteen years between those two Decembers were years of astonishing change: in 1944 no one expected independence to come to Kenya nineteen years later, not even Jomo Kenyatta, who returned to Kenya in 1946 after many years spent in England, where he had been a member of the group of intellectuals, which included Kwame Nkrumah, who were dedicated to the cause of African independence.[1]

The most politically minded Europeans hoped for independence with European predominance and in 1946 the President of the European Electors' Union declared that the Union aimed at the "lessening of direct influence of the Colonial Office in the internal affairs of the Colony"[2] and that the Europeans intended to make European power "the predominating factor in the whole of East Africa"[3] and the Union's Conference agreed that it was time to get rid of "the fooling about by the Colonial Office".[4] At the same time Francis Khamisi, the Hon. General Secretary of the Study Conference of the Kenya African Union, maintained that Kenya was "a black man's country" and that Africans "must see that it remains so for ever";[5] and in London Kenyatta had recently written that "Africans will never be satisfied until they enjoy full self-government".[6] Whether European power was to be "the predominating factor in the whole of East Africa" or whether Kenya was to be a "black man's country", one fact was beyond dispute: the final responsibility lay with the Imperial Parliament and the Colonial Office.

Before Kenya was seen by the first explorers Britain had had experience of colonies of British people and of dependencies inhabited by other races. Failure to appreciate that settlements of British colonists would demand self-determination had led to the revolt of the American colonies in 1776. The British Parliament's acceptance of Lord Durham's recommendation for internal self-government for Canada in 1839 averted a similar disaster there and led to Dominion Status for the "White" Dominions of the Commonwealth. In the nineteenth century Britain was concerned with the administration of India and became responsible for the government of dependencies in West Africa and Asia. These were territories where what Sir Keith Hancock calls "the settlers' frontier" did not create the problems which arose in the United States and what, if one thinks of climate rather than of actual geographical location, one might call the non-tropical countries in the British Empire. Kenya lies across the Equator, but its agricultural areas are largely sub-tropical or temperate; but they were territories where "the traders' frontier" and "the planters' frontier" raised issues of trusteeship and imperial responsibility. In North America the indigenous population was small, small enough to be exterminated or confined in "reservations", and the theory of "manifest destiny" was advanced in the United States to justify the conquest of the West. In her own Empire Britain relinquished her trusteeship for "native" peoples in New Zealand in 1856, in South Africa in 1910, and in Southern Rhodesia in 1923. In New Zealand in 1840 the Imperial Government believed that guarantees given to the Maoris by the Treaty of Waitangi would be respected by the settlers and safeguarded by the law, but in fact "the settlers' frontier took control of New Zealand's destinies",[7] and in 1856 the "imperial authority, by conferring self-government upon the European settlers, surrendered its trust".[8] In South Africa the black population was large, the white comparatively small. It was hoped that the grant of independence in 1910 would cause the white population to assume the moral obligations of trusteeship, but the selfishness of power disappointed the idealists. The same miscalculation was made in Southern Rhodesia in 1923, but in Kenya, although, to quote Margery Perham, "there can be no doubt that the dominant influence was provided by white settlement",[9] responsibility for the trusteeship of the indigenous population was retained by Britain.

When Burke insisted that British rule in India was "in the nature of a 'trust' for the benefit of the Indian people"[10] and when Macaulay declared in the House of Commons that when the people of India were justified in demanding "European institutions", it would be "the proudest day in English history",[11] they were speaking in terms which their audience could understand. The law of trust in England grew up outside the common law as part of the law of equity. It obliged a trustee to accept obligations to look after the welfare and property of someone else, usually a minor, on whose coming of age the trust would cease. It is a law dealing with the actions and responsibilities of individual men, but it could not fail to affect public life and, when Britain became an imperial power, to play a part in moulding her ideas of her responsibilities towards dependent peoples.

In Kenya the responsibilities of trusteeship for the indigenous people could not be isolated from obligations to the immigrant races, many of whom had been encouraged by Britain to go to Kenya and whose work and skill and capital were of use to Britain in the discharge of trusteeship. In 1945 for historical reasons life in Kenya was organised on racial lines. Such a social structure could not provide a permanent base on which to build a nation and in the period after the Second World War the Colonial Office and the various Secretaries of State hoped that it would be possible so to foster racial co-operation that an inter-racial or non-racial democracy could ultimately be the recipient of independence. At the beginning of the period that possibility seemed to be generations away. Economic disparity, discrimination and colour bar divided the races so widely that the thought of a common and equal citizenship seemed to be an ideal to be realised only in some far future.

Representation in Legislative Council and in local Government was based on racial communities, salary scales were decided by a communal structure, and discriminatory practices existed in many places. Within each broad ethnic group there were many divisions. Afrikaners and British, for instance, approached political affairs with different outlooks; Hindu and Moslem Asians were not united; and tribal differences prevented the attainment of African harmony throughout the Colony. In this study 'race' means the four categories used by the Government: Africans, Arabs, Asians and Europeans.

The word 'European' included all those whose original roots were in Europe, even though their genealogy had passed through the United States, Canada, Australia, South Africa or elsewhere. There were rare occasions, however, when it was used only in connection with people coming directly from Europe, as when the Office of the Minister of Legal Affairs and Attorney General wrote that registration of births and deaths was "compulsory as regards persons of European or American or Asiatic origin or descent".[12] This was an exception, however, to the normal inclusion of Americans in the European category.

Among Asians after the partition of India at the time of Independence in 1947 the main religious differences were reinforced by national allegiancies and, although for official purposes they were all classed as Asians, the various Asian communities were very different from each other in matters of custom and religion and also in their feeling of loyalty towards Kenya.

The coastal strip, the Protectorate, not the Colony, of Kenya, was held on lease from the Sultan of Zanzibar, whose scarlet flag flew over Fort Jesus, the sixteenth century Portuguese fortress, in Mombasa; and an Arab Administration under the Liwali of the Coast was woven into the Government Administration with its Provincial and District Commissioners. Many of the Coastal Arabs felt a strong loyalty to the Sultan and regarded themselves as British Protected Persons with a culture and traditions of their own. All Arabs, whether on the Coast or up country, were represented in Legislative Council as a separate community. They had long been the principal landowners on the Coast. Under the colonial regime they had, however, become less and less politically significant, but their land-owning position on the Coast and the administrative system pertaining there caused friction between them and the Africans. After Independence, however, the Arabs were accepted more as an indigenous than an immigrant community, even to the extent of an Arab, Farid Hinawy, being appointed the first Kenya Ambassador to Congo, Kinshasa, from where he later went to Cairo as Ambassador to the United Arab Republic. In 1956 Michael Blundell wrote to Wilfred Havelock that Africans were "rather bitter" because European politicians had been "paying attention to the Arabs whom the Africans consider completely useless and decadent". And he went on to say that "the Arabs have the same feelings about the Africans".[13] Arab educational standards were in general low and in 1948 Sir Philip Mitchell, the Governor, planned the building of a Moslem Institute in Mombasa, which, he hoped, would help the Arab community to reach higher levels of education and achievement. In the meantime it seemed to the Indian leader, A. B. Patel, that politically "the Arab is treated as a nonentity".[14]

Africans were of four broad ethnic groupings—Bantu, Nilotic,

Hamitic and Nilo-Hamitic. The Hamitic strain is widespread. The pure Hamites are found only in the north east, but the Kalenjin group of tribes, the Nandi-speakers and the Masai, are Nilo-Hamites. The Nilotic Luo do not have Hamitic blood, but the Bantu tribes, to quote C. G. Seligman, are "hamiticised to a varying extent" and he claims that "Many of the Bantu Akikuyu are no more pure negroes than are the half-Hamitic but sedentary Nandi . . ."[15] Many of the Kamba in the east and the Luyia in the west have strong Hamitic facial characteristics. This book is not an ethnic or anthropological study and the general description or classification of 'African' must suffice. There were also the Somalis who regarded themselves as a separate community. Their fervent devotion to Islam intensified their communal consciousness and, although they were classed as Africans for general purposes, such as wage scales, they were frequently referred to as a separate community, normally within, but at times distinct from, the general category of 'Africans'. The Chief Secretary, for instance, when commenting in 1955 on the Townships Ordinance, reported that "The Governor may make rules for African (including Somali) locations and villages"; but at the same time, when discussing Immigration Control, Ordinance 51, he wrote, "In the Ordinance 'African' is defined as any person who is a member of an African tribe indigenous to the East African Territories, and includes a Swahili, but not a Somali". And the Municipalities Ordinance dealt, said the Chief Secretary, "with the power of Municipal authorities to make provision for the return of destitute Africans (including Somalis, Malagasis and Comoro Islanders) to their homes". Immigrants from Madagascar and the Comoro Islands were, like the Somalis, included for general administrative purposes as Africans, even though their peculiar ethnic distinctions were recognised.[16]

The first census after the Second World War was taken in 1948. The African population was given as 5,219,865 and the non-African population was 154,846:—

Asian	97,687
European	29,660
Arab	24,174
Other	3,325
Total	154,846

The census of 1962 showed an increase. The African population had
risen to 8,365,942 and the non-African to 270,321:—

Asian	176,613
European	55,759
Arab	34,048
Other	3,901
Total	270,321

In 1948 the British population among the Europeans was 27,546
and in 1962 it was 48,207. In 1962, the year before Independence,
the make-up of the European population was as follows:—

British	Italian	American	South African	Irish	Dutch	German	Others	Total
48,207	1,687	1,066	823	545	540	526	2,365	55,759

The British amounted to 87 per cent of the European population.
Many of the Europeans were born in Kenya and many felt strongly
that they were Kenyans. The figures were:—[17]

	1948	1962
Local Born	6,744	11,582
Foreign Born	22,916	44,177
Total	29,660	55,759

In December 1944, the Second World War was drawing towards
its end. The Allied Forces had landed successfully in France and
relieved the pressure on the Russian front and, although fierce
fighting still lay ahead, the winds of victory were beginning to blow
from the West and from the East towards the heart of Germany.
A little later the War with Japan would come to an end. Soldiers
from the various theatres of war would return to their homes in
Great Britain and America, on the continent of Europe and in Africa,
but nothing would ever again be the same as it had been before the
War. This was as true of Kenya as of anywhere else. "We are at the
birth of a new age", wrote an African in 1946.[18] Before the War
Britain expected the colonies to pay their way, but in 1940 a new
sense of responsibility for the welfare of colonial peoples was shown
in the Colonial Development and Welfare Act passed by the British
Parliament. Towards the end of the War the ultimate aim of British

colonial policy—self-government—was given a new sense of urgency. India was on the threshold of Independence and that step into a new era for the Commonwealth and Empire would open the door for colonial progress along the same path. "Politically", Oliver Stanley, the Secretary of State for the Colonies, told an American audience in March 1945, "our aim is that of the maximum practical self-government within the Empire at the earliest possible time".[19] This aim applied to all British colonies.[20] It is not surprising that the question of when the people of a dependency were ready to govern themselves should be disputed and that independence should not come completely peacefully. A sense of responsibility in the trustee and an impatient confidence in the ward were bound to create friction; but the goal was clear. In Kenya, however, there was a factor which complicated the issue. Who were the people to whom the grant of self-government was to be made?

European Settlement

A fundamental issue in colonial Kenya was competition between the two historical meanings of the word 'colony'. The settlers thought of a colony in the classical sense of a projection from a mother country of people who would found new settlements and live the type of life which they had known in their original homes: colonies like the Greek settlements in Asia Minor and the thirteen colonies along the Atlantic seaboard of North America or the colonies which developed into the nations of Canada and Australia. At the same time, however, the concept of dependencies, for whose ultimate development Britain was responsible, was being advanced by the Colonial Office. The struggle between these two ideas was basic in the history of Kenya, and, wrote Sir Andrew Cohen, "the measure of inconsistency between the dominion and the trusteeship policies remained unsolved".[21]

In the earliest days, even before the end of the nineteenth century one or two people had seen the possibility of European settlement, developing the Highlands of Kenya as an area growing wheat as well as sub-tropical crops and feeding cattle and sheep of European breeds; but European settlement began on a larger scale with official encouragement as a result of the construction of the railway. This was built as the Uganda Railway to link Uganda with the sea and for strategic purposes to give Britain command of the headwaters of the Nile. Between the port of Mombasa and Kisumu

on Lake Victoria, from where communication to Uganda was by
boat, lay 500 miles of undeveloped country. The Uganda trade was
not large enough to pay the cost of maintaining the railway and the
British Government was never anxious to spend money on maintaining colonial projects. As Kenya had no mineral resources to exploit,
the only source of revenue lay in the development of agriculture,
providing commercial exports, along the western half of the line,
where conditions were suitable, and so in the production of revenue
from freight charges to Mombasa. In Uganda, a country of sub-
tropical conditions, the Africans, with some help from the Government, were able to make an economic success of cotton-growing
by peasant cultivation, but in Kenya, in the dry Rift Valley round
Nakuru with its cold nights and on the heights of Molo and Mau
Summit, large-scale agriculture requiring considerable capital
investment was needed.

In the early years of the century Sir Charles Eliot, the Commissioner, as the Governor was called in the days of the East African
Protectorate, was determined to found a "White Man's Country"
over the whole Highland area from Mount Elgon to the border of
Tanganyika. ". . . the interior of the Protectorate is a white man's
country", Eliot wrote in 1904 soon after his resignation, "and so
I think it is mere hypocrisy not to admit that white interests must
be paramount, and that the main object of our policy and legislation
should be to found a white colony".[22] Colonel Richard Meinertzhagen, who spent four observant years in Kenya from 1902 to
1906, saw the inherent danger and wrote about Eliot,

"He amazed me with his views on the future of East Africa. . . .
He intends to confine the natives to reserves and use them as
cheap labour on farms. I suggested that the country belonged to
Africans and that their interests must prevail over the interests
of strangers. He would not have it, he kept on using the word
'paramount' with reference to the claims of Europeans. I am
confident that in the end the Africans will win and that Eliot's
policy can lead only to trouble and disappointment".[23]

In 1906 Lord Elgin, the Secretary of State, agreed to what amount-
ed to a White Highlands policy, which came to be known as "the
Elgin pledge". This was not revoked when, later on, the Imperial
Government asserted its responsibility for trusteeship, but although
Eliot and the settlers were intent on creating a country where the
interests of the Europeans should be paramount, immediately

afterwards the Foreign Office in instructions to Sir Donald Stewart, Eliot's successor, was insisting that "the primary duty of Great Britain in East Africa is the welfare of the native races".[24] The fundamental debate started in those early days. A solution did not seem to be urgently required. The Imperial Government did not think that the Africans would be able to accept political responsibility for a very long time and never laid down clear guidance for advance with any idea of a time table for African and Indian partnership in running the Colony. Sir Philip Mitchell saw the weakness and wrote in his retirement, "there was no colonial policy, for Secretaries of State changed every eighteen months or so; so no one ever disciplined a Governor and no Secretary of State would ever force a row with settlers".[25]

"Imperialism", Hancock warns, "is no word for scholars".[26] Marx and Hobson and Lenin accused the imperial powers of metropolitan exploitation, of acquiring colonial territories at the instigation of investors who needed new areas in which to invest their surplus capital. Hancock, however, has pointed out that in the British context "the empire of investment showed a marked lack of concern with the political Empire".[27] In 1914 £1,779,995,000 was invested inside the Empire and £1,934,666,000 outside it.[28] The great evil was seen when, as in the Congo under King Leopold, there was a sinister combination of monopoly capitalism and Governmental power.[29] Sir Andrew Cohen concluded that in British West Africa "it was the anti-slavery movement, the humanitarian factor, which led to the involvement from which all the rest followed",[30] and Hancock saw there, "a more rational and humane collaboration between Europeans and Africans" than in such territories as the Congo.[31] In West Africa, to use Hancock's phrases, the missionaries' frontier caused the initial penetration and opened the way for the traders' frontier. In Kenya the missionaries' frontier took the initiative, because, as Hancock appreciated, "David Livingstone went to Africa".[32] The traders' frontier followed with the arrival of the British East Africa Company and, at about the time when in 1895 the Company surrendered its charter and the British East Africa Protectorate was proclaimed, the settlers' frontier made its first, small appearance.

The problems which were to face the new territory were the problems of a plural society. The settlers' frontier established a community which acquired power and privileges and, largely to

support its position, discrimination grew up in the colony. The
need for labour, the danger of exploitation of Africans in order to
secure it, economic requirements for development by the immigrants
and the personal freedom of the natives—such were the problems
which would have to be solved. Kenya was not the creation of
financiers in London, who needed new fields to which they could
transfer their capital to be used for the exploitation of the native
inhabitants and the enrichment of the alien financiers themselves.
It was not an example of "privately owned industrial and financial
monopoly in action".[33] There was no great agricultural industry
equivalent to the cocoa production of Ghana, no crops grown by
native peasants reaching the outer world through exporters who set
the price paid for the African grower's produce and at the same time
were the importers who regulated the price of the goods sold to him.
There were no copper mines exploiting the labour of Africans for
the benefit of investors in the capital cities of the West. This is not
to suggest that Kenya would have been different in this respect
from other areas if opportunity had arisen. The shortlived gold rush
at Kakamega in the early nineteen thirties, when the Government
allowed prospectors to work claims in land which had been deline-
ated at Luyia Reserve, showed that it was probably lack of
opportunity rather than a moral sense which saved Kenya from
exploitation.

There was in fact little in Kenya to attract the financiers of the
western capitals. A country with scant mineral resources and no
large areas suitable for plantation cultivation had only a limited
appeal for them. A large proportion of the coffee estates were
privately owned. So were a few of the tea estates, such as Gregor
Grant's 500 acres at Kericho which was the result of many years of
frugal living and the ploughing back of profits. Tea estates made a
small total in comparison with Ceylon or India and the sisal estates
on the Coast were not on a large scale. The chief investors were
European farmers and the settlers' frontier advanced at the settlers'
own expense. A survey undertaken by the Royal Institute of International Affairs and published in 1937 estimated that up to 1934,
£35,171,000 of external capital had been invested in Kenya and
Uganda, of which more than £27,000,000 were supplied by the
British Government, and supplied far from willingly. In addition
£28,000,000 had been invested by individual European farmers.[34]
This enabled them to experiment and develop an agricultural

industry and much of it was lost in the process. In the nineteen thirties many farmers were impoverished by the world slump and some even greased their tractors with the butter which they could not sell. Many of the settlers had additional capital in Britain, but they were making their homes in Kenya and few were concerned with making large incomes there in order to send money to Britain. The great majority were colonists in the classical sense, who for various reasons—adventure, joy of creating something new, the enjoyment of a perfect climate, a desire for greater independence than could be found in Britain—intended to live and die in Kenya and to create a future there for their children. They hoped to make money, but they intended to use it in Kenya, not to send it to Europe. Kenya was not a colony against which Lenin's accusation of metropolitan monopoly capitalism exploiting an indigenous population could rightly be applied. It was not a colony which fulfilled Hobson's theory of "Aggressive Imperialism", which he saw a "a source of great gain to the investor who cannot find at home the profitable use he seeks for his capital" by providing him with opportunities for "profitable and secure investments abroad".[35] The accusation which *could* be made was that a capitalist community of employers in Kenya itself used its power to maintain its economic superiority and that, because the employers were white and the employed were black, a colour bar operated against all Africans and prevented the elite from reaching the higher economic levels and receiving the social respect of the Europeans.

The adventurous enthusiasm of the settlers and their willingness to risk their personal capital in experiments to overcome the unpredictable hazards of agriculture in the tropics were of inestimable value in the development of a country which lacked mineral resources and conditions for large-scale production of exportable tropical crops. The fundamental problem in Kenya was how to reconcile their ambitions with trusteeship of the indigenous Africans, into whose land the West intruded. Colour bar and discrimination were fostered to maintain a privileged position for the Europeans, and Britain, as trustee, was obliged to ensure that the Africans, as they advanced in education and the skills of the modern world, were not held back by European domination. That was a negative task. There was a more positive hope: that the European community would be able to help the trustee in the obligations of trusteeship. Too often, however, the Europeans, who claimed a share in trusteeship, wanted to maintain a position of isolated superiority and dominance, but, as Mitchell wrote early in his period of office as Governor, the Imperial trustee and the Kenya Administration could not "concede a specially privileged position to a small group of Kenya farmers and politicians".[36]

Among the early settlers were some men of humble origins like James McQueen, a village blacksmith from Scotland, and John Boyes, whose father was a shoemaker.[37] Eliot was disappointed at the poor response in Britain to the idea of settlement in Kenya and in 1903 he sent one of his senior officials to South Africa to try to attract immigrants to Kenya. At that time the depression following the Anglo-Boer War was causing hardship among the Afrikaner farmers and the response to Eliot's invitation was unexpectedly great. In 1904 they began to arrive in Kenya and most of them trekked on with their ox wagons to the wide, veld-like plateau of the Uasin Gishu. The influx continued for several years and reached its height in 1908, and until 1912 the farmers from South Africa outnumbered those from Britain. But from the earliest times there were also settlers from upper class families in Britain with money and social position, who set about farming on a grand scale, amassing great acreages of land and spending their wealth on experiment and development. Among these aristocratic settlers was Lord Delamere, who soon became the leading figure among the Europeans of Kenya. Hugh Cholmondeley, 3rd Baron Delamere, was born in 1870. After several big game hunting trips to Somaliland, he organised a journey to the south and in 1897 entered what was later to become Kenya Colony. On his return to England he tried to settle down on his estate in Cheshire, but returned to Kenya to live permanently. He became the leader of the Europeans in the political field and the most important figure in the development of agriculture in Kenya. He died in 1931. "There was hardly an industry in which he had not experimented, a society to which he had not belonged, a political issue in which he had not joined".[38] In 1909 the Governor, Sir Percy Girouard, described these settlers with few exceptions as men "of unusual education and social standing".[39] Their social standing and wealth had a persuasive touch about them and all the Commissioners, or Governors, Eliot, Stewart, Sadler, Johnston and Girouard, succumbed to their requests, even at times against the instructions of the Secretary of State.

The settlers worked from the earliest times to gain a position of political power. In 1906, with the support of the Commissioner, they won from the Secretary of State agreement to the formation of a Legislative Council, and a constitution was provided, comprising a Governor with Executive and Legislative Councils, in the latter of which unofficial members were to be included. The Africans were only just emerging from a life untouched by modern influences and the Indians were not deemed acceptable for inclusion in the Legislative Council, the unofficial members of which would therefore be Europeans. After this first success the Europeans steadily increased their position of power and privilege. In 1915 they succeeded in getting a Land Bill passed in Legislative Council, which, though avoiding legal discrimination and the creation of legal *apartheid*, provided machinery for securing it in practice both in the Highlands and the towns. This Land Bill came soon after the publication of the *Report of the Native Labour Commission 1912–1913*. Then Lord Delamere had made the settlers' attitude plain to the Commission when he said that an African's small capital needs could be provided by a year's wages "and so as a result of a year's work he had established himself on a farm for life without any necessity to work for a European again, which was certainly wrong and could be done by no one else on earth".[40] Such a state of affairs, he suggested, was harmful to the European settlers, whose interests should be paramount.

Here was the leader of the settlers proclaiming a doctrine directly opposed to the spirit of trusteeship. It was contrary to the instructions of the Colonial Office but in keeping with the thought of pioneers of the classical type of colonies. The spirit of anti-government independence, the spirit of the frontier, sought, as George Bennett aptly expressed it, "to assert itself in the main street in Nairobi",[41] where, for instance, in 1906 E. S. Grogan and some Afrikaners flouted the law by publicly flogging three Kikuyu servants outside the Magistrate's Court, for allegedly insulting a white woman, instead of referring the matter to the Administration.[42] It lived on into the twenties and even longer. The belief that the Governor and the Administration, being British, ought to make the advancement of European interests their primary concern seemed axiomatic to many of the early settlers. Lord Cranworth put this point of view very clearly when he wrote: "I say that though as a matter of course both the native and the Indian should receive fair and equitable treatment, the first and prime consideration should be the well-being and prosperity of the British colonist".[43] The extreme right wing among the Europeans continued almost to the end of the colonial period to think that Kenya was *their* country in which Africans also happened to live. Even as late as 1956 when Princess Margaret visited Kenya, the right wing magazine, *New Comment*, claimed her as the *Europeans'* Princess instead of as the sister of the Queen of all the inhabitants of Kenya.[44]

When Lord Delamere said that it ought to be made necessary for Africans to work for Europeans, he was speaking with the voice of the pioneer, within, not external to, the colony, who was himself willing to suffer hardship in order to transform the bush into productive farms. He and his friends were not overseas capitalists seeking to exploit primitive natives in the tropics in order to swell the coffers of metropolitan financiers. They were trying to create a new country, of which they were a part. They were, however, to be the privileged section and they thought it reasonable to expect the Government to use the power of taxation to force Africans to work on their farms, because without African labour their purpose could not be achieved. In the early days some Governors were unduly influenced by European pressure and in 1925, the Secretary of State for the Colonies found it necessary to state categorically that "the provision of compulsory labour for private employers is absolutely opposed to the traditional policy of His Majesty's Government".[45]

At that time two Government officers, Norman Leys and W. McGregor Ross, exposed the evils of "persuasion", sometimes practised by chiefs and others whose livelihood depended on pleasing the Administration. The missionaries did the same and some members of the Administration itself were opposed to earlier directives from higher authority. The missionaries in Kenya were true to their traditions. In the eighteen fifties in New Zealand, when the New Zealand Company was arguing that the Treaty of Waitangi was not binding and "the settlers' frontier" was expanding at the expense of honour, it was the missionaries in New Zealand and missionary circles in Britain who protested against this lack of good faith. "We can trace in their protests", Hancock wrote, "the evolution of the doctrine of trusteeship".[46] It was missionaries above all others who were responsible for the Secretary of State's declaration of trusteeship for the Africans in Kenya in 1923. They helped to keep alive a spirit of human relationships which ultimately tempered the strength of racial discrimination. The purely nominal

punishment awarded to Grogan and his friends in 1906 was remembered and so were the scarcely greater sentences passed on Europeans
who had murdered African farm workers. Norman Leys saw the
source of the evil in "the idea of racial dominance, the idea that
Africans exist only to labour for our profit" and believed that many
such crimes are inevitable whenever men are given both political
control over a subject people and the opportunity to profit by their
labour".[47] It was a situation like that of the mid-nineteenth century
in the West, when the rich had both political and economic power
over the working classes. The solution lay either in democratising
society, as had been the case in Britain, or in revolution as in the
communist countries. J. H. Oldham, Secretary of the International
Missionary Council, a committed Christian with detailed knowledge
of Kenya, had faith in the former solution and believed that "white
settlement is a desirable spur to progress".[48] Evil cannot be condon-
ed, but its glare often obscures the more ordinary decency of less
eventful lives. Oldham believed that, although abuses must be
rooted out, "The white race . . . is the guardian of values that
are essential to the welfare of the black race as well as of its own".[49]
When Africans became employers themselves it was often found that
they were fully influenced by the profit motive and that in the best
of western values lay the curb on exploitation.

The composition of the communities in a plural society affects the
problems and strains which beset it. In Kenya the Europeans were a
capitalist society. The Asian community varied from rich commercial
families to artisans and junior clerical workers. The history of the
immigrant communities in the first four decades of the twentieth
century created the conditions facing the Africans as they entered
into the new era which followed the Second World War. The labour
of the Africans and the capital, skill and work of the immigrant
communities were twin foundations of the colony's economy; but
in 1945 at the end of the War the four races, Africans, Arabs,
Indians and Europeans, seemed to the new Governor to be communities with "political capacity in more or less inverse ratio to
their numbers".[50] The agricultural development of the country
had been a European achievement and the settlers, joined by the
European business community, had worked themselves into a
position of political power which enabled them to influence Governmental decisions in their favour and in directions which still further
increased their political strength. They aimed at "a form of self-

government", wrote Mitchell, "based on a legislature in which the
European as such is to be entrenched in power by the terms of the
constitution and has a majority over all other races combined",[51]
and four years later, in 1949, the Electors' Union announced in its
Kenya Plan that its aim was "The greatest possible executive control
by the European community" and went on to say, "Thus it will be
seen that our undeviating purpose is the control of our own affairs.
All else is subservient".[52] Twenty-six years earlier, however, in 1923,
the very year in which Southern Rhodesia had been given almost
complete internal self-government, the Imperial Government had
proclaimed that in Kenya African interests would be paramount.
In that year in their eagerness to forge a weapon to use against
Indian demands to be allowed to farm in the White Highlands the
Europeans created a boomerang which recoiled on themselves
and "the engineer" was "hoist with his own petard". In addition
to demands to be allowed to own agricultural land the Indians asked
for unrestricted immigration. Plans agreed between the Foreign
and India Offices in 1922 caused such consternation among the
Europeans that plans were made to capture the railways, the posts
and telegraphs, and the Governor. These illegal plans, like Grogan's
illegal act in 1906, did not bring stern punishment. The Imperial
Government, always apprehensive of the influence and power of the
Europeans, was afraid that there might be serious trouble in Kenya
and called together in London the conference which resulted in the
issue of the White Paper, *Indians in Kenya*.

The Declaration of the Paramountcy of African Interests

  The Europeans' feeling of success when the Secretary of State, the
Duke of Devonshire, issued the White Paper indicated the strength
of their self-confidence. They were jubilant at its refusal to allow
Indians access to the White Highlands and a general equality with
Europeans, but they did not take seriously the declaration which
it contained of the paramountcy of "the interests of the African
native races" nor its assertion that "His Majesty's Government
regard themselves as exercising a trust on behalf of the African
population, and they are unable to delegate or share this trust, the
object of which may be defined as the protection and advancement
of the native races".[53] Even critical writers like Ghai and McAuslan
admit that the failure of the early settlers to achieve their aim of a
Rhodesian form of society, although owing something to the

Indian presence, was due "first . . . to the realisation in London
that an important ingredient of the imperial mission in Africa
was the protection of the indigenous peoples".[54]

The Devonshire Declaration of the paramountcy of African
interests in the White Paper of 1923 had a curious origin. The
Indians conceived the doctrine in an attempt to promote equality
between themselves and the Europeans. The Europeans approved
of it because it gave grounds on which to base opposition to Indian
demands for unrestricted immigration and was accompanied in the
White Paper by a clause barring Indians from occupancy of land in
the White Highlands. The missionaries pressed for it at its face
value. Its inclusion in the White Paper was largely due to
the advocacy of Dr. John W. Arthur, the head of the Church of
Scotland Mission at Kikuyu, and above all to the work of the
brilliant diplomatist and "wire puller", J. H. Oldham, Secretary of
the International Missionary Council of the Conference of
Missionary Societies.[55]

It has sometimes been claimed that the doctrine of native paramountcy was negatived by the acceptance of the *Dual Policy*,
propounded by the Hilton Young Commission of 1928 which said,
"By permitting immigration and the alienation of land to non-
natives on the one hand and on the other by declaring itself a
trustee for native interests (White Paper of 1923) His Majesty's
Government has already accepted a 'Dual Policy'. There is an
obligation to the natives and there is also an obligation to the
immigrant communities, neither of which can be ignored".[56]

The Imperial Government could not fail to recognise the great
contribution made by the Indians to the economic development of
Kenya. The economy of the Colony would have collapsed if the
Europeans and Indians had been removed. The plural society was
a fact. It was not the *Dual Policy* but the upsetting of the balance in
ways which discriminated against Africans and supported European
racial privilege that obscured the obligations of trusteeship. But
whatever changes there were in political plans and whatever lapses
there may have been, one fact remained constant: the Imperial
Government accepted full responsibility for trusteeship. The
Europeans in Kenya could help the trustee, but the responsibility
remained in London. Professor Rosberg has pointed out that in
1923 the Devonshire Declaration "appears to have been a moral
principle rather than a basis for practical politics" and "did not lead to

any radical departures in the formulation and conduct of policy".[57]
Its value lay in underlining the principle of trusteeship and standing
as a declaration which could later be cited as defining a principle
which had to be observed in the formulation of policy.

Composition of the European Community

The composition of the European community did not change
very much in character in the period between the two World Wars,
the Kaiser's War and Hitler's War, as they were often called in
Kenya. The commercial community grew larger, but the influence
of the farmers continued to predominate, although a few leading
businessmen were in the inner circle of European politics, and
immediately after Hitler's War the Leader of the European
Elected Members, Sir Alfred Vincent, was a businessman, not a
farmer.

After the first World War a soldier settlement scheme attracted a
considerable number of men of the officer class in Britain. Fifteen
hundred settlers left Britain for Kenya in November 1919. By the
time the depression of the nineteen thirties made Kenya no longer a
country to attract British people who wanted to settle in agriculture,
the European farming community was in the main composed of
men from the landed and professional classes in Britain, who had
been educated at British public schools. Sir George Pickering,
once Regius Professor of Medicine and the recent Master of
Pembroke College, Oxford, has described them as schools "which
followed Arnold's methods in moulding a new kind of cosmopolitan
gentility, which at its best was characterised by convictions of
personal integrity, corporate loyalty and paternalistic service".[58]
In nineteenth century Britain there were self-seeking landlords and
employers, terrible slums and the selfish attitude which sent the
Tolpuddle Martyrs to the penal settlements, but there were also landlords who had a sense of paternalistic duty towards their tenants
and employees and, although the fashion of today is to pour scorn
on Lady Bountiful, she had her place—as did of course the Church—
in an age before the State accepted the obligation to care for the
sick and aged. Although the Kenya settlers often took with them
the pride and self-sufficiency of their background, many of them
took also a sense of responsibility for those whom they employed.
The farm dispensaries run by farmers' wives and other services
rendered to their employees and their families at the farmers'

expense were the twentieth century equivalent in Kenya of old traditions in Britain.

In Kenya the best of the settlers, albeit a minority, believed that by living the British way of life and showing it as an example to the Africans among whom they settled they would be able to build a country in which the untamed earth would be transformed into productive farms and the native people would gradually be raised to the standards of the western world. They saw all round them an illiterate population and they felt that, just as they had created the wheat fields and the dairy farms from the forest and the bush, so it was they who in the fullness of time could create a new nation, in which they would lead the Africans towards a better life. The majority, however, in the early days were mainly concerned with sport and profit, as Lord Cranworth put it in the title of a book.[59] All the settlers wanted freedom from anything beyond the broadest control by the Colonial Office, freedom to live their lives and bring up their children in their chosen way. Most settlers, both good and bad, came from families which had for generations employed servants and been in the upper levels of the social hierarchy in Britain, families whose gracious style of living was made possible by the existence of other, less affluent, levels of society. An education for their children superior to that available to the general mass of people was a privilege which they took for granted and many of them were refugees from the rise of socialism at the end of the nineteenth and beginning of the twentieth centuries. They were used to authority and had never brought themselves to appreciate the implication of the British Government's statements that it alone had the responsibility of trusteeship for the Africans, and that the Europeans of Kenya could not exercise a dominant role in all aspects of the life and development of the colony. Right up to the fifties European politicians continued to proclaim that, as the Electors' Union's Outline of Policy said, ". . . the European community desire to play an increasing part in the direction of the internal affairs of the Colony, aiming at a system of Government free from the direct influence and intervention of the Colonial Office over African problems".[60]

"The British way of life" was often spoken of with little thought of what it might demand. At best it was not just a way of social living in which members of the upper classes could enjoy certain graces and forms of etiquette. It meant the basic principles of the

national culture resulting from centuries of experience. Among its
most fundamental principles were "respect for the human personality,
for liberty, for tolerance".[61] Human personality does not depend on
colour or race nor on privilege or caste; but in Kenya "the British
way of life" was often put forward as a slogan to uphold a pretended
right to a position of privilege. Communal distinctions obscured
moral principles and colour hampered the recognition of the
individual human personality. Sir Philip Mitchell wrote, as he
looked back on his long period of colonial service, ". . . it must
surely be seen that the great, the overwhelmingly great, problem
overshadowing all else, is the human problem".[62]

Mitchell was a devout Christian and in his approach to the
problems of East Africa he was moved not only by the political
sense of the civil servant, who had reached the highest level in the
Service, but by the Christian belief in the worth of every human
soul. He appreciated the value of European settlement, economically
and culturally, but he saw, as Oldham had seen in his controversy
with General Smuts in 1929, that their need of African labour and
their reasonable desire to make an economic success of their farms
and their businesses made it impossible for the Europeans "to
take the detached, comprehensive and far sighted view that is
necessary" and that trusteeship and responsibility for the general
progress of Kenya were "an imperial task of the first magnitude
and importance".[63] In 1939, when he was Governor of Uganda, the
Secretary of State suggested his accepting the Governorship of
Kenya, but he turned down the offer. The Governorship of
Tanganyika was what he wanted.[64] In the end, however, when his
wartime duties in the Pacific were over and he returned to East
Africa, it was to accept the post in Kenya with all the inter-racial
problems which had daunted his imagination in the past. "I drafted
a letter to Malcolm MacDonald", he had written in 1939, "thanking
him for his telegram about the Kenya Governorship but saying that
I thought they knew I was not a candidate, for much the same
reasons as led me to refuse the post of C.N.C. in 1931—that greatly
as I like Kenya and many of the people in it the prevailing attitude
to Asians and Africans is one I cannot stand—or rather could not
qua Governor".[65] He was clear about the Governor's responsibility
as representative of the Imperial Trustee.

Towards the end of his Governorship Mitchell said that he had
all the time been like a man walking on a tightrope. If he leant too far

towards the Africans, he displeased the majority of the Europeans, and, if he did too much for the Europeans, he was apt to be accused of discrimination by the Africans. With the Asian community also to consider, the Governor's role was delicate.[66] Always there was the conflict between the responsibilities of trusteeship for the Africans and recognition of the contributions made by the immigrant communities.

After the War it was clear that many European farms were too large for the resources available to their owners and the European settlers and the Electors' Union wanted more European immigration in order to make closer, more intensive farming possible and to strengthen British influence in the Colony. The bi-partisan policy in Britain was in favour of strengthening white settlement provided this could "be done without prejudice to the rights of native people".[67] In Kenya the Europeans, who demanded that the White Highlands should be kept entirely for European ownership, claimed that the area was the European Reserve, just as other areas were the Kikuyu Reserve or the Kamba Reserve, etc. They forgot that there was one great difference. In a tribal reserve all the resident inhabitants, with such exceptions as Asian traders, were members of the tribe and, although the Chairman of the Local Council was the District Commissioner, the members were all Africans. In the White Highlands, however, there were many more Africans than Europeans, but the Europeans were strongly opposed to any African representation in local government. They needed African labour but rejected any idea that Africans might own or lease land in the White Highlands, where they felt they should be a source of labour without any democratic rights. Mitchell wanted more European immigrant farmers, because he wanted more intensive farming by trained farmers, but he would have liked the Board to inaugurate an African tenant scheme on Crown land in the White Highlands. He could not understand why Europeans should see no objection to having African squatters living among them but should be so strongly opposed to the idea of having Africans as tenants of the Highlands Board.[68] Persuasion was the only possible way of bringing about a change in policy, unless the Secretary of State issued a new directive, and Mitchell did manage to get Sir Alfred Vincent, the European leader, to agree to "do what he could to try to persuade the Highlands Board to lease unused land for native occupation",[69] but nothing came of this. Many farms were only partially developed

and some Europeans, like Blundell, saw how harmful this was to
the economy of Kenya and to the cause of European settlement,
but it was generally held that the only possible solution lay in a
large increase of European farmers. For some years before the
eruption of Mau Mau, Blundell had advocated measures to ensure
the proper use of land. Soon after the Declaration of a State of
Emergency in October 1952 one of his constituents wrote to him to
praise his judgment in this. "I shall long remember your remarks
made at a Solai Association meeting some years ago at K. Ireland's
house when you condemned big undeveloped farms and land
lying idle. By golly you were right".[70] It seemed to people like the
Governor that this attitude, which allowed the system of resident
labourers or squatters, but refused to allow Africans of better
quality to become tenant farmers, was as irrational as that of the
farmer who had African servants to cook his food, wash his clothes
and clean his rooms, but, when an African chaplain was going to
conduct a service for African servants in his house, stood at the
doorway of the room with a flit pump of anti-fly mixture and flitted
the congregation as they went in.[71]

The European Elected Members noted with some disquiet a
statement made in the House of Commons in London in 1948 by
the Secretary of State for the Colonies. If land on European farms
were unused and if in consequence it were taken away from a
European farmer, "does this mean", he was asked, ". . . that that
land will be available only to other white farmers?". "No", replied
Creech Jones, "but most of the legislation will be modelled on
legislation in this country".[72] When Creech Jones visited Kenya in
1949 the Elected Members wanted an assurance on the "Security"
of the White Highlands.[73] The powers of the Highlands Board were
confirmed and in fact the Board continued to administer the "White"
policy. But it was often forgotten that the continued "whiteness"
of the White Highlands was the result of administrative practice,
not of law. It was the powers, not the policy, of the Board which
were established by law. But because the Board had legal powers the
Governor could not normally overrule it. Instructions of former
Secretaries of State had laid down a "white" policy which another
Order-in-Council could, however, annul.

"The first comprehensive census of non-African agriculture in
Kenya since the War was taken in 1954".[74] Of the 7,576,900 acres
3.6 per cent was forest land and 13.2 per cent was called "other

land". Steep land and "vlei" and other areas of very poor soil were included in this, but more intensive farming reduced the area of "other land" in the following years and brought it down to 9.3 per cent or 998,000 acres in 1958, when there were 3,540 "farm units" as follows:[75]

Size of Holdings in Acres	Number
20– 199	615
200– 499	510
500– 999	803
1,000– 1,499	531
1,500– 1,999	299
2,000– 4,999	501
5,000–48,999	271
50,000 and over	10

The very large farms, like the enormous Ol Pejeta ranch on the Laikipia Plateau, were in areas of low rainfall where as many as ten to fifteen acres were needed to feed a single head of cattle.

It was not till 1956, when the inter-racial St. Julian's Community wanted to buy a house within the boundary of the White Highlands, that the Highlands Board was forced to depart from its completely European attitude. That was at a period of rising African power when, from a political as well as a moral point of view, the Governor had to send the Board's refusal back for reconsideration. Two years earlier Blundell had reached the conclusion that land on European farms which was still not fully developed by 1960 would have to be acquired by the Highlands Board and used for tenant farming by tenants of all races.[76] During Mitchell's period as Governor conditions were very different and a declaration of war on the European community would have been political folly. But Mitchell was no believer in the permanence of European domination, although he did not think that Africans would develop with anything like the speed with which they did in fact progress. He believed that the members of each race should respect those of the other races and his aim was that all should "share alike in the life, political and cultural, of the community to the extent of their capacity".[77] He made it clear at the very beginning of his Governorship that "the Settlement report was only one leg of a tripod, since native and Asian development projects must also be worked out."[78]

The chances of achieving true inter-racial co-operation were much affected by the character of the European community. In the years following the Second World War there was only a small increase in the number of European farmers. The Europeans who arrived in Kenya then were mainly in the commercial world and the professions, some intending to stay, at any rate for the duration of their working lives, but others on temporary assignments. Interracial tensions were aggravated by a great increase of the urban population. This was due to the influx of Africans into the towns in search of work and to the growth of services such as Posts and Telegraphs and Railways and Harbours, for which Europeans, largely not of high administrative calibre, were required for junior posts, and to the expansion of European business which necessitated a large addition of junior European staff. Inadequate housing and low wages in the towns fostered new African resentments and the urban African often came up against an urban European, with little sympathetic understanding of African problems. N. S. Carey-Jones, Deputy Director in Development Administration in the University of Leeds and formerly Permanent Secretary of the Ministry of Lands and Settlement in Kenya, contrasts the earlier immigrants, many of whom went to Kenya with a tradition of obligation arising from a privileged position, with the post-war immigrants. "Many of the new immigrants", he writes, "clearly lacked the gentleman's principles but were quick to grasp his privileges".[79] The man who is economically and socially secure is likely to be more considerate than those who feel the need to fight continuously to retain their position. This is a general fact, not restricted to Kenya. M. S. Lipsett, Professor of Government at Harvard, has noticed that in the United States the progressive members of society "have been American Tory radicals—men of upper-class background and values".[80] In such a town as Kitale the Europeans were mainly people in minor positions. The Town Council was dominated by Europeans and in 1952 there was not even an African social hall there. A neighbouring farmer was struck by the poverty of the Africans and "the conditions under which they lived" and wrote that "the Town people seem to be incapable of taking an interest in the welfare of their employees".[81]

It was not only the newly arrived townspeople, however, who were illiberal in their outlook. Some of the post-war farmers also were unsympathetic to the other races. When Michael Blundell was fighting for the inclusion in Government of Asians and Africans in the mid-fifties, he wrote to Oliver Woods of *The Times* and Patrick Monkhouse of the *Manchester Guardian* an account of the situation in Kenya, in which he said about the Rift Valley:

"I find that almost every South African is against me and the rest of the opposition is concentrated around new settlers who have only been in the country for the last five to eight years. Almost every member of the F.I.P.[82] who is prominent is a new settler. . . . They have not got used, as many of the older settlers such as myself, to constant association with the other races and in particular the African".

". . . in the eight years during which I have been in politics 20,000 new Europeans have come into the country. Very few of them understand how the Government works, most of them are wage earners and not capitalists".[83]

The murder of the Ruck family by Mau Mau in January 1953 caused great anger among Europeans. It was a bestial crime perpetrated on a family who had been helpful and sympathetic to their African employees and neighbours, but that only made them more liable to be murdered by Mau Mau, because a sympathetic European was an impediment to the creation of hatred. The murder was followed by a march by Europeans to Government House to demand stringent measures against Mau Mau. They left Government House when it was arranged that a meeting should be held in the Memorial Hall at 6 o'clock that evening. Blundell wrote an account of the march to Government House and of the evening meeting and described the composition of the crowd.

"The crowd", he wrote, "both at G.H. and in the Hall was an interesting cross-section of the European population of Nairobi. There was a great mass of decent, reasonable citizens who had come there under false pretences, having been told that the Elected Members wanted them to do so. There were also a great number of South Africans and especially women who were extremely bitter. Next I noticed a number of Continental Europeans, no doubt recent settlers, who were extremely inflammable and vocal, and lastly there was a small number of extremely discontented and possibly dangerous men and women, who for the time being had quite lost control of their reason".[84]

When Delamere led a march of protest to Government House in 1908, settlement was comparatively new and the settlers were imbued with the spirit of the pioneer who is irked by Government restraints.

The "recent settlers" who marched to Government House in 1953
disregarded the historical developments of the previous forty-five
years and failed to see, or refused to recognise, that Kenya was no
longer a pioneer country, in which a small white community could
dominate primitive "natives".

Just as some of the older settlers had been "refugees from the rise
of socialism in Britain"[85], so some of the post-Second World War
immigrants went to Kenya because they were tired of restrictions
at home. Many of the older settlers had come to appreciate that the
Africans must be helped to develop educationally and economically
and under the leadership of Lord Francis Scott, who was anxious
that the Elected Members should take an interest in African Affairs,
constructive policies might possibly have been devised in the early
nineteen forties; but the War claimed the major part of the country's
attention. However, experiences in the field caused many European
officers to admire the African troops under their command and
liberal attitudes became more prevalent. During the controversy
over national registration by universal finger-printing the violent
opposition came largely from recent immigrants. The old settlers
and businessmen were far more ready to fit in with the conditions of
life in Kenya than were the new arrivals, who were unable to adapt
their habits of thought and their prejudices to circumstances in
which they had never found themselves before.

A comparison of the Censuses of 1948, the first after the War, and
1962 shows that the European population had doubled during those
twelve years:—

	1948	1962
British	27,114	48,207
Non-British	2,546	7,552
Total	29,660	55,759
Nairobi	10,830	21,477
Total urban	17,065	34,865
Local born	6,744	11,582
Foreign born	22,916	44,177
Total	29,660	55,759

The increase in the number of non-British residents needs qualify-
ing by remembering that in 1948 Irish and South Africans were
registered as British but that by 1962 they were classed as non-
British and were included in the figure of 7,552 in 1962 but had not

been included in the figure of 2,546 in 1948.[86] The most significant increase was in Nairobi, which grew steadily during the years between the end of the War and the attainment of independence. It was the commercial centre of East Africa and much capital, both European and Asian, was invested in it.

Urban housing was in great shortage after the War. For Europeans this was inconvenient: for Africans it was desperate. In Nairobi and elsewhere commercial offices and light industries brought employment, but housing of Africans did not keep pace with the growth of jobs and the hope of employment attracted far more Africans to Nairobi than could in fact be absorbed. There had been a housing shortage for years. "By 1941 it was reported that 6,000 Africans had nowhere to sleep in Nairobi".[87] As the city grew in commercial importance, the problem increased. In 1950 "the technical officers of the City Council", who had long since ceased to talk about rooms for Africans, estimated that in the Nairobi City Council's locations there was a deficiency of over 10,000 "bed spaces".[88] And "bed space" sometimes implied such overcrowding that the last man to go to bed could not put his mattress on the floor until the door had been shut and he could use the few feet of floor against it. Lack of a place to sleep in caused many an African to view his European or Asian employer with less than friendly eyes, especially as the Municipal Council was entirely under European control. Inadequate representation on municipal and other local councils was a major cause of African resentment and, together with an unsatisfied desire to hold the chairmanship of African councils, contributed to the growth of Mau Mau.

On many farms—by no means all—there was a friendly relationship between the settler and his family and the farm workers, but the newer urban life was less personal and the African clerk and office boy were more ready to question the situation than were the simpler and unsophisticated farm labourers. Vernon Bartlett, a British journalist of perspicacity and liberal views, writing in 1953, said that "The White settlers of Kenya deserve kinder things than are generally said about them". He explained that "These genuine settlers are outnumbered and outvoted by town dwellers and artisans, many of whom have had much less experience in dealing with people of another race. They have not made compromise much easier, and compromise above all is essential in a plural society".[89] The number of settlers was small. In 1948 there were 1,921 European

farmers and a total of 2,871 Europeans engaged in agriculture.[90]
Wives and children brought the number of Europeans resident on
farms to approximately 10,000. During the following years the
number of farmers did not change very much and they were
increasingly outnumbered by others, who, as J. E. Goldthorpe wrote,
"being transients have little reason, or desire, to become closely
involved in the life of a country which is for them a workplace
rather than a home".[91] It was the 2,000 farmers with the addition of
those members of the commercial European community who had
decided to make Kenya a permanent home for themselves and their
families who had a real involvement in the development of Kenya
and any valid claim to be regarded as co-Trustees with the United
Kingdom for the African people, with whom their lives were so closely interwoven. They were a small part of the total European
electorate, but a true assessment of the European outlook is
impossible unless notice is taken of the liberalism, springing often
from paternalism, which was slowly increasing among these white
"Kenyans".

The Asians

The existence of a small educated and economically prosperous
European community among an African population a hundred times
larger was certain to produce many problems. The situation was
further complicated by the presence of an Indian community three
times the size of the European community. The contribution of the
Indians to the development of Kenya was of enormous value, but
their success brought on them the jealousy of both Africans and
Europeans. The latter feared the competition of the richer Indians
and the possibility of their being granted land in that part of the
Highlands which they were determined to keep "White", and the
Africans became jealous of the Indians' monopoly of small trading
and artisan crafts and junior office jobs, which in the earlier years
they were entirely incapable of undertaking themselves. When
the West entered into Africa, tribal society became exposed to new
influences and new needs. Work for wages, small though they were,
drew Africans away from the customary, regulated life of the tribe
and produced simple desires for consumer goods. It was the Indians
who, by hard work and a willingness to face adventure and danger
in the pursuit of trade, satisfied these wants, and it was they who
through skill in crafts and artisan pursuits, such as carpentry, metal

work and building, made development possible. Their skill was handed down from father to son and their family networks produced an efficient pattern of wholesale and retail trade. They satisfied needs which no one else was able to fulfil and, because Africans wanted these services but were themselves unable to supply them, the Indians inevitably secured a virtual monopoly. Then, as the Africans began to progress along the same lines, the success of the Indians in supplying services which the Africans needed but had been themselves unable to supply roused African jealousy and demands for restriction of Indian commercial enterprises.

At the same time Indian success in trade caused apprehension among the Europeans, and Indian demands to be allowed to farm in the Highlands met with universal European opposition. Indian aims had never been concealed. One of their early leaders, A. M. Jevanjee, even said,

"I would go so far as to advocate the annexation of this African territory [Kenya] to the Indian Empire, with provincial government under the Indian Viceroy, and let it be opened to us, and in a very few years it will be a second India."[92]

The Report of the Royal Commission of 1953–54 said,

"There had from the earliest times been Indian traders settled at the coast and, as the development of the hinterland went ahead, many of these moved inland. . . . The emergence of a "White Highlands" policy was at the outset due rather to a fear of Indian settlement than to considerations of being swamped by Africans."[93]

The Indians' wish to own land and to farm in the White Highlands was always opposed by the Europeans. In 1951 a pamphlet written by the Electors' Union stated that "land in other areas has been set aside for their agricultural use, but which, except in the very smallest numbers, they have had apparently no inclination to settle and develop".[94] This was rather like saying that, after the Europeans had enjoyed the meat, the Indians showed a lack of gratitude by not thankfully gnawing the bones which were offered to them. The European *apartheid* policy on land largely confined Asians to the towns and trading centres. In the African Reserves after the Second World War economic considerations were beginning to arouse African resentment at the presence of Indians even in the trading centres, and the opinion was sometimes voiced that the Indian should quit "step by step his trading centres in the heart of the

Reserves and confine himself to the towns".[95] The African writer of this letter became somewhat unrealistic in his demands at a time before African transport companies could have met all African needs. "All transport by Indians within the Reserves", he wrote, "should cease and no licences of any sort be issued to Indians trading in native produce. Thus the Indian shall be confined entirely to the big towns". A similar suggestion was made in 1949 by the Abaluyia Welfare Association.[96] Throughout the colonial period, however, Asian shops remained everywhere and Asians carried on transport business in the Reserves. The Government of India protested frequently against discrimination and, as the Government in London did not want to antagonise the Government in Delhi, the situation was often delicate.

Sometimes Africans and Indians made common cause against the Europeans. "The Indians work harder, perhaps with more guile, to enlist their sympathies",[97] wrote Negley Farson. European social exclusiveness without doubt gave an impetus to such collaboration, but the Asians' attempts to win African friendship were ultimately unsuccessful. B. A. Ohanga, who later became the first African Minister in the Kenya Government, said of the Indian National Congress and its pretended love of Africans, "Economically the Indian plays no mean part in the field of African exploitation while socially he enjoys perpetual indifference".[98] Their failure to win the friendship of the Africans caused the more far-sighted of the Asians to realise that the British presence in Kenya and British responsibility for all the races in the Colony were their safeguard against the Africans as they rose in education and technical skill. In 1949, for instance, a meeting of Africans at Eldoret voted in favour of turning Asian traders out of the area, but the Government declared that it would be unfair to get rid of Asian traders "just because African traders are now coming into the field".[99] Already before the Second World War Indians had acquired wealth and, when new towns were being built and plots for shops sold by auction, it was almost impossible for an African to outbid the Asians who arrived to establish themselves in these new markets. Moreover, the Asians had behind them great experience of trading and a network of wholesale buying, often through other members of their families, which enabled them to undercut any African who might venture to compete. And so, although often Africans and Asians could get along together more easily than either could associate with Europeans, one of the important factors in the years after the Second World War was a growing African bitterness at their exclusion from the retail trade. This situation continued throughout the colonial period. In 1953, for instance, African traders at a meeting held in the British Legion Club at Nakuru said that "they would be able to sell far more cheaply if they were not forced to purchase on a wholesale basis from Asians. They all complained", wrote the Municipal Welfare Officer, "that they are cheated at every possible opportunity and they experience great difficulty when buying in small quantities. It is the latter factor which forces them to buy at very near retail rates from Asian shopkeepers who act as wholesalers for the sale of goods in small quantities".[100] In November 1945 African soldiers, recently returned from service overseas, passed a resolution to stop further Indian immigration—a resolution fully in keeping with African thought.[101]

The Indians had tried in the past to win African favour and had given considerable financial help to African causes. In 1921, during Harry Thuku's campaign against an increase in Hut and Poll Tax, M. A. Desai, the editor of the *East African Chronicle*, had written articles in his paper on behalf of the Africans and had given Thuku an office on his premises. In 1945 no less than £650 of the £1,000 needed to pay the expenses of a delegation sent to England by the African Study Group were given by Indians,[102] and the Governor noted that African politicians were "certainly being largely influenced by the least desirable kind of Kenya Indian politicians".[103] Indian Members of Legislative Council spoke from time to time on behalf of African interests, but the Africans were anxious not to accept help of that kind. In 1945, Archdeacon Beecher, representing African interests, said that such Africans as he had been able to consult empowered him to say that "so far as they and their friends were concerned, no authority had been conveyed to the Hon. Indian members of their Council to voice opposition on their behalf".[104] As late as 1954 Indians were still making similar attempts to win African gratitude and were still being rebuffed as when Eliud Mathu told Legislative Council that the Indian members "had no mandate" to speak on behalf of the African community;[105] and the Indians never won the gratitude or friendship of the Africans.

Economic rivalry was not the only cause of friction between the races. Always in Kenya, as elsewhere, human emotions played a vital part. When an African said "You have hurt my pride", he meant that his human dignity, his right to be respected as a human being, had been affronted and all too often he had to suffer indignities arising from other men's feelings of racial superiority. A frank admission is given in a paper delivered by an Asian at a meeting of the American African Studies Association in Chicago in October, 1964, that the Asians "supported and even helped create" African nationalism and gave "a lot of money to African leaders", but "Yet the more perspicacious and objective among the Asians . . . readily admit the wrongs their people had done to the Africans: the exploitations of the Africans in the *duka*, in the bush and the cities, the discourteous treatment given to them by Asians, the open flaunting of disrespect towards African culture and the African physiognomy".[106]

The Asians, then, were an urban community. They were traders and artisans in the townships and were not employed in farming, with the exception of ownership and technical posts on sugar estates near Kisumu and sisal estates in the Coast Province. The sugar estates near Kisumu were not on the scale of the Indian sugar estates in Uganda, near Jinja, but they were an important item in the economy and were the fore-runners of the later, largely post-Independence, development of sugar at Kibigori, Chemelil, Songhor and Muhoroni. The original culture of sugar in the area, however, the estate at Miwani, was the work of an Australian, George Russell Mayers, who started growing sugar near Kibos in 1921 and later sold to Indians and himself moved to Nandi Hills to grow, first coffee, and later tea.[107]

In 1948 there were 97,687 Asians in Kenya and in 1962 there were 176,613 of whom 164,992, which is 93.1 per cent, were urban, while at the same time only 5.3 per cent of Africans were urban. During the fourteen years from 1948 to 1962, when censuses were taken, the Asian population of Nairobi increased from 41,810 to 86,453 and of Mombasa from 25,580 to 43,713. During these years Africans, unable to make a living in the Reserves, flooded into Nairobi and Africans, already in Nairobi, were striving to rise in the economic structure, but everywhere Asians, usually with better skill and education, stood in their way. Without the restrictions placed on Asian immigration the pressures would have been even greater. As it was, the increase in the Asian population was due mainly to the Asian birth rate in Kenya. In 1948 there were 47,429 local born Asians, (48.6 per cent of the total) and 50,258 (51.4 per cent) foreign born and in 1962 there were 88,978 (61.7 per cent) local born and 67,635 (38.3 per cent) foreign born. A large number of the 67,635 were already living in Kenya in 1948 and the scale of immigration was low. It was not Asians in professional and managerial positions whom Africans regarded as rivals at that time. It was the artisans and Asians in clerical posts and shop keepers against whom their envy was turned, because these held positions which Africans felt they themselves could adequately fill.

A glance at the categories of Asian employment in 1962 shows the extent of their problem.

Economically Active Adult Asian Males

	Percentage
Professional and Managerial	23.0
Technical and Supervisory	4.1
Clerical and Sales	42.1
Craftsmen and Skilled Manual Workers	26.0
Semi-skilled and unskilled and unclassified	4.8
	100.0%

The Statistics Division of the Kenya Ministry of Economic Planning and Development pointed out that "in all the age groups over 45 years the numbers of Craftsmen and Skilled Manual Workers were greater than the Clerical and Sales Workers whereas in all age groups below 45 those in the latter heavily out-numbered those in the former. This general shift from Skilled Manual work to Clerical and Sales work may be regarded as reflecting the increasing amount of education experienced by the younger generation of Asians".[108] The Africans' struggle for more education was partly due to their realisation that without it they could not hope to be accorded social recognition or economic advancement and the ability to compete with the "white collar" Asians.

After the Second World War the richer members of the Asian communities "experienced a tremendous boom. What had been potentially the most affluent group in East Africa now definitely turned into the richest. . . . In urban East Africa, more than 75 per cent of all buildings and real estate and about an equal proportion of investments belonged to Asians".[109] The richer Asians were able to pay for overseas education for their children. This created new problems. Asian doctors were a valuable addition to the medical profession, but Asian lawyers, some called to the English Bar and others qualified as advocates in the courts of India, naturally expected that appointments as magistrates and judges should be open to them but were met by African and even Asian fears that they would not be impartial.[110]

Opposition to Asian Immigration

After the Second World War the increase of African resentment at the economic position which Asians had acquired for themselves in the lower and middle ranges of society and European antagonism at all levels were united in opposing Indian demands for unrestricted immigration. In the middle of 1945 the Governor told some leading Indians that in all countries Governments "had a duty to protect their own populations from unemployment due to excessive immigration: that there were close on 20,000 Indian children in Kenya and the community was breeding fast and that in their own interest I could not allow unrestricted immigration, quite apart from the fact that the natives objected strongly and every petition I received raised the point".[111] Some Asians saw the danger of unemployment.[112] Matters were made especially difficult immediately after the War because, as Mitchell told an Indian delegation, "the Government of India took the line that they would not allow 'selective immigration'; unless we took every Indian who wanted to come, we could have none, so the answer would of course be none".[113]

In 1945 the Governor discussed the question of Indian immigration with representatives of various Indian communities. The followers of the Aga Khan and all the other Moslems thought that all further Asian immigration ought to be stopped, but the Hindus took the opposite view and went so far as to consider trying to get all Indians "to refuse to co-operate with Government, resign from all Boards and Committees and Legislative Council".[114] They did not in fact do so, but the proposal that they might do so showed how wide was the gulf which divided the Asian community within itself, and the Hindus did manage to pass a resolution in the East Africa Indian National Congress protesting against restrictions on Indian immigration.[115]

The Government's fear of unemployment among artisans was clearly shown in the decision to repatriate all Italian prisoners of war, although there were many who were valuable craftsmen and who wanted to stay in Kenya. In July 1946 it was decided that they must all be returned to Italy because there was already some un-employment among Asian artisans and among some Europeans also and the Government's trade schools would soon be turning out considerable numbers of African carpenters and masons.[116] A few months later, however, the Governor said that he saw no objection to the employment of some high grade Chinese electricians, earning £25 to £30 a month. They would not compete with anyone, but he refused to allow "ordinary labour to be recruited in China".[117] The same arguments applied to would-be immigrants from India.

In 1949 a Select Committee on Indian Education issued a Report to which S. V. Cooke, Member of Legislative Council, added a note, in which he pointed out that the Asians were expected to double in number in the next thirty years and that the Africans whose numbers were also increasing fast, would enter into "stern and unrelenting competition" with them. In the Rhodesias the white artisans barred the progress of the Africans, but in Kenya it was the Asians whom the Africans saw just above them at every turn, and tensions, arising from economic causes, existed between Africans and Asians rather than Africans and Europeans. In the interests of the Asians themselves Cooke pleaded that Asian immigration should be strictly controlled.[118]

Their hard work and enterprise had given the Asians a leading position in trade and the artisan life of Kenya. The Africans became increasingly jealous of them and the Europeans to a great extent despised them socially and feared their economic competition and growing numbers. Their business ethics were suspect and made them disliked. In 1945 an Indian Member said in Legislative Council during a debate on crime in Kenya, "I do not want to incur the unpopularity of my own community by saying that they are receivers of stolen property, but they certainly have that reputation".[119] And it was frequently believed that Asian traders kept three different sets of books: one for the shareholders, one for the manager, and one for the Income Tax Department.[120]

They were told that they were not welcome in the Colony, but, when they turned to India for support, accusations of disloyalty to Kenya were levelled against them. "Whenever we have run to our mother country for help, we have always been blamed", said Dr. Rana. "Why do you Indians go and take your complaints to the

Government of India? and my reply is that when a baby is in
difficulty what can he do but run to his mother. India is our Motherland".[121] This insistence on India as the motherland was unwise,
although it was understandable. The Europeans who dominated
politics opposed all Indian claims to equality and so gave the Indians
no encouragement to regard Kenya as their home and India merely
as the land from which their culture derived. They could not claim
that they were British "colonists" with some responsibility for
assisting the Imperial Trustee to further African progress. To
identify themselves completely with Kenya was almost impossible,
but their failure to do so was one of the causes of their unpopularity
with Africans. In this respect the Moslems and above all the Ismaili
followers of the Aga Khan were wiser than the Indians. Both
Liaquat Ali Khan and the Aga Khan told their followers to "identify
themselves fully with Kenya, forget their original homes, and put
down local roots by investing in land and property locally".[122] But
their loyalty to Kenya remained suspect. Throughout the colonial
period on the anniversary of Indian Independence and on all other
festival days and holidays Moslems and Hindus alike decked their
shops with Pakistani or Indian flags and never flew the Union
Jack or any form of Kenya lion. Certainly the Indians were more
prone than the Moslems to engage in anti-British politics. The
Commissioner for the Government of India became the friend of the
African nationalist politicians and A. B. Patel told Alderman Allah
Ditta Qureshi that Nehru had "instructed" him "to support all
African demands and claims".[123] Fortunately Patel was too wise to
obey this instruction from Delhi, but the fact that the Indian Prime
Minister thought that he had the right to give instructions to Indian
politicians in Kenya throws an interesting light on the Indian view
of the plural society.

The "New" Africans

During the Second World War African soldiers fought in
Abyssinia and South East Asia and met British, South African
and Indian officers and private soldiers there and in Kenya itself.
". . . we have travelled far in new lands", wrote an African corporal
on his return, "have had contact with strange peoples, their customs
and all, and above all at all times discussed various matters with
our superiors, i.e. British Officers and N.C.O.s".[124] In addition to
such contacts and experiences they were subjected by General Sir

William Platt to a policy which was revolutionary in its effect. As a military commander he had to create as efficient an army as possible and his liberal views were in line with his military policy. "Education", said a leading article in the *East African Standard*, "must clearly be the basis on which he would rely for the raising of the military and technical standard of the African element of his forces".[125] Ninety-five per cent of the soldiers under his command were illiterate and the Army Education Corps was formed to teach them to read and write. The alphabet was taught by scratching on the sandy ground, and the earth provided the exercise books in which they learned to write. When General Platt left his command in January 1945, the *East African Standard* commented that he had "helped to awaken the African to a sense of his own latent capacity".[126]

During the nineteen forties, although not as a result of the War, the University College of East Africa at Makerere in Kampala was being transformed from being little more than a technical school to a college whose students were to sit for the External B.A. Degree of London University, and African secondary education in Kenya, though small in quantity, was reaching high levels in quality. At the same time as the soldiers were returning from overseas a new class of Africans, better educated than the Africans of pre-War days, was coming onto the scene. Most Europeans remained for many years ignorant of the growing African elite, whom they had few opportunities of meeting; and much bitterness was caused by the sense of frustration felt by the better educated Africans who craved for a recognition of their progress, which they seldom received, and by the discontent of the demobilised soldiers, who found no opportunities of employment in the Reserves and drifted into the towns, where they swelled the numbers of the homeless and un-employed.

Early in 1946 Elspeth Huxley visited Kenya after an absence of seven years. A broadcast talk which she gave in March showed how she found the Kenya of 1946, the post-war Kenya, to be very different from the Kenya of the nineteen thirties. To her, visiting Kenya from the outside, much was plain which was not appreciated by Europeans living in Kenya itself and dangers and needs which were obvious to her were not recognised by the European farmers and business community, who quite naturally were unable to stand back and see themselves and their surroundings in a dispassionate

manner. First of all Mrs. Huxley pointed out that it was "absurd
to mean only Europeans when one talks about the 'people of
Kenya' ". As speeches made during the political turmoil of 1946
showed, that particular absurdity was not all uncommon in the
White Highlands. "It struck me very much", Mrs. Huxley continued,
"that a whole new generation of Africans has grown up, and the
Europeans seemed as a rule to know all too little about them".
Opportunities for Europeans and the "new" Africans to meet were
few, but without personal contacts changes in attitude were not
likely to be significant, and, as Mrs. Huxley saw, the need was for
"more bridges" crossing the racial gulf.[127] Lack of imagination and
racial pride too often produced statements that (as they might be
summarised), because it took Great Britain two thousand years to
progress from the days of Queen Boadicea to the days of Queen
Victoria and from Stonehenge to the Muthaiga Club, it would take
the Africans of Kenya almost as long. At the same time it is true that
the rate of African educational progress was remarkably fast and
was an achievement which not even the most liberal Europeans
would have dared to predict in 1945.

In 1946 Creech Jones, at that time Assistant Secretary of State for
the Colonies, visited Kenya and concluded that Africans needed "a
process of education and economic growth" to build up their "sense
of social responsibility and public duty."[128] The provision of money
for the education of Africans showed one of the difficulties of a
plural society. Because the Africans were poor, although they
probably paid in direct and indirect taxation a greater proportion of
their substance than Europeans did, the total sum arising from
taxation of Africans was considerably less than the money paid by
the immigrant races. The process of developing parliamentary
government gave great power to the European Elected Members
of the Legislative Council and they insisted on maintaining the
standard of education which they would have expected their children
to receive in Britain. The amount of money voted for the education
of Africans was extremely small, but to increase it substantially
would have required heavy taxation of the immigrant races or large
grants from Britain. The former would have endangered the growth
of the economy: the latter would have been unacceptable to the
British Parliament. Without the European community there would
have been even less money in Kenya to meet the requirements of
trusteeship. The need was for liberalising, not abolishing, the

immigrant communities. At about the same time Eliud Mathu said
with realistic appreciation, "Our contribution as Africans towards
better race relations in Kenya lies in improving our economic
position, our educational standards and our standard of living".[129]
By doing so they could reach a standard approximating to European
standards and make social contact easier, but it was also necessary
for Europeans to acquire knowledge of African traditions and
values and to temper their inherent feeling of white superiority.
Kenyatta saw the need for an improvement in African standards
of public duty and integrity. In March 1948, for instance, he told a
public meeting at Nyeri that "Africans were getting themselves a
bad name by preferring thieving and thuggery to honest work"
and he pointed out that African progress was being hampered
by "the tendency of those who had to handle money, L.N.C.[130]
rate-collectors, for example, to steal the money with which they
had been entrusted".[131]

Equal pay for equal work was naturally an object of African
endeavour, but in order to achieve it a sense of responsibility and
financial rectitude had to be shown. As Meredith Hyde-Clarke, the
Labour Commissioner, a sincere advocate of African progress, said
in 1948, "But equal pay for equal work cannot be based on mere
ability to do the job, but . . . it means the obligation to go on doing
it day after day, week after week, year after year, and doing it with
integrity".[132] And at the same time the Chief Native Commissioner
reminded Legislative Council of the "deplorably low standard of
integrity among Africans in the Civil Service". Every week he had
to agree to "the writing off of this and that amount which has been
stolen by a member of the African Civil Service".[133] There was something of a vicious circle here. Integrity and reliability seemed to the
Government and to the members, mainly Europeans, of commissions
on salaries and wages to be a prerequisite for equal pay, but the
knowledge that, however well they might do a job, they would
get little more than half the salary which a European would get
for the same work seemed so unjust to the Africans that the maintenance of high standards may have seemed to some to be of
secondary importance. Mathu pointed out in Legislative Council
that "as a member of the standing Finance Committee" he knew
that some Europeans and Indians in the Civil Service were dishonest
also.[134] This was certainly true of the Public Works Department
whose stores offered great temptations, but, although such bad

examples had to be condemned, it was impossible to deny that
there was more corruption among Africans. The frequent failures
of African co-operative societies were particularly evident. After
the War, when it was hoped that the soldiers would be able to use
their gratuities to make a good start in civilian life, attempts were
made to persuade traders to combine and purchase goods wholesale, but "Most of these co-operatives failed owing to the dishonesty
of their officers", reported the Commissioner for Community
Development.[135]

Government files, official reports and newspaper accounts give a
long story of lapses from financial integrity, but none give so telling
a picture as the condemnation of a man, so widely loved and
respected that, when he died in 1966, the business of Parliament
was suspended to allow Members to attend his funeral and a cortege
of cars over two miles long took the mourners from All Saints
Cathedral to Kikuyu, where they found a crowd of six thousand
humble Africans gathered at the grave-side. Carey Francis, the
great Headmaster of the Alliance High School, never condemned
without cause, but during the War he wrote in a memorandum
on African terms of Service, "There is corruption everywhere,
among Chiefs, and interpreters, District Commissioners' clerks,
medical orderlies—yet African voices are not raised in protest;
most of them would do the same if they had the chance".[136] Lack of
sympathetic understanding caused poverty and unequal pay to be
overlooked by most Europeans, but the extent of dishonesty could
not be disregarded when Africans themselves and their European
friends and helpers were emphatic in denouncing it. Such a state of
affairs gave support to those who contended that many of the
regulations and practices which Africans regarded as discriminatory
were merely realistic, and Africans with high standards suffered
because of the faults of others.

Among the general mass of Africans poverty was the main cause of
discontent, but among the better educated tensions were due
fundamentally to spiritual and mental causes, to human feelings and
emotions, and racial considerations entered into them at every turn.
Racial tensions were caused above all by the European sense of
superiority and by the desire of the better educated Africans to be
accepted by Europeans as "civilised" rather than backward tribal
people and by a similar feeling of social slight on the part of the
Asians. There was at the same time a growing desire among Africans

(a desire long felt by Asians) to be allowed to own land in the White Highlands, which was opposed by the Europeans' contention that they would be unable to preserve their way of life unless the White Highlands remained inviolate. In the period of history which opened after the War the European position of political power and racial dominance was to be attacked by African pressures which had been only slightly recognised in earlier years, and the dominant position of the Asians in trade and crafts was to arouse increasing envy. In the new period of development human relations were to be of greater importance than at any time in the past.

1. Kenyatta told Malcolm MacDonald, Kenya's last Governor and Governor General in the year between the attainment of Independence and the establishment of a republic, that he had not expected to see Independence in his lifetime. (Interview with Rt. Hon. Malcolm MacDonald, O.M., 27 May, 1972).
2. E.A.S. 25 Jan. 1946.
3. ibid, 1 Feb. 1946.
4. ibid, 8 Feb. 1946.
5. ibid, 8 Feb. 1946.
6. Jomo Kenyatta: *Kenya: The Land of Conflict*, p. 23.
7. W. K. Hancock: *Survey of Commonwealth Affairs*, Vol. II, part I, p. 57.
8. ibid, p. 62.
9. Margery Perham in Vincent Harlow and E. M. Chilver, ed.: *History of East Africa*, Vol. II, p. 1i.
10. Sir Reginald Coupland: *India A Restatement*, p. 43.
11. T. B. (later Lord) Macaulay in House of Commons: Hansard Vol. XIX, 10 July, 1933, col. 536.
12. Office of Chief Secretary, Deposit No.8/1400 II: Births and Deaths Registration Ordinance; in Kenya National Archives.
13. Blundell to Havelock, 7 June 1956, Havelock file H.14 in Kenya National Archives.
14. E.A.S. 12 Oct. 1945. Report of Indian National Congress.
15. C. G. Seligman, *The Races of Africa*, pp. 53 and 160.
16. All these quotations are from the *Review of Discriminatory Legislation Prepared in Accordance with a Motion Accepted by the Legislative Council on the 3rd December 1953* (Papers Laid Vol. VI, 1955(56)). There is a copy in the Library of the National Assembly and another in the Library of the Kenya National Archives. The Departmental Memoranda from which the Review was compiled are in Office of the Chief Secretary, Deposit No. 8/1400, II in the Kenya National Archives.
17. *Kenya Population Census 1948 and Kenya Population Census 1962.*
18. E.A.S. 16 Feb. 1946.
19. E.A. & R. 29 Mar. 1945, p. 689.
20. e.g. ". . . it is up to us . . . to ensure that as quickly as possible people are trained and equipped for eventual self-government". H.C.D. Vol. 391, col. 49, 13 July 1943. (Oliver Stanley)
21. Sir Andrew Cohen: *British Policy in Changing Africa*, p. 22. Hobson calls "the creation of free white democracies" *colonialism* and the government of dependencies *imperialism*. (J. A. Hobson: *Imperialism*, p. 125, revised).
22. Sir Charles Eliot: *The British East Africa Protectorate*, p. 103.
23. Colonel R. Meinertzhagen, *Kenya Diary* 1902–1906, p. 30.

24. F.O. 2/833 Landsdowne to Stewart, 8 July, 1904, quoted in George Bennett: *Kenya: a Political History*, p. 16.
25. Sir Philip Mitchell's Diary, 16 Jan. 1956.
26. W. K. Hancock, op. cit. p. 1.
27. ibid, p. 26.
28. ibid, p. 26.
29. ibid, Part 2, p. 80.
30. Sir Andrew Cohen: *British Policy in Changing Africa*, p. 10.
31. W. K. Hancock, op. cit. Part 2, p. 181.
32. ibid, Part 1, p. 71.
33. Leonard Barnes: *Soviet Light on the Colonies*, p. 8.
34. Royal Institute of International Affairs: *The Colonial Problem*, pp. 276, 284.
35. J. A. Hobson: *Imperialism*, revised edition, 1938, p. 55.
36. Sir Philip Mitchell's Diary, 21 Aug. 1946.
37. J. A. Hunter and D. Mannix: *African Bush Adventures* has interesting accounts of them and other early settlers.
38. Elspeth Huxley: *White Man's Country*, Vol. I, p. 320.
39. Quoted in M. K. P. Sorrensen: *Origins of European Settlement in Kenya*, p. 120.
40. *Report of the Native Labour Commission 1912–1913*, p. 109.
41. George Bennett: *Kenya: A Political History*, p. 22.
42. *Correspondence relating to the flogging of natives by certain Europeans at Nairobi, Cd. 3562* (1907).
43. Lord Cranworth: *A Colony in the Making*, p. 9.
44. *New Comment*, No. 30, 26 Oct. 1956.
45. *Kenya: Compulsory Labour for Government Purposes, 1925*, (Cmd. 2464) p. 15.
46. Hancock, op. cit., p. 57.
47. Norman Leys: *Kenya*, p. 166.
48. J. H. Oldham: *White and Black in Africa. A Critical Examination of the Rhodes Lectures of General Smuts*, p. 31.
49. ibid.
50. Sir Philip Mitchell: *African Afterthoughts*, p. 219.
51. ibid, p. 217.
52. The Electors' Union: *Kenya Plan*, p. 14.
53. *Indians in Kenya, cmd. 1922* (1923).
54. Y. P. Ghai and T. H. V. N. McAuslan: *Public Law and Political Change in Kenya*, p. 42.
55. There is a detailed account in Robert G. Gregory: *Sidney Webb and East Africa*.
56. *Report of the Commission for Closer Union for the Dependencies in East and Central Africa (The Rt. Hon. Sir E. Hilton Young, G.B.E., D.S.O., M.P., Chairman) Cmd. 3234, 1929*, p. 36.
57. Carl J. Rosberg: "Political Conflict and Change in Kenya", *Transition in Africa*, ed. Gwendolen M. Carter and William O. Brown, p. 110.
58. Sir George Pickering: *The Challenge of Education*, p. 29.
59. Lord Cranworth: *A Colony in the Making* (1913) revised as *Profit and Sport in British East Africa* (1919).
60. Electors' Union: *An Outline of Policy*, p. 24.
61. J. V. Taylor: *Christianity and Politics in Africa*, p. 95.
62. Sir Philip Mitchell: "Africa and the West in Historical Perspective", *Africa To-day*, ed. C. Give Haimes, p. 24.
63. J. H. Oldham, op. cit., p. 14.
64. Sir Philip Mitchell's Diary, 6 Nov. 1939.
65. ibid, 6 Nov. 1939.
66. Conversation with R. A. Frost, 1952.
67. *Imperial Policy. A Statement of Conservative Policy for the British Commonwealth and Empire*, 1949, p. 35.
68. Sir Philip Mitchell's Diary, 27 Nov. 1945.

69. ibid, 16 Oct. 1945.
70. Dick Edmunds to Blundell, 2 Nov. 1952, Blundell 11/2.
71. Bishop Obadiah Kariuki told this story to Miss Clarke of the St. Julian's Community: Miss Clarke's Diary, 18 May 1957.
72. H.C.D. Vol. 452, col. 415, 16 June 1948. The European Elected Members Organisation discussed the matter on 7 Aug. 1948: Minutes of E.E.M.O. Meeting, 7 Aug. 1948.
73. European Elected Members Organisation: Minutes of Meeting, 2 May 1949.
74. *Kenya Agricultural Census 1955 (Highlands and Asian Settled Areas)* East African Statistical Department, June 1957 (Mimeographed) p. 1.
75. ibid.
76. Blundell to Kendall Ward, 14 Apr. 1955. Kendall Ward deposit in Kenya National Archives.
77. Sir Philip Mitchell's Diary, 9 Sept. 1948.
78. ibid, 16 Dec. 1944.
79. N. S. Carey-Jones: *The Anatomy of Uhuru*, p. 6.
80. M. S. Lipsett, *Political Man*, chapter 9, section 2, "Upper Class Liberalism".
81. E. C. Del Kirk to Michael Blundell, 20 July 1952, Blundell 3/1.
82. Federal Independence Party.
83. Blundell to Oliver Woods and Patrick Monkhouse, 15 Aug. 1956, Blundell 5/3.
84. Blundell, 12/4.
85. L. J. Beecher.
86. *Kenya Population Census 1962*, Vol. IV.
87. S. H. Ominde; "Population Movements to the Main Urban Areas of Kenya", *Cahiers d'Etudes Africaines*, Vol. V 4e Cahier, pp. 593–617.
88. George A. Tyson: *African Housing and Allied Problems.*
89. Vernon Bartlett: *Struggle for Africa*, p. 174.
90. *Report on the Census of the Non-Native Population of Kenya Colony and Protectorate Taken on the Night of 25th February, 1948*, p. 114.
91. J. E. Goldthorpe: *Outlines of East African Society*, p. 140.
92. Quoted in Elspeth Huxley: *White Man's Country*, Vol. II, p. 121.
93. *East Africa Royal Commission 1953–1954 Report, Cmd. 9457*, pp. 18–19.
94. Electors' Union: *Notes on the Political Economy of Kenya.*
95. E.A.S. 1 Feb. 1946 (letter).
96. ibid, 13 Dec. 1949.
97. Negley Farson: *Last Chance in Africa*, p. 31.
98. E.A.S. 19 Oct. 1945.
99. ibid, 26 Aug. 1949.
100. Letter to Blundell, 22 July 1953, Blundell 16/3.
101. E.A.S. 2 Nov. 1945.
102. E.A. & R. 7 Mar. 1946, p. 670.
103. Sir Philip Mitchell's Diary, 1 Dec. 1945.
104. L.C.D. 4 July, 1946, col. 59.
105. ibid, 15 Dec. 1954, col. 1147.
106. A. Bharati, Professor of Indian Studies at Syracuse University, U.S.A. *Maxwell Graduate School of Citizenship and Public Affairs, Syracuse University. The Program of Eastern African Studies. Occasional Paper No. 12.*
107. Letter from his son, Roy Mayers, 8 Nov. 1970.
108. *Kenya Population Census, 1962*, Vol. IV, Statistics Division, Ministry of Economic Planning and Development, March 1966.
109. A. Bharati, op. cit. p. 1.
110. e.g. letters in E.A.S., 7 Jan. 1949.
111. Sir Philip Mitchell's Diary, 2 June 1945.
112. e.g. "Jobless Kenya-born Asian", in E.A.S., 9 Sept. 1949.
113. Sir Philip Mitchell's Diary, 28 Feb. 1945.
114. ibid, 28 Feb. 1945.
115. E.A.S. 12 Oct. 1945.
116. Sir Philip Mitchell's Diary, 26 July 1946.

117. ibid, 11 Feb. 1947.
118. *Report of the Select Committee on Indian Education, 1949.*
119. L.C.D. 16 Nov. 1945, col. 232.
120. E.A.S. 27 July, 1956.
121. L.C.D.: 20 July 1945, col. 115.
122. Alderman Allah Ditta Qureshi to Kendall Ward: Kendall Ward deposit in Kenya National Archives.
123. ibid.
124. E.A.S. 2 Nov. 1945.
125. ibid, 19 Jan. 1945.
126. ibid, 19 Jan. 1945.
127. Broadcast talk: E.A. & R. 28 Mar. 1946, p. 744.
128. E.A.S. 2 Aug. 1946.
129. Speech at Mwakinyungu, printed in *Pan Africa*, June 1947, p. 13.
130. Local Native Councils.
131. E.A.S., 26 Mar. 1948.
132. L.C.D., 19 Aug. 1948, col. 324.
133. ibid, cols. 308–9. File P/Fin. 4/6 and District files like DC/NKU/2/2 and DC/NYI/2/2 in the Kenya National Archives give many examples.
134. L.C.D., 20 Aug. 1948, col. 354.
135. T. G. Askwith: *Some Observations on the Growth of Unrest in Kenya*, 24th Oct. 1952. (Mimeographed).
136. Memorandum by Carey Francis submitted to the Committee on Arab and African Terms of Service, quoted in L. B. Greaves: *Carey Francis of Kenya*, pp. 82–83.

2

SOME POST-WAR PROBLEMS

Problems of Trusteeship

Sir Philip Mitchell took the Chair in Legislative Council for the first time on the 3rd January, 1945. The Indians welcomed him as a man who, as Governor of Uganda, had shown himself to be impartial and free from racial bias. The Indian Leader, A. B. Patel, speaking in Legislative Council, said, "From what I have heard and know of your Excellency's work in adjoining territories, one hopes that in the advancement and development of this Colony the Indian community and other communities residing in it will have fair play and justice during your period of administration".[1] Some Europeans were suspicious, because he had served in Tanganyika under Sir Donald Cameron, whose liberal views were far from popular with the majority of Europeans in Kenya. The Africans were pleased by his appointment because in Tanganyika and Uganda he had shown himself to be free from prejudice against the coloured races. He combined a liberal attitude with great experience of East Africa. The former caused some apprehension among Europeans: the latter gave him a sense of realism as representative of the Imperial Trustee.

British trusteeship was assailable from two directions. Two courses were possible. Was Britain's task "one of transforming colonial society into a modern western civilisation, however long that task might take"? Or ought Britain to purify and preserve "the traditional order of native society"?[2] A trustee ought to have a policy, but Britain has been chided by some critics for doing what she thought was "best for the African" rather than doing what the Africans thought was best for themselves.[3] No doubt, if the British Government had adopted an opposite policy, there would have been accusations of neglect of the duty of "modernising" the ward. It was natural that a colonial power should base its policy on its own system of government and its own system of law. In Kenya there were abuses and discrimination, but it was the British parliamentary system which enabled Africans to gain political power and to pass without disruption to Independence.

Some writers have advanced a third alternative. They suggest that Britain's duty was to sweep away the capitalist system, which had been developed, and create a socialist society instead. Ahmed Mohiddin of Makerere, for instance, wrote in 1969 that "Independence was granted on the basis of the continuation of the system, and not on its destruction",[4] and Ruth First seems to have regarded Mau Mau as a national peasant revolt to which the British Government ought to have conceded an extreme socialist pattern of life.[5] "The idea behind land consolidation in Kenya", wrote Mohiddin, ". . . was to create a class of property-owning Africans who could be relied upon to maintain and safeguard the emerging liberal society in its economic aspects".[6] He thought it wrong that, after Independence, Kenyan Ministers should not have advocated the adoption of a communist system but should have shown an "anti-communist bias in some of their speeches".[7] The Swynnerton Report on African agriculture was anathema to him and so was Sir Philip Mitchell's aim of establishing "a civilised state in which the values and standards are to be the values and standards of Britain, in which everyone, whatever his origins, has an interest and a part".[8]

The Colonial Office, Secretaries of State and those members of the British public who gave thought to colonial affairs, agreed that development in Kenya should be according to British democratic principles, although the details varied in accordance with the ideas of the different political parties in Britain. In Kenya itself, as in Britain and elsewhere, group interests were often in conflict with the ideal, but Africans frequently admitted the value of the leadership which the Europeans, most of whom were British, could give. The problem in the years between the end of the Second World War and Independence, as the Imperial Government saw it, was how to substitute partnership for privilege and co-operation for discrimination without losing the standards and principles underlying what was regarded as "the British way of life". It was an ideal requiring co-operation and tolerance and mutual respect. In 1945 there did not seem to be an abundance of these requirements. Leading European politicians were alarmed at the bad state of race relations, and the Governor mentioned "an apparent deterioration between the various races in the Colony".[9] Debates in Legislative

Council and speeches at political meetings during the political
crises over the Membership system, Papers 191 and 210, and
National Registration did not give any hope that the politicians
would set an example of a spirit of co-operation. The Governor did
not hold a high opinion of the European Elected Members and
described them as "little, frightened, narrow, heathen men with
nothing to offer but words, tricks, schemes and spite",[10] still in 1951
as Creech Jones had found them in 1946, "obstinately full of racial
bitterness, narrow and unhelpful".[11] Outside the political arena,
however, there were hopeful signs, but, as was the case during the
fifties also, the growing spirit of goodwill received little recognition
and did not catch the newspaper headlines. The Imperial Government, the Trustee, was ill informed on this vital matter and observers
overseas did not recognise the extent of the advance of liberal
opinion.

The advance of liberal opinion required the lessening of discrimination, which existed to maintain the privileged position of the
Europeans. There were certainly some practices which differentiated
between the races which could be justified on economic or other
grounds. Asian carpenters and other artisans, for example, were
more skilled than African craftsmen in the nineteen forties and,
if African craftsmen had received the same wages as Asians, many
would have been unemployed. But other forms of discrimination
existed in order to maintain European privileges. There were few
discriminatory laws: discrimination was imposed by regulations and
administrative practice. Although some discriminatory practices
could have been made illegal, the ending of much of the discrimination which existed could only be achieved by a change of heart.
When Sir Philip Mitchell was considering the events of 1950 he saw
some grounds for hope. "I believe", he wrote, "I may have made
some progress with the things that matter here—the restoration of a
Christian approach to public affairs, the growth of trust and liking
between the races, and even the diminution of the power for mischief
of angry demagogues".[12] Mitchell believed that what Kenya most
needed was a new outlook, a new approach to politics, a replacement of communal selfishness by inter-racial harmony.

African Poverty and Overcrowding

The great economic disparity between all Africans and all
Europeans produced a general feeling of superiority in the European

community and ill will among many of those Africans whose
educational standard could have won for them better economic and
social conditions if there had been no discriminatory practices
which kept them in an inferior position. Among Africans in general
the poverty and hardships experienced in Nairobi were matched by
poverty and overcrowding in some of the African Reserves. British
administration had brought an end to tribal warfare, and agricultural
and veterinary science and administration had overcome the worst
dangers of famine, while medical science had brought about a great
decrease in the death rate and so a great increase in the population.
Tribal individualism prevented the removal of population from an
overcrowded area to one with land to spare, as, for instance, in
Bukusu country immediately north of the overcrowded Maragoli
and Kakamega Reserves. If European farms had been sequestered
for African subsistence farming, a purely temporary relief would have
been obtained at the expense of the main source of Kenya's revenue.
African soldiers had returned from the War and their hopes of a
golden future had not been realised and they were felt to be in "an
ugly temper".[13] Overcrowding in the Reserves drove many Africans
to seek work in the towns, where they often found themselves among
the unemployed. In Nairobi they became useful subjects for the
propaganda of the secret movement of discontent which was
growing up among the Kikuyus there. Poverty and lack of housing
were leading factors in the increase of crime which caused great
concern among Government and Unofficial Members of Legislative
Council of all races alike.[14] The reaction among the European
population as a whole was to equate Africans with crime, which
made them even less able to appreciate the progress being made by
the African elite.

The effects of overcrowding in the Reserves were aggravated by
sub-division of holdings and by inefficient agriculture. A conservative
peasantry found it hard to adopt new methods in order to meet
new needs. In the Kikuyu Reserves the organisers of Mau Mau
opposed such work as terracing which was needed to combat soil
erosion. Whatever the causes may have been, the standard of
agriculture was low. According to the Provincial Agricultural
Officer of the Central Province in 1952/3 the percentage of land
well farmed was in Kiambu District, 2.40 per cent (6,750 acres),
in Fort Hall District, 5.75 per cent (13,911 acres), and in Nyeri
District, 6.93 per cent (11,522 acres).[15] The Reserves were grossly

overcrowded, in some places carrying 1,000 people to the square mile. Kenya had reached the stage when some people would have to live unconnected with the land, but industrial development posed great problems for a country with few mineral resources, and urban life would require not only employment but adequate wages and a system of social security for old age. Better subsistence agriculture was needed in the Reserves, but there was also a use for the kind of farming developed in the White Highlands where capital and knowledge were producing a large output of commercial proportions.[16] The value of European farming was such that the Fabian Colonial Bureau, which was not the best friend of European settlement wrote in 1954, "The economic arguments against African settlement in the White Highlands are powerful. Much of the pressure on African lands is due to African neglect".[17]

There seems to have been an unwillingness to believe and act on indications of discontent. Neither the Colonial Office nor the Administration nor the European Elected Members showed appreciation of the need for urgent action to raise the standard of the urban African workers to at least subsistence level. The Municipal Affairs Officer in Nairobi wrote a report which showed that the wages paid by the Municipal Council were not sufficient to feed a man and a small family on a diet of posho (maize flour) with meat and vegetables once or twice a week, but wages were not increased to the required level. In 1947 Dr. H. C. Trowell, specialist physician, Uganda Medical Service, and Lecturer in Medicine at Makerere, conducted a clinical examination of 500 Railway employees in Nairobi as part of a report under the Director of Surveys. The Colonial Office suppressed the main part of the report until after the Railways had put up wages and rations; but with the Director's approval, Dr. Trowell published his own findings in the East African Medical Journal, and as a result he got into very hot water from the General Manager of the Kenya and Uganda Railways and Harbours. He found that working conditions were excellent and housing was above the urban average but inadequate for what "privacy and decency demand at least for a married man".[18] The number of calories which wages could buy was not sufficient for prolonged hard work; but "the psychological strains which may inhibit efficiency" were most serious of all.

". . . sitting and talking with the workers in their homes", wrote Dr. Trowell, "one became aware of a very grave discontent which, unless constructively guided and relieved, may well, in my opinion, threaten the civil peace. The mood is one of resentment and disappointment, it has the appearance of being ominous. When asked to state their grievances they return with monotonous regularity to the question of wages and of poverty."[19]

The Governor himself did see that the question of poverty and over crowding must be tackled. His previous service had been largely in Tanganyika and he had been Governor of Uganda. He believed that remedies for these evils ought to be sought on an East African basis. No doubt he remembered that between Busia and Iganga in eastern Uganda a group of Nandis from Kenya had been happily established for many years. He thought that the overcrowding in the Kikuyu Reserves could be alleviated by moving some of the Kikuyus to land which could be made available in Tanganyika and Uganda. He wanted a Royal Commission on Land and Population to be appointed on an East African basis and he put his proposals to Andrew Cohen of the Colonial Office in June 1951.[20] Six months passed and in January 1952 he wrote a despatch on the subject.[21] There was further delay and the British Government's decision to appoint a Commission was not announced till October 1952 and the Commission did not fly to Kenya till the end of February 1953, by which time the Mau Mau civil war was raging.

African Suspicion

In January, 1948, S. V. Cooke proposed a motion in Legislative Council alleging that Africans had lost confidence in the "higher administration" and had become so suspicious of the Government that in schemes of obvious benefit for Africans they immediately began to wonder what was "behind them". Cooke quoted from the last Report of the Registrar of Co-operative Societies that "the African to-day tends to regard with suspicion any advice offered to him by the Europeans".[22] The Kamba Reserve, for instance, had become badly eroded and schemes of reafforestation or at least of shelter belts were required; but there was much opposition to planting because agitators told the people that the lines of trees were in fact to be the boundaries of new European farms which would be stolen from the Reserves. This opposition to a measure which was needed for the improvement of the Kamba land was typical of the suspicion found in many other parts. In the Fort Hall Reserve most of the forest had been cut down by the Kikuyus, but in and around 1930 much was replanted with black wattle to provide fire wood, charcoal and timber for building. The planting of this valuable timber was strongly opposed by the Kikuyus and it was only by prolonged effort that the Administration was able to get it established. Twenty years later the value of wood, charcoal and bark exported was £120,000 a year.[23] Similar suspicions were found in Tanganyika. In the 1930s, writes Dr. Mair, "the offer by the Government of European seedling trees, to be planted along river banks as a protection against erosion, was refused on the ground that once planted they could be made a pretext for claiming the ground on which they stood".[24]

Unfortunately such suspicion was not always due only to the innate conservatism of the peasant. In the past African trust had been betrayed and memories are long. The Masai had suffered in such ways and the Nandi, having been informed that the boundaries, fixed in 1907 after the Nandi War, circled land which "is theirs for ever",[25] found two areas taken from them for European soldier settler schemes after the First World War. According to the Nandi District: Political Records in June 1907 the "Boundaries of the Reserve were drawn up and in November a "Deputation of Nandi representatives were officially informed that the land within the Reserve was theirs for ever" and the boundaries were approved in the Provincial Commissioner's office on October 3rd 1911; but in 1920 the "Alienation of 100 square miles was sanctioned". The soldier settler schemes at Kaimosi and Kipkarren were a violation of that earlier promise, but in spite of that, when war broke out with Germany in 1939, there as a "remarkable demonstration of loyalty from ex-askaris of the last war, offering their services."[26] "A vast crowd of several hundred presented themselves for enrolment and all sorts of subterfuges were resorted to in an endeavour to have the good fortune to be selected".[27] Ninety *moran* were enlisted. At the same time Senior Chief Elijah Cheruiyot said to the District Commissioner that in the First World War many Nandi young men gladly served the Flag and that once again at a time of great danger to Britain the young men wanted to serve, but the Nandis hoped that this time they would not find that more of their land had been taken away from them.[28] Such episodes made all the more difficult the work of the Agricultural Officers and others. "To win the hearts of the people is the secret of extension work",[29] wrote one Agricultural Officer. Only so could suspicion be overcome.

Increasing Tension

In the late nineteen forties tensions were seen in parts of the
Central Province, and in the West of Kenya there were disturbing
signs of ill will also in areas where it had not been apparent before.
In the Kitale area, a District of European farms, and in the neighbouring Uasin Gishu round Eldoret the authorities felt that the
Africans had completely lost confidence in the Europeans. The
Dini ya Msambwa was active, cases of arson occurred on several
European farms and black and white speckled hens, which signified
strife among the Bukusu tribe, mysteriously appeared on farms
around Kitale. In the adjoining Nandi Reserve signs of ill will
were particularly surprising, because the Nandi were among the
most friendly of tribes in spite of the alienation of their land. The
priests of the big Roman Catholic Mission near Kapsabet, the
District Headquarters, found that, whereas formerly they had never
had any need to take food with them on their tours in the Nandi
Reserve, because they had always been supplied, often without
payment, with chickens, eggs and milk, in 1950 they could sometimes
not even *buy* food from the Nandi people.[30] In Naivasha, where
Mau Mau was growing rapidly in secret, the District Officer reported
that "a disturbing feature" was "the number of unprovoked assaults
by Africans on Europeans recorded during the year".[31]

The growth of discontent among Africans aggravated the fears of
Europeans. Many were afraid that, as the Africans became better
educated and demanded greater and increasing shares in the government of Kenya, the European community would become either a
protected minority or be submerged altogether. And in addition to
this fear was the dread felt by most Europeans that, if the races
mixed together socially, the result would be inter-marriage. The
social exclusiveness of the Europeans and the world-wide feeling of
white superiority were very galling to the few educated Africans
and the greater number of educated, and often rich, Asians, who
owned a large proportion of the land and buildings in the commercial
quarters of Nairobi and Mombasa and in most of the smaller towns.
The fact that in spite of their economic position the Asians were
in a minority in Legislative Council and in the Municipal Councils
of Nairobi and Mombasa was made all the more bitter when they
saw that both in Kampala and Dar-es-Salaam the Mayors were
Asians, while in Nairobi they were never able to win even the
Deputy Mayorship.

The violence of political feeling was seen during the first few years of Mitchell's Governorship by reactions to three major proposals, one for reorganising the Government of Kenya, one for constituting a more efficient East African organisation than the East African Governors' Conference, and one for instituting a system of national registration in Kenya. The reaction to these proposals was in each case racial and it was clear that without a sense of inter-racial co-operation, which did not exist in the nineteen forties, there could be no hope of a peaceful passage to an independence in which the different races each had a part to play.

The Membership System

On his journey from Fiji, where he had been Governor, to London, where he was to meet Colonel Oliver Stanley, the Secretary of State, Mitchell worked on plans for reorganising the Government of Kenya. Two things seemed to him to be wrong. Too much of the Governor's time was taken up by attendance in the chair at Legislative Council and he proposed that a Speaker should preside instead. It seemed to him to be entirely wrong that Unofficial Members should be free in Legislative Council to attack measures proposed by the Government after they had taken part in discussing them in Executive Council, where they shared all the secrets and confidences of the Government. He therefore proposed a Membership system in which individual members of Legislative Council, either Official or Unofficial, should be responsible for various matters, such as Law and Order, Education, and Agriculture, and should either support Government proposals in Legislative Council or resign.

These proposals were published in June, 1945. The Europeans were jubilant, but the other races were appalled, because the Unofficial Members would certainly all be Europeans and, although they would have to be loyal to Government policy, it was feared that their affinity of interests with their European constituents would put the making of policy and the details of its execution more securely in European hands. That was bad enough, but, when it was announced that Sir Ferdinand Cavendish-Bentinck was to be Member for Agriculture, Indians and Africans were aghast. He was regarded as one of the most uncompromising of Europeans and his Department was to deal with agriculture throughout the Colony, in African and European areas alike. To the Indians he was above

all the man who had always fought against their owning land and
engaging in agriculture at all.[32] Indians and Africans joined forces
in opposing the Membership system and, as Sir Alfred Vincent,
the Leader of the Europeans in Legislative Council, pointed out,
the African Press showed a "strange similarity" with the Indian
Press.[33] Indians had facilities which Africans did not have money to
acquire, and to further their common struggle they put their printing
presses at the service of African journalists.

Mitchell was sincerely impartial and he understood the traditions
of British politics. When he appointed Cavendish-Bentinck as
Member for Agriculture he made it quite clear that "unofficial"
freedom must be given up. "He must be a member of the Government and if he did not agree with the Government he must resign
before he could recover his freedom of action",[34] Mitchell wrote.
Immediately after Mitchell's arrival in Kenya European efforts
were exerted to persuade him to allow civil servants to join the
Electors' Union. He had to refuse and he "gave them some of the
obvious reasons".[35] It is significant that leaders of the European
political party, which was in the circumstances a racial party,
should have ever imagined that civil servants could be members.
The normal rules of impartiality seemed to be forgotten or perhaps
the truth is that they were unable to see that civil servants had to be
impartial and no more able to join the political party of their own
race than that of another race. The Governor's "obvious reasons"
were apparently not understood, because a few months later they
asked him to help them to prepare the Union's Statement of Policy.
"I had of course to say", wrote Mitchell in his diary, "that it was
a political document and I could have no part or share in it, nor
responsibility for it; for ex hypothesi I am entirely impartial and
unconnected with any party and my 'policy' was embodied in my
oath of office".[36]

A. B. Patel was Leader of the Indian Elected Members. His
honesty and sincerity produced a pleasant sequel to his opposition
to Cavendish-Bentinck's appointment. Four and a half years later,
when it was announced that Ernest Vasey was to succeed Sir Charles
Mortimer, who was a civil servant, as Member for Health and
Local Government, Patel said, ". . . though the Indian members have
always looked with a certain amount of suspicion upon unofficials
crossing the floor and taking over a post—as I had the honour to
express on behalf of Indian members when Major Cavendish-

Bentinck was appointed as Member for Agriculture and Natural Resources—from experience it has been found that once an unofficial member crossed the floor there is no need to entertain that suspicion because they are immediately within the fold of the Government benches and therefore they are not likely to be influenced as we had anticipated then by the unofficial side".[37]

Papers 191 and 210

The storm roused by the introduction of the membership system was successfully weathered. Then, exactly a year after Mitchell became Governor, his ideas for superseding the East African Governors' Conference by an organisation better fitted to carry out functions which had to be performed on an inter-territorial basis, having been discussed with his fellow Governors, were published in London as a Non-Parliamentary Paper on 12th December 1945.[38] The Europeans of Kenya were roused to violent expressions of opposition, because the proposed Central Legislative Assembly, which would have power of legislation over all the Territories on certain common subjects, would contain two Europeans, two Asians and two Africans from each Territory. Such parity with Asians and Africans was an idea which Europeans in Kenya regarded as both dangerous and degrading. The Paper was published under a Labour Government, but Mitchell had discussed his ideas a year earlier with Colonel Oliver Stanley, a Conservative Secretary of State for the Colonies, and with his Parliamentary Under-Secretary of State, the Duke of Devonshire, and he found that "it plainly made a very good impression on Stanley".[39] And Stanley said afterwards that he was largely responsible for the main lines of the proposals.[40]

The long run of Conservative Governments in Britain before the War had been advantageous to the European settlers, because the settler lobby in Conservative quarters at Westminster was strong, and the settlers also profited from their key position in the economy of Kenya. Labour victories after the War were welcomed by Africans, but in the end it was a Conservative Government which granted independence in 1963 and a Labour Government which agreed that Paper 191, which was welcomed by the Africans and had been approved in principle by a Conservative Secretary of State, should be cancelled and replaced by Paper 210, which was applauded by the Europeans and condemned in the strongest terms by the Africans.

Paper 210 gave the Europeans an extra seat by providing for the
selection of a member by the whole Council. At that time the choice
would undoubtedly have fallen on a European and the Africans
saw in this provision a scheme to give the Europeans a permanent
majority. "Two ten", as it was called, became "a term of abuse
among Kenya Africans".[41] Neither the Africans nor the Europeans
appreciated that in time African representation in Legislative
Council would increase and that the picture would be very different
one day. Creech Jones and Mitchell in fact wanted then and there
to increase the number of Africans in Legislative Council.[42] This was
probably not publicly known but, when in April 1947 Mitchell
published his Despatch, Number 44, in which he proposed a reorganisation of the Government which would give an Unofficial
majority in Legislative Council, the *East African Standard* saw
what the future had in store. As the Africans advanced educationally
and economically, a leading article pointed out, their progress
would "require an ever-increasing ratio of representation", and in the
end the European community would become "constitutionally a
racial minority".[43] Pressure from without and violence within
accelerated the process, but the course was clearly set in 1947.

National Registration by Finger-Printing

Since 1919 all Africans had been compelled to carry an
identification card, called the *Kipande*, at all times when they were
not in an African Reserve. None were exempt and the better educated
Africans naturally regarded this obligation as a humiliation and
as discriminatory, because it was a form of identification peculiar
to Africans. At last in March 1947 the Government gave preliminary
consideration to a report on the subject, which recommended that
the *Kipande* should be replaced by a national registration system.[44]
Among illiterate people finger-printing is the best, possibly the
only efficient, means of identification and the European Elected
Members supported the Chief Native Commissioner when he asked
that everyone in Kenya should be registered in that way. "I submit",
he said, "that if the registration is non-racial, the identification
must be non-racial".[45] All Members voted for the Bill, which was
then introduced, with the exception of the Indians who said that
finger-printing would be "a source of irritation to the great majority
of the Europeans and Asians living in this country".[46]

The Europeans in Kenya accepted the idea of universal registration by finger-printing until a lawyer in Nairobi, a certain W. T. Shapley, founded a society, called the Society of Civil Liberties, to oppose the registration of Europeans in that way. Public meetings were held all over the country and a violent correspondence was started in the Press. Some of the most hysterical outbursts came from post-war immigrants, like one who painted a lurid picture of Europeans being hauled off to police stations and subjected to treatment made infamous in Europe by the Gestapo.[47] A few weeks later a "Not So New Settler" wrote to point out that this violent new settler should remember that there were differences between Kenya and Britain and that he should not forget that he had come to "a colony of mixed races" and that he ought to learn something about "the background of registration in the country to which he had chosen to come".[48]

In response to pressure in the constituencies the European Elected Members began to waver. Two of Blundell's constituents wrote to him to say that "the people who are *for* finger-printing remain too silent" and "trouble is they are not so assertive and clamorous as the others".[49] Right up to the eve of Independence the extent of moderate and progressive European opinion was obscured by the vociferousness of the reactionaries. Legislative Council became the scene of bitter debates of a racial character.

Some Europeans became childishly insulting on many occasions. After Eliud Mathu's long struggle to have the *Kipande* abolished, for example, had been successfully concluded his fellow members in Legislative Council, European and Asian alike, offered him their congratulations. In his speech of thanks he told them that he had received an anonymous letter from someone in Nanyuki. Had the writer given his name and address, Mathu said, "I would have invited him to my place for a cup of tea." The letter was in the form of a limerick.

"There's a nigger called Mathu, they say,
"Who mutters in Leg. Co. all day!
   "I'm the black son of Ham,
   "But God knows *who* I am,
   "Since they've taken my *Kipande* away."

Mathu's polished and witty speech was a fitting answer.[50] Finally all the European Elected Members, except Erskine, voted against compulsory finger-printing and for an amendment which provided an alternative for the literate, while the African and Asian Unofficials

and Erskine voted for the Bill. The result was ten Unofficial votes
for and ten Unofficial votes against an amendment. The Government,
which had no wish to change the universality of finger-printing as a
means of identification, therefore decided to leave the Ordinance
unaltered, and another debate, ranking with those which Mitchell
described, as "racial dog fights",[51] followed. In fact, large numbers
of Europeans registered willingly and not long afterwards the
Emergency was declared and new regulations had to be issued. The
episode showed how possible it was for a European pressure group
to persuade the European Elected Members to change their minds
even in face of their principles and how strong the European feeling
was that other races were of secondary value.

There were many Europeans to whom "the people of Kenya"
meant the European residents unless otherwise qualified. The
Governor understood why the Europeans made the debate so bitter.
He wrote in his Diary that "all there is to it is indignation that
Government should have turned down the European Elected
Group".[52] The Electors' Union passed a resolution, with which the
Elected Members agreed, that "the Government of Kenya by its
action in overriding the decision of Legislative Council expressed
by a clear majority in regard to the Glancy Report on the Registration of Persons Ordinance has proved to all people of good will
and sincerity that the present system of Government is neither
workable, tenable nor acceptable and is one in which no fair minded
person can retain any confidence".[53] To those racially minded
Europeans the nine black and brown faces on the Unofficial benches
were mentally invisible and only Derek Erskine was seen by them
as being in opposition. The same sort of mental blindness was shown
in 1952 when Chief Inspector Tamason arap Barmalel became the
first African to be in charge of a police station in the White Highlands. At Koru Europeans would go into his office, see him in his
Inspector's uniform and ask, "Is there anybody here?". After a
while, however, when it was realised that he knew the law and the
regulations well and that he was both firm and courteous, he was
treated exactly as they had treated his European predecessors.[54]
It was through practical experience that racial prejudice was gradually overcome among an increasing number of the Europeans of
Kenya.

Signs of Liberal Thought

That would take time. Politics in the late nineteen forties were strongly racial and frequently bitter. Politicians had to have regard to their electorates, on whose votes they would depend at the next election. But the careful observer could detect signs of a new outlook among some Europeans, indications that the electorate, and so the politicians, would come to be divided into die-hards and progressives. In 1946, immediately after the end of the War, Donald Purves, a settler at Njoro, thought that there were many Europeans "who are already doing much and are anxious to do more for the uplift of the African, so that he may eventually play his full part as a partner in the cultural life, administration and development of Kenya:"[55] and scattered about the White Highlands were men and women who had a sense of responsibility for the development of the Africans, not because they were Africans, but because they were fellow human beings. The existence of a new spirit of goodwill was noticed by C. E. (later Sir Charles) Mortimer, the Commissioner for Local Government, Lands and Settlement. "Never before in my twenty years in Kenya," he told the Nairobi Rotary Club in 1944, "have I found so much good feeling towards Africans as exists today. There is a new spirit abroad amongst the settlers of Kenya. I would like to stress the importance of this spirit of co-operation between African and European for their mutual good and the benefit of the country as a whole."[56] It is perhaps significant that this speech was reported in the first number of *The Kenya Guardian*, the official magazine of the Electors' Union.

As education produced its effect among Africans, the younger Africans quickly made their mark in the cultural life of the Colony. Gregory Maloba became the best sculptor in Kenya, African teams competed successfully in the national Drama Festival, and African artists, mainly trained in the Art School at Makerere, which Mrs. Margaret Trowell had developed, became recognised in Nairobi. Two years after Purves wrote this letter the first Africans were admitted into the officer grades of the Administration and, earlier, the removal of discriminatory restrictions led to economic developments such as the production of high quality coffee and tea grown by Africans. In all these activities European help and encouragement were of the greatest value, not only the help provided by civil servants, like the officers of the Agricultural Department, but the interest shown here and there by individual European farmers and townspeople. In 1946 their number was small but "mony a mickle mak's a muckle" or, as the Swahili proverb says, *"chembe na chembe ni mkati"* (a crumb and a crumb is a loaf), and, as Africans increasingly showed what they were capable of doing, refusal to recognise their progress became more and more unrealistic. Then some Europeans became willing to regard Africans and Asians as partners in Kenya, but the majority of the small European community were still unwilling to share their privileges and were afraid that their way of life would be diluted by outside influences. They feared that, if their small community surrendered its exclusiveness, it would be unable to retain its character and deluded themselves into believing that legal enactments would give them security in their isolation.

European Attitudes in Different Areas

Philip Mason in the Burge Memorial Lecture in 1960 remarked that "it is easier to be tolerant if you feel safe".[57] The long-established settlers in the Rift Valley, who had mellowed over the years, had become prosperous and could afford to be liberal. Looking back over the period of the nineteen fifties, Blundell estimated that throughout the Rift Valley as a whole about three fifths of the farmers were increasingly willing to accept liberal change, although around Kitale the die-hard element was preponderant. East of Nairobi in the Ukamba constituency near Machakos there was a large liberal element. Many of the estates there were of great size, as was necessary in a district with low rainfall, and excellent relations existed between many of the settlers and the Africans in the adjoining Reserve.

In parts of the areas of Kiambu and Ruiru near Nairobi, there were many flourishing European coffee estates. There were European farmers there with a liberal attitude of mind, who had got to know the African Chiefs in the nearby Kikuyu Reserve and entertained them to tea in their homes. These settlers and Chiefs used to meet together to discuss wages and conditions on the coffee estates. Meetings were held twice a year with the Chiefs, who normally each brought six men with him to discuss any problems connected with the estates.[58] These settlers gave an ambulance to the Reserve and some took an interest in the welfare of the African peasantry, A similar situation existed on the eastern boundary of the Uasin Gishu adjoining the Elgeyo Reserve on the rim of the Rift Valley

near Eldoret, where an Elgeyo farmer, Kite arap Tiren, had developed an excellent farm with a tractor, his success being due to the
advice given to him by two European farmers at Moiben, Mr. A.
Wright and Mr. J. Few. Mr. Wright showed continuous interest in
his Elgeyo neighbour and a very happy relationship existed between
them and continued after Independence. The Report of the Royal
Commission of 1953–1955 noticed the situation at Machakos,
where the committee set up by some of the settlers to help the
Kamba farmers was appreciated by the Africans, who said that the
Europeans "were of real help to them", and it mentioned a European
settler at Mbulu in Tanganyika who lent farm machinery to his
African neighbours, who "welcomed the help of this particular man
because his competence as a farmer and his attitude of interest in
helping them forward was already well known to them". Such
examples, said the Report "can be matched all over East Africa".
The Commission believed that "few matters can be more important
than the stimulation of a public spirit of co-operation", and they
went on to enunciate one of the basic facts of the history of East
Africa in the period between the War and Independence. Co-
operation, they said, "must have its origin in the seed of personal
behaviour".[59] Unless account is taken of the work and influence of
individuals, the history of Kenya in these years cannot be fully
understood.

The farmers of Ruiru and Moiben lived adjoining or near the
African Reserves. It was indeed only settlers whose farms lay near
the edges of the White Highlands who had much opportunity of
meeting the leading Africans in the Reserves, but over the country
as a whole only a few of them took any active interest in the welfare
of the African peasantry nearby. For European farmers who lived
far from the Reserves contact with the African areas from which
their farm workers were drawn was impossible.

In the Nyeri District the atmosphere was far less happy than at
Ruiru, Moiben and Machakos, and for several years before the
Mau Mau outbreak farmers were considering the possibility of a
Kikuyu rising. As early as 1950 the strategy to be adopted by the
Kenya Police Reserve, if the Kikuyu decided to invade the European
farms, was discussed at settlers' meetings. At one such meeting, held
in the polo club at Mweiga, it was agreed that the wives and children
should be left on the farms while the husbands defended the various
bridges and roads. A visitor, who was present at the meeting,

suggested that the only constructive course was for the settlers to begin as soon as possible to win the goodwill of their African neighbours and to help them to become more prosperous and happier in their conditions of living: in short, to engage in the kind of social work which would be normal if rich and poor were not distinguished by being white and black. The settlers expressed agreement with his views as long term policy; but fishing in the Gura, Sagana and other rivers remained the only activity in which they engaged in the African Reserve.[60] The District Commissioner at Nyeri, whose District of Kikuyu Reserve marched with the European farms, came to the same conclusion about the settlers there. "I do not think one settler in a hundred", he wrote, "had set foot in the Reserve. They had gone through to Nairobi on the main road and had fished in the Chania and Gura rivers, but I do not think there was one who knew what life and agriculture in the Reserve really meant".[61]

In the West was the Nyanza constituency, which in the early fifties included Kericho and Nandi Hills. In these tea-growing areas the electorate was largely composed of employees of tea companies, who intended to retire on pension in Great Britain. They had no fears about the future of their farms or families, because they had no farms and their children would be educated and usually work in Britain. In Kisumu European businessmen realised that their trade depended mainly on Asians and Africans, because Europeans were few, and so they had to be well behaved towards those whom they needed as clients. Moreover, John Riddoch, the leading businessman in Nyanza, was a man of progressive thought, a friend of Asians and Africans, who exerted a liberal influence on his fellow Europeans. The Coast was far removed from areas of European settlement and emotions arising from alienation of land; and "seaside sanity" was a calmer background than the heights of Molo or the Kinangop. S. V. Cooke was five times elected to Legislative Council by the Europeans of the Coast, but he would probably have been defeated if he had stood for the Trans-Nzoia seat.

Signs of a New Spirit of Co-operation

After the Second World War many Africans began to question what they had previously accepted and some Europeans acquired a new sympathy and understanding. A few were willing to admit that political power would ultimately pass to the Africans, although a communal outlook and a belief that the Europeans could remain the leading community, entrenched in power in an independent Kenya, were still preponderant in European thought in the late forties. Immediately before the War the leader of the European Elected Members found almost all his colleagues indifferent to African needs, but in the years immediately following the War the first stirrings of a new, liberal spirit was seen in European political circles. European officers had served with African soldiers in Abyssinia and South-East Asia. Admiration and friendship had produced a new interest and sympathy in African problems. Major Frank H. Sprott and a few of his friends remembered what they regarded as, "the poor deal which the British Tommy had had after the First World War" and they were determined to try to save the returning African soldiers from suffering in the same way. The problem of employment was particularly difficult, because others had been trained to take their places when they went into the Army and they could only be taken back if these others were dismissed and, as there was no shortage of labour, the danger of unemployment was acute. Sprott and his friends saw that something must be done at once and he decided to go into politics and devote himself especially to African affairs. He founded the African Affairs Committee of the Electors' Union and, although only a few members concerned themselves with this new Committee, none opposed it and it gradually won recognition as an essential part of the European political organisation.

To Sprott colonialism meant "a long-term trusteeship with the obligation that the final stage would be a common roll".[62] Major and Mrs. Sprott had a farm at Karen near Nairobi, carved out of the forest in the early days by Major Sprott's father. No one could regard him as a crank, newly arrived in Kenya and ignorant of the Colony and its races, and the fact that he was able to become a leading figure in the Electors' Union was an indication of the existence after the War of an element of liberalism within the European community. He was a valuable link between European politics and those who were trying to foster a spirit of co-operation and understanding which would influence the makers of political decisions. The speed of African progress was remarkable and no one expected that the trustee would so soon be able to give independence to the ward, but it is significant that the founder of the African

Affairs Committee of the Electors' Union saw in a common roll the ultimate goal of political policy.

Here and there other signs of a new attitude among Europeans were seen—signs of a recognition of African progress and its implications. In August 1946, for example, the Hon. Mrs. Grant, a settler at Njoro, wrote a letter to the *East African Standard*, in which she said:

"I think any one with vision can see that the Africans are going to take an increasingly active part in the administration of the Colony, and it is right that they should. We settlers have got to realise that in future nearly all public offices will be filled by Africans—however distant that future may be."[63]

It is true that few would have expressed such a non-racial view in 1946, but Mrs. Grant was on the Council of Makerere and could see that higher education of Africans would lead to more senior positions in all walks of life. The realists in the post-War period were those who accepted this fact, not those who hoped that European dominance would last for ever.

Effects of a Resident European Community

If there had been more knowledge and understanding on the part of the Imperial trustee and the European community and if the resident Europeans, who claimed a share in trusteeship had not remained so aloof and had not so often had a master-race mentality, many mistakes might have been avoided. An ultimate African majority in Government and administration, however little the European community may have appreciated the fact, was the inevitable goal of trusteeship. In the task of preparing the Africans to hold the highest administrative posts the existence of a settled European population was both an asset and a hindering factor. If there had not been European and Asian communities with considerable education, the Government would have had to rely far more on the African population. The Legislative Council would have contained more African members and Africans would have had to be trained earlier and in greater numbers for responsible work. On the other hand the constant pressure exerted by the Europeans made the Civil Service probably the most efficient in any African colony and so, although African participation was smaller in quantity and later in time than it would otherwise have been, the quality attained was good.

A senior African civil servant said soon after Independence that he thought that the Africans of Kenya were more mature than the Africans of the neighbouring territories and he attributed this to the fact that "so many Europeans had lived among them for so long". It had not been the presence of European settlers in Kenya to which the majority of Africans objected. Their struggle was against European privilege and discrimination, against African exclusion from the White Highlands, against the master-race mentality. After the War there were indications of the existence of a spirit of goodwill and a European awareness, small though it was at first, that the Europeans' future lay in co-operation with the African community, not in a perpetual attempt to remain the master race. The most remarkable fact in the last period of colonial Kenya was the growth of a spirit of inter-racial goodwill. It was not due to chance but was the result of conscious effort, in which many agencies and individuals played a part.

1. L.C.D., 3 Jan. 1945, col. 428.
2. Kenneth Robinson: *The Dilemmas Of Trusteeship*, pp. 85-6.
3. e.g. Y. P. Ghai and J. P. W. B. McAuslan: *Public law and Political Change in Kenya*, p. 173.
4. Ahmed Mohiddin: "An African Approach to Democracy", *East Africa Journal*, February 1970, vol. VII, No. 2, p.7.
5. Ruth First: *Barrel of a Gun*, p. 46.
6. Ahmed Mohiddin: "Sessional Paper No. 10. Revisited", *East Africa Journal*, March 1969, vol. VI, No. 3.
7. Ahmed Mohiddin: "An African Approach to Democracy", op. cit. p. 7.
8. Sir Philip Mitchell: *African Afterthoughts*, p. 275.
9. L.C.D. 22 Oct. 1946, col. 15.
10. Sir Philip Mitchell's Diary, 31 Dec. 1951.
11. ibid, 20 Aug. 1946.
12. ibid, 31 Dec. 1950.
13. ibid, 3 Apr. 1946.
14. e.g. L.C.D. on 9 Jan. 1945.
15. Letter from Provincial Agricultural Officer, E.A.S., 17 Apr. 1953.
16. Cf. *The Earl of Portsmouth:* A Knot of Roots, p. 262.
17. Fabian Colonial Bureau: *An Opportunity in Kenya*, p. 12.
18. This was exactly what the Carpenter Report (*Report of the Committee on African Wages*) found seven years later to be a general condition of African urban conditions.
19. H. C. Trowell, M.D., F.R.C.P.: "Medical Examination of 500 African Railway Workers", *East African Medical Journal*, Vol. XXV, No. 6, June, 1948.
20. Sir Philip Mitchell's Diary, 3 June 1951.
21. ibid, 25 Jan. 1952.
22. L.C.D., 8 Jan. 1948, col. 686.
23. T. G. Askwith, Commissioner for Community Development: *The Problem of Youth*, June 1952, p. 2.
24. L. P. Mair: *Native Policies in Africa*, p. 139.

25. Nandi District: Political Records, vol. I Section 1. Year 1907–1908, p. 17 File DC/NDI/3/1 in Kenya National Archives.
26. All quotations from Nandi District: Political Records, Vol. I DC/NDI/3/1.
27. Annual Report for 1939. DC/NDI/1/4.
28. The DC concerned to R. A. Frost in 1950.
29. Handing over Notes: T. Hughes-Rice to G. Gamble, Nyeri District, 15 Feb. 1951, File DC/NYI/2/1 in Kenya National Archives.
30. Report by R. A. Frost, August 1950, Frost papers.
31. Annual Report 1951, Naivasha District, Nakuru Division, written by E. E. C. Russell, D.O. Naivasha. ADM/15/1, Kenya National Archives.
32. Major (later Sir) Ferdinand Cavendish-Bentinck, heir presumptive to the Dukedom of Portland, was the European Elected Members' Secretary and Whip in the thirties and in 1934 "he managed to organise them effectively for the first time". (George Bennett: *Kenya a Political History*, p. 85). He became the champion of the Europeans who disliked the moderation of Lord Francis Scott. Mitchell called him in the thirties "a rather Bolshy politician", presumably because he did not toe the Government line. (Diary, 2 July 1936).
33. L.C.D. 20 July 1945, col. 184.
34. Sir Philip Mitchell's Diary, 19 Jan. 1945.
35. ibid, 22 Dec. 1944.
36. ibid, 25 July 1945.
37. L.C.D. 10 Jan. 1950, col. 741.
38. *Inter Territorial Organisation in East Africa. Colonial 191.*
39. Sir Philip Mitchell's Diary, 29 Nov. 1944.
40. H.C.D. vol. 425, col. 267, 9 July 1946.
41. Carl G. Rosberg and John Nottingham: *The Myth of Mau Mau: Nationalism in Kenya*, p. 222.
42. Sir Philip Mitchell's Diary, 21 July 1946.
43. E.A.S. 4 Apr. 1947.
44. Sir Philip Mitchell's Diary, 14 Mar. 1947. Dr. L. P. Mair saw the main purpose of the *Kipande* as being to facilitate the "tracing of deserters under contract" (*Native Policies in Africa*, p. 89).
45. L.C.D. 24 July 1947, col. 122.
46. ibid, 24 July 1947, col. 130.
47. E.A.S. 11 Mar. 1949.
48. ibid, 1 Apr. 1949.
49. A. B. Sysdorff and T. H. Chettle to Blundell, May 1949: Blundell 9/1.
50. L.C.D., 24 July 1947, col. 133.
51. Sir Philip Mitchell's Diary, 10 July 1946.
52. ibid, 16 Feb. 1951.
53. European Elected Members Organisation, Minutes of Meeting, 9 Feb. 1951, Blundell 14/1. The Glancy Report was *The Report of a Commission of Enquiry Appointed to Review the Registration of Persons Ordinance, 1947, and to Make Recommendations for any Amendments to the Ordinance that he may consider Necessary or Desirable. (Sir B. J. Glancy, Commissioner).*
54. Information given by Tamason arap Barmalel in 1952 and confirmed in an interview in 1970. He is now a Member of Parliament.
55. Donald Purves to Sir Angus Gillan, Controller of the Empire Division of the British Council: British Council Headquarters file EA/8/1.
56. *The Kenya Guardian*, No. 1 May 1944.
57. Philip Mason: *Race Relations in Africa*, the Burge Memorial Lecture, delivered at Church House, Westminster, 31 Mar. 1960, S.C.M. Press, London.
58. Interview with C. V. Merrett of Ruiru 12 Apr. 1970.
59. *East Africa Royal Commission 1953–1955. Report (cmd. 9475)* p. 381, para. 3.
60. Information in a report written by R. A. Frost, Frost papers. The visitor was Wallace Chisholm of the British Council.
61. O. E. B. Hughes: *Memorandum on Nyeri District, 1949–1952.* A copy

is in the Frost papers.
62. Interview with Major F. H. Sprott, 20 Feb. 1970.
63. E.A.S. 16 Aug. 1946.

3

ATTEMPTS TO PROMOTE INTER-RACIAL CO-OPERATION AFTER THE WAR

A Conference on Race Relations

Immediately after the end of the War people in both official and unofficial positions felt that it would be important in the post-War Kenya to study race relations and understand the changes which would result from wartime experiences. Among them were the new Governor, Sir Philip Mitchell, C. E. Mortimer, the Commissioner for Local Government, Sir Geoffrey Northcote, a former Governor of Hong Kong, who had retired to Kenya and had organised the Government Information Services during the War, Major Frank Sprott and Mrs. Olga Watkins, the European Elected Member for Kiambu in Legislative Council. They realised that the War would have important effects and that relations between the races would be affected by the experiences of Africans who had served overseas or had had contact with Europeans in Kenya itself on more equal terms than anything experienced before the War. Dr. Reinhallt-Jones, the founder and Director of the South African Institute of Race Relations, was asked to visit Kenya and to describe the work of his Institute to a Conference which was held in Nairobi in August, 1946. Among others who attended were the two African members of the Nairobi Municipal Council, Muchochi Gikonyo and Francis Khamisi. A resolution advocating the immediate formation of an Institute of Race Relations in Nairobi was passed unanimously,[1] and in a Communication from the Chair in Legislative Council in October the Governor said that he welcomed the proposal in view of the concern felt by the Government at "an apparent deterioration in relations between the various races in the Colony".[2] Only two years earlier Mortimer had told the Nairobi Rotary Club that a new spirit of goodwill and "co-operation between African and European" was to be seen. In 1946, however, there was "an apparent deterioration in relations". Wartime experiences had caused Africans to question the state of race relations in Kenya and the bases of

European privilege; unemployment was found where a golden future had been expected; and the rigidity of salary differences between the races injured relations between the better educated and the Government.

The work of the South African Institute, which Dr. Reinhallt-Jones described to the Conference in Nairobi, was concerned with "the collection and dissemination of factual information on the non-Europeans"[3] and with creating opportunities for inter-racial meeting as in the Durban International Club. Both types of activity were needed in Kenya. Political power was in European hands, but few Europeans had any real knowledge of the customary thought and background of the Africans or of the hopes and aims of the new elite and the older political leaders. Africans wanted more responsibility, but Europeans were apt to think that they really wanted to get rid of the immigrant races. The Indians were uncertain about their position and their future and were themselves divided into sub-communities with a great variety of background and outlook. The European electorate, who were politically the most powerful section of the population, controlled the policies of their representatives, but their politics were based on prejudice and communal selfishness rather than on authoritative understanding of the complicated problems of a plural society. Power had enabled the Europeans to be socially exclusive. They needed the work of the other races but not their company. For them inter-racial co-operation demanded the relinquishment of a position of privilege. They were required to give what the other races were anxious to take. Knowledge was required, but the individual elector had no means of acquiring it and the small staff of the Electors' Union, although more progressive and realistic than the majority of the electorate, was not large enough to undertake scientific studies of the other races, which would supply the information required for the construction of wise policies.

An Institute of Race Relations could have supplied some of the information needed by undertaking factual studies, publishing pamphlets and providing speakers. Its Director could have tried to get unbiased information studies by the higher ranges of the Administration in Nairobi, whose sources in the provinces at times suffered from Service bias. Such an Institute could perhaps have acted as a link between the African and Asian politicians and the Government and the European Elected Members; but, although the

Conference had unanimously accepted the proposal to found an
Institute of Race Relations and the Governor had welcomed it, an
Institute was not formed. Instead the United Kenya Club, an
unofficial venture, was founded and the Colonial Office advised
the provision of "primarily cultural facilities".

The United Kenya Club

The United Kenya Club was the first voluntary association
providing facilities for social mixing on equal terms by members of
the different races. The founders of the Club,[4] wanted to provide a
place where they and other people could meet as friends in a town
where no other meeting place was available. The Club house was a
rather dilapidated wooden building in Whitehouse Road (later
Haile Salassie Avenue) with two rooms and a kitchen. Dr. Mary
Parker, who visited Nairobi in 1950 wrote about the Club with
sympathy but failed to see beneath the statistical surface. ". . . so
far as I could discern", she wrote, "its active membership is limited to
Government and Municipal European employees more specifically
concerned with African affairs, one Asian Government employee
in the Social Welfare Department, a number of Asiatics of a political
turn of mind, a few philanthropic idealists both European and
Asian, and finally a number of educated Africans mostly in Government, Municipal or British Council employ".[5] As there were few
educated Africans at that time who were not in Government employment, most of the African members of the Club were Government
servants, but three prominent African members were journalists and
several were in business, and all the Europeans were practical people,
among whom there were not the "philanthropic idealists" whom
Mary Parker thought she saw. The Asians were no more of "a
political turn of mind" than most educated people and the European
Government servants were all people of standing with a wide circle
of friends among the settler and business communities whom they
were likely to influence. The weekly lunches with a speaker had some
value but more valuable were the smaller daily lunches, when a
few members of each race met each other as friends.

In 1952 the Club moved to a building designed for it on Hospital
Hill. These better premises attracted a greater number of Asians and
the Club became more and more an Asian Social Club with a large
weekly lunch meeting, at which speakers, often distinguished
speakers, addressed an audience composed of Europeans, Asians

and a few Africans; but it was not unusual to see African residents, for whom lunch each day was covered by their weekly payment, leave before the talk. From the African point of view the value of these weekly lunches lay in the provision of a platform for leading Africans like Tom Mboya, where they could address senior Europeans and Asians, many of whom would have been less likely to attend lunch meetings in the simple wooden Club building in Whitehouse Road. In the middle and later fifties the new Club was almost the only place in which such Africans could put across their point of view. The Club continued to fulfil a useful purpose, but it became something different from the Club of the Whitehouse Road days. Then it was the only place where members of the various races could meet together as equals in surroundings which were adequate for the Europeans who wanted to go there but not economically embarrassing to the Africans and where friendships were made which have lasted up to the present time. But, even then, it was felt that the African membership was disappointingly small. One of the main reasons for this was that Africans "were diffident about meeting members of the other races whose economic position [was] so much higher than theirs".[6]

The British Council

On 20th September, 1946, the Governor wrote to the Director of the British Council in London to say that, when Creech Jones was in Kenya earlier that year, they had discussed the possibility of the British Council starting work in the Colony.[7] The Colonial Office had also written to the British Council in September to say that Creech Jones was impressed by the urgency of establishing an Institute "to provide cultural facilities and promote inter-racial understanding". The Colonial Office appreciated "the urgent need for developing improved race relations" and thought that this could best be tackled through an organisation which "would aim in the first place at establishing primarily cultural facilities".[8] The requests received from the Governor and the Colonial Office were quickly acted on and a Representative of the council, Richard Frost, landed at Mombasa on 23rd May 1947. His instructions were simple. He was told that the Secretary of State wanted a Cultural Centre and National Theatre established in Nairobi, where there was at that time no place other than the United Kenya Club where educated members of the different races could meet, and that he was to see what the British Council could do in East Africa.

The Kenya National Theatre

The Kenya National Theatre was the first national theatre to be built in the Commonwealth. It was the first part of a Cultural Centre and was officially opened by the actor, Sir Ralph Richardson, in November 1952, but the Emergency prevented the rest of the Centre from being financed and built till some years later. In 1947 a campaign was being organised, and some money had already been raised, by the European National Theatre Movement Trustees for the building of a theatre. This would have been a purely European affair and would probably have led to a similar venture being undertaken by the Asians. To the surprise of everybody one society after another agreed to join together in a common enterprise. There was to be no interference with the internal policy of any society. Multi-racial societies or societies confined to a single race would all be welcome, but their representatives would all have to sit together round a common committee table and the theatre and other buildings would be open to all on a basis of cultural standards alone. It was possible as early as December 1947 to ask the Governor to appoint an inter-racial committee "to make definite plans for this project", and Brigadier-General Sir Godfrey Rhodes accepted the position of Chairman.[9] In July 1948 the British Council Representative went to London and gave an account of progress to Andrew (later Sir Andrew) Cohen, who at that time was head of the African Department of the Colonial Office, and to Creech Jones, the Secretary of State. He returned to Kenya with a promise of £50,000 from the Colonial Development and Welfare Fund for building a theatre, after which money was to be raised locally for a Cultural Centre. Creech Jones promised to go personally, if necessary, to Sir Stafford Cripps, the Chancellor of the Exchequer, to obtain the money. The Governor wrote several despatches, Creech Jones did have to ask the Chancellor of the Exchequer personally for the grant, but the promise was kept.[10]

After Independence Ezekiel Mphahlele, a distinguished South African writer, who had founded the Chemchemi Cultural Centre in Nairobi, upbraided the original organisers of the Cultural Centre for siting it where they did. It was too far, he maintained, from the "working class" areas of the City.[11] This criticism failed to understand the basis of the work done in previous years to improve race relations. The National Theatre was built where it was built because those who planned the scheme, including Thornly Dyer, the architect who designed the Parliament Building and conceived the master plan for Nairobi, wanted to build the National Theatre in the "snob" centre of Nairobi. The instruction given by the Secretary of State to the British Council Representative was to build a National Theatre and Cultural Centre where people of culture and position could meet. At that time no Africans were able to live anywhere near the site which was selected, but that site was chosen because it was hoped that in due time the residential *apartheid* would be brought to an end and Muthaiga, Westlands, the Hill and other areas, which were then open only to Europeans, would become districts where leading people of all races would live. As it was not to be a 'working class' theatre, it was built in the middle of 'well-to-do' Nairobi. It was hoped that the Centre would be the headquarters of drama and music and that from there the arts would be taken out to other districts. 'People's theatres' could be established elsewhere, but the National Theatre and Cultural Centre were to be at the centre of Nairobi.

Under the terms of the Charter, which was the work of Sir Philip Mitchell, any society or institution, which was not political, could be affiliated to the Cultural Centre and have a representative on the Board of Management, if the Governing Council regarded it as of a sufficiently high standard. Quality alone was to be the determining factor. Race and colour had no part in it whatsoever. The British Council offered to act as Honorary Secretaries and continued to do so till two years after Independence.[12]

The East Africa Conservatoire of Music

When the Cultural Centre was built, it provided offices, teaching and practice rooms, and a concert hall for the East Africa Conservatoire of Music and other performers, and the Conservatoire was able to move from the wooden huts which it occupied in Kirk Road. Dr. J. R. Gregory, a medical practitioner, a man always devoted to public service and at one time Mayor of Nairobi, was the first Chairman of the Conservatoire and was annually re-elected to that office. The date of the founding of the Conservatoire was due to the fact that a Polish violinist, Dr. B. Fruhling, was living in Nairobi at that time and was available to teach the violin. When it was founded in 1944 its first pupil was a Goan.[13] He was quickly followed by a number of Europeans and in 1950 two Africans were enrolled, one for piano and one for singing. Other Africans soon applied to be enrolled, but most were not able to pay the fees. The British Council came to the rescue when the Representative persuaded his Headquarters to take the unprecedented step of allocating a small sum of money for the provision of bursaries, not for study in Britain, but for paying fees at the Conservatoire in Nairobi. The Conservatoire's Articles of Association required it to function on strictly non-racial lines and when Nat Kofsky arrived from Cape Town as Director in 1951, he found African, Asian and European students playing together in the students' concert. "This, I believe", he wrote later, "to be perhaps the Conservatoire's greatest contribution to the Kenya of today".[14]

Inter-racial Concerts

In December 1947 the British Council organised the first public concerts at which Europeans and Africans appeared in the same programme. As the *East African Standard* explained to its readers, the object was "to encourage music among the Africans" and "to bring Europeans and Africans together on a cultural basis".[15] Two concerts were held during the weekend before Christmas, one in the Hall in the Kaloleni location and one in the Memorial Hall in Pumwani. The choir of the African Boys' School at Kisii, who had won the inter-schools choral competition in Nyanza, were brought to Nairobi and the African choir of St. Austin's Mission in Nairobi was joined by the Director of the East Africa Conservatoire of Music and other European musicians. The audience too was composed of Africans and Europeans. The *East African Standard* commented very favourably on the performance of the Kisii choir which "reached an unexpectedly high level of quality".[16] They stayed at the European Prince of Wales School as the guests of Mr. Philip Fletcher, the Headmaster. The boys of the School were away on holiday. Even so, the Headmaster felt that it would be unwise to put the African boys in a dormitory and they slept in the gymnasium. He put the two African masters in a prefect's study, but an Afrikaner master, who was still in residence, protested so strongly that the Headmaster felt it wise to move the two African masters to the gymnasium. He could not ignore the Parents Committee, which contained members who were bitterly opposed to any sort of mixing with boys of other races. One of them heard that the Headmaster had wanted to accommodate two African masters in a prefect's study and strongly upheld the protest made by the junior master. "Don't you realise, Mr. Fletcher", she said, "that they might have brought all sorts of terrible diseases into the school?"[17] Even to have them in the gymnasium was a bold step, but boldness was needed to overcome prejudice.

Three years later, when Sir John Russell, an eminent agricultural scientist, was in Kenya on a lecture tour organised by the British Council, he gave a number of lectures to inter-racial audiences, including one in the hall of the Kenya High School, which at that time was in fact a European Girls High School, in Nairobi, where the audience was composed of boys and girls from the senior forms of the schools of all three races in and around Nairobi. Miss Janette Stott, the Headmistress, was, like the Headmaster of the Prince of Wales School, a person of liberal views and by 1950 there was sufficient liberal opinion in Kenya to make it possible for her to allow the school hall to be used by an inter-racial audience.[18]

Farming—a Common Interest

Although in the later nineteen forties it was possible for people of all races to join together for musical performances, the Kenya Arts and Crafts Society and the Photographic Society remained exclusively European, mainly because their meetings were to some extent of a social kind. Participation in activities of mutual interest was the basis on which racial prejudice could be overcome. Farming was an activity common to Africans and Europeans alike and it was possible to use it as a means of bringing people of different races together in friendly meetings. In April, 1948, members of the Kitui Local Native Council paid a visit to the large agricultural estate owned by Sir Frank O'B. Wilson near Machakos and found this opportunity of seeing a highly developed farm of great interest and value.[19] It was not a social visit. At about the same time Eliud Mathu, Member of Legislative Council, asked to be allowed to stay with some European farmers to see something of European agriculture, but nothing came of that suggestion.[20] The idea of having an African as a social guest was something which at that time few Europeans would consider.

In 1949 the British Council used a common interest in farming to bring Europeans and Africans together. The Representative invited some leading members of both races, with their wives, to a tea party in the Pumwani Memorial Hall in Nairobi and showed three films on farming and small-holding in England. The films were interspersed by talks given by the Director of Agriculture, the Representative of the British Council and David Waruhiu, the first British Council Bursar from Kenya, who had been studying small-holding work in Devonshire. Among the guests was Major Frank Sprott, who had recently formed the African Affairs Committee of the Electors' Union. He and some other European farmers who were at the party were so much impressed by David Waruhiu's talk that they wrote to the British Council to say that they would like to help African farmers in the Kiambu District. The Representative took them to tea with Chief Magugu at Kamothai in the Gatundu Division, a farmer whose up-to-date methods of rotation on a small acreage had been mentioned in the Department of Agriculture's Report for 1947. From this occasion and on the basis of a common interest a friendly relationship grew up. Chief Magugu visited Major and Mrs. Sprott at Karen and other farmers of both races were drawn into the circle.

Major Sprott was President of the Kenya National Farmers' Union. In 1950 two Kipsigis farmers, Chief arap Tengecha and George arap Belyon, were invited to attend the Union's Conference in Nairobi.[21] Six years later African farmers were allowed to be members of the Union and the *East African Standard* noted with approval the spread of visits between farmers of the two races.[22] This development had been going on steadily since 1950 when the Union urged Europeans to give their help to African farmers and asked the British Council to help the Union's local secretaries to arrange meetings between farmers, as was done, for instance, in 1951 when European farmers in Sotik were put in touch with African chiefs in the neighbouring Kisii Reserve.

In the years after the end of the Second World War the work of building bridges across the chasm which separated the races was based on functional rather than social lines. It was only in the fertile and antagonistic imagination of people like a writer in *Comment* that the builders of bridges provided "tea parties and round games with the intelligentsia",[23] and that much of the time of the British Council was spent in trying to persuade settlers to ask their garden boys to tea or in playing Beethoven to the Masai and teaching Morris dancing to the Nandi. When people with similar interests were brought together to pursue or discuss the subjects in which both were interested, the wide social and economic disparities between the races were forgotten and common interests could help to bring about a realisation of a common humanity. Seeds planted in the late nineteen forties produced plants which were not without value in the campaign to improve race relations in the fifties.

The Royal East African Automobile Association
During this period economic considerations came to the aid of non-racialism. In December 1949 the Royal East African Automobile Association at an extraordinary general meeting decided by a vote of 28 to 4 to admit non-Europeans to membership. In moving the resolution Colonel E. R. La Fontaine said that the main object was a financial one. Although the Association had considerable funds, they were nothing like enough to provide what was needed. "Membership might now be extended to non-Europeans, provided it was done on a selective basis through a balloting committee."[24] Selected Asians were wanted because economically they were on a level where association became possible. In time Africans would be car-owners also and able to join the Association.

Other Attempts to Improve Understanding
In the late nineteen forties and early fifties Government and educationalists became concerned about the intellectual loneliness facing the 'new' Africans, who were returning to Kenya from Makerere and overseas and those others, not quite so well educated, who were leaving secondary schools with success in the School Certificate examination. Frustration and bitterness were likely to follow unless those who became educated were recognised as having reached a higher level than the general mass of Africans and were not "trousered apes" as one European, writing to the *East African Standard*, seemed to believe.[25] P. Wyn Harris, the Chief Native Commissioner, told his colleagues in Legislative Council that "men of goodwill of the three races must resolutely, by example, cultivate good race relations". He stressed that Africans would study in Britain, would "receive a university education" and, unless there was a change from the practices then existing, would be "debarred from the very civilisation which we have taught them to admire and share" and that that would create "great hatred between the races, hatred for which we will be responsible".[26] Two years

after the Chief Native Commissioner made this plea the African
Affairs Committee of the Electors' Union was saying the same thing.
Europeans, they said, must give time to Africans, help African
farmers and get to know those Africans who had been to England
for education. If an African who has been to Britain for education,
they asked, "is to have no further contacts with Europeans on his
return from England, what is he going to do for his cultural
progress"?[27] This plea for establishing social relations with the
new African elite was made only five years after the end of the War.
Before the War it would have been unthinkable. Africans with such
education did not then exist and, even if they had existed, it is
extremely unlikely that any Europeans would have asked them into
their homes; but in 1950 it was possible for the Europeans' political
organisation to ask its members to dispense with the colour bar
where cultural interests made social meeting possible without
being artificial. There were also older, more experienced, though
less academically well educated, Africans who were in public
positions but who had little social contact with any Europeans.
Nevertheless, when the Secretary of State visited East and Central
Africa in 1949, he told the Governor that "the atmosphere of
Nairobi was much better than Salisbury and Lusaka and we had",
wrote Mitchell, "Indians and Africans really taking part in
affairs".[28]

It was a period of contradictory trends. The Administration
and some European politicians were perturbed by an apparent
deterioration in race relations, but at the same time influences
like those generated by the African Affairs Committee of the Electors'
Union, the United Kenya Club, the Churches and various societies
and organisations were beginning to bring leading members of the
different races into touch with each other and so to create a background of understanding and goodwill which was essential for
co-operative political advance.

In 1950, the Dean of Makerere toured Kenya to try to persuade
Europeans to take an interest in the schoolmasters who had been
educated at Makerere and who often felt lonely, because their only
contacts outside school were with Africans much less educated than
themselves. Soon afterwards Mrs. Trowell, the head of the Art
School at Makerere, visited some of the principal schools in Kenya
to discuss instruction in art. She took with her one of her African
Assistants, Joseph (Sam) Ntiro, a Chagga from northern Tanganyika.

They both stayed at Njoro with the Hon. Mrs. Grant, who was a member of the council of Makerere and whose enlightened outlook has already been referred to. While they were staying with Mrs. Grant, Mrs. Trowell was invited to a small cocktail party at the home of Mr. and Mrs. Donald Purvess and to her surprise Ntiro was included in the invitation. A number of settlers were at the party and, when it was over, the host said to Mrs. Trowell, "I am so glad you brought Mr. Ntiro. The Dean of Makerere spoke at the Njoro Club recently about the educated Africans and none of us had ever met one. So when we heard you were bringing one to Mrs. Grant's, we thought we'd hold a party to meet him and see what he was like. We are all astonished. He is charming and so cultured and interesting".[29] Subsequently Joseph Ntiro held a one-man exhibition of paintings at the Piccadilly Gallery in London and became High Commissioner for Tanganyika in the United Kingdom. Mr. Purvess and his friends were not activated by a patronising spirit. They wanted information about African progress and were ready to recognise what they saw. Through such contacts knowledge of change was acquired and passed on to a wider circle.

At about the same time John Dugdale, the Minister of State for the Colonies in the British Government, visited East Africa. "I remember", E. B. Hosking, a former Chief Native Commissioner, wrote in the *Kenya Weekly News* some years later, "that Mr. Dugdale expressed his astonishment to me when he found Africans lunching with the rest of us at an official luncheon given in his honour at Eldoret. None of us had given it a thought as the Africans were Municipal or Legislative Councillors and had as much right there as any of us."[30] Hosking did not mention, however, that an Afrikaner who had been invited to the luncheon, declined the invitation because he refused to sit down, as he said, with "Kaffirs and Indians".[31] Those Europeans who wanted to meet the few Africans who were members of Municipal Councils could do so without difficulty, but most of these were not among the best educated Africans but belonged to an age group who had not had opportunities of acquiring education. It was much more difficult to find occasions for meeting the more highly educated and cultured Africans like Joseph (Sam) Ntiro. Invitations appearing apparently at random would have been received with suspicion. If these men were schoolmasters, the majority would be living and working either in the towns or in the Reserves, far from European farms, and natural opportunities for the settlers to meet them could be few.

Humphrey Slade, who was later to become the elected Speaker of the House of Representatives of independent Kenya, pointed out in 1950 that to overlook the wide cultural differences between the races was only harmful to progress and said that he believed that at that time some discriminatory measures were necessary and beneficial. He cited, for instance, the control of the sale of liquor to Africans and the preservation of Hindu and Moslem laws of marriage and succession. But, with that proviso, he wrote that some people of each race "even now show their capacity to overcome the natural social barrier of colour and to share responsibility with other races".[32] The pity of it was, however, that too few Europeans extended a hand of friendship to those of the other races who had overcome the cultural barriers which divided them.

This was true also in official circles in the Reserves. It was clear to a man like O. E. B. Hughes, who was District Commissioner at Nyeri before and during the earlier stages of the Emergency, that 'European leadership' in the Reserves was a meaningless phrase unless European Government officers in all Departments mixed in a friendly way with Africans. He believed that all the European officers in a District, officers of the Administration, the Agricultural, Education, Medical and other Departments, ought to consider their work as extending beyond their official duties and including friendly contact with the higher grade Africans around them, and he constantly urged them to bring their African colleagues into their circle of friendship. The District Commissioner, however, had no authority over the officers of other Departments. He was the Chairman of a team and, as such, could only ask and try to inspire. Some officers of all Departments were co-operative and genuinely enjoyed friendship with educated members of the other races, but some remained aloof. Sometimes lack of social mixing in the Districts was due to prejudice or social laziness on the European side, but often economic reasons were a bar. R. E. S. Tanner has written about the same difficulty in Tanganyika. "Except for the small group of officials in his own Department, over whom he had direct control [the District Commissioner] was bound to be out-numbered by officials in technical departments, over whom he had no direct control, and yet whose co-operation he had to obtain both for the running of Government business and for the social peace of the Community".[33] The racial salary scales more than anything else made social mixing in Government circles difficult: economically the races were so far apart. Another difficulty was that in the late nineteen forties there were few, very few, educated African women and so it was almost impossible for an African Assistant Officer in any Department to entertain his European colleagues and their wives, while in the case of Asians the pattern of domestic life made such entertainment even more impossible.

An important feature of this period was that many officers of the Administration, some European members of Legislative Council and other politicians, and some Europeans in other walks of life *were* concerned about race relations and were trying to improve them. By doing things together people were beginning to understand each other and overcome prejudice. Although the numbers were small in 1950, there were some Europeans who believed that there could be no happy future for Kenya unless discrimination based on race could be replaced by divergences based on quality and that the leadership, which Africans were willing to concede to Europeans, was not tainted by a master race mentality. Among farmers, businessmen, Government servants, missionaries and leaders of churches were men and women who were working to overcome prejudice and fear and ignorance. The small inter-racial group who, led by the inspiration of W. Kirkaldy-Willis, F.R.C.S., wrote a little book called *His Kingdom in Kenya* under the pseudonym of Adelphoi, may be taken as an example. Politically there was little harmony, but elsewhere there were signs of the growth of inter-racial co-operation and goodwill. In April 1950 a fete was held in Nairobi to raise funds for the Coryndon Museum and Dr. Leakey summed up the spirit of co-operation it evoked by writing to the *East African Standard:*

"Finally may I be allowed to say that I believe that this fete and pageant have provided our City of Nairobi with an outstanding example of the way in which all races and all creeds, all ages and both sexes can co-operate in a common cause whole-heartedly. Not only was I myself struck with the wonderful spirit of inter-racial co-operation and unanimity but numerous visitors including quite a few from outside Kenya said to me how amazed they were at the co-operation between the races which were so evident at this fete".[34]

1. E.A.S. 9 Aug. 1946.
2. L.C.D., 22 Oct. 1946, col. 15.
3. Gwendolen M. Carter: *The Politics of Inequality: South Africa since 1948*. p. 336.
4. Among the founders of the Club were S. V. Cooke, T. C. Colchester, T. G. Askwith, W. Kirkaldy-Willis, Hassan Nathoo and B. M. Gecaga.
5. Mary Parker: *Political and Social Aspects of the Development of Municipal Government in Kenya with Special Reference to Nairobi*, p. 25. (Mimeographed).
6. Richard Frost: 'Nairobi' *The Geographical Magazine*, Nov. 1950, p. 287.
7. British Council Headquarters file, EA/8/1.
8. ibid.
9. Richard A. Frost: *The British Council in East Africa, 1947–48: Two Broadcast Talks*.
10. The inscription on a plaque at the entrance of the Cultural Centre is curiously inaccurate. It reads, "In 1949 it was decided to bring together in one centre all those societies which were interested in music, drama and the arts and which contributed to the cultural life of Kenya. The inspiration behind this idea was the then Governor of Kenya, Sir Philip Mitchell, G.C.M.G., M.C. In 1952 the National Theatre was opened by Sir Ralph Richardson as the first part of the Kenya Cultural Centre." The credit for the idea must certainly go to Sir Philip Mitchell. In 1947 he asked that it should be put into effect and £50,000 for the building of the Theatre was promised by the Secretary of State in 1948.
11. This was referred to in E.A.S., 18 Apr. 1969.
12. A copy of the Charter is in the files at the Cultural Centre.
13. Letter from Dr. Gregory, 6 Apr. 1972, Frost Papers.
14. E.A.S. 27 May 1966.
15. ibid, 19 Dec. 1947.
16. ibid 25 Dec. 1947.
17. Information supplied by Philip Fletcher in December 1947 and confirmed in an interview on 28 Aug. 1969.
18. British Council Annual Report for East Africa, 1950–51.
19. E.A.S. 9 Apr. 1948.
20. ibid, 14 May 1948.
21. ibid, 14 Oct. 1950.
22. ibid, 16 Mar. 1956.
23. *Comment*, No. 9, 12 Nov. 1949.
24. E.A.S. 16 Dec. 1949.
25. ibid, 26 Mar. 1948.
26. L.C.D. 18 Mar. 1948, Cols. 224–225.
27. E.A.S. 16 June 1950.
28. Sir Philip Mitchell's Diary, 14 May 1949.
29. Note dated 4 Sept. 1950, by R. A. Frost, Frost papers.
30. K.W.N. 22 Jan. 1954, p. 22.
31. Report dated 4 Sept. 1950, by R. A. Frost, Frost papers.
32. E.A.S. 22 Sept. 1950.
33. R. E. S. Tanner: 'European Leadership in Small Communities in Tanganyika prior to Independence', *Race*, Vol. VII, No. 3 Jan. 1968.
34. E.A.S. 14 Apr. 1950.

4

NEED FOR GREATER KNOWLEDGE

Inadequacy of Information

Although efforts to bring educated Africans, leading Asians and Europeans into touch with each other and to improve race relations were being consciously made in the late nineteen forties and were to bear fruit in the following decade, distrust was increasing in other directions. This was largely due to lack of knowledge and understanding and sympathetic consideration of African progress and aspirations and to what one District Commissioner described as "the crass ignorance about the Reserves of the settlers and about the Highlands of the Kikuyus".[1] There were also the prevalent lack of courtesy and consideration in human relations, which were a constant source of friction.

Lack of knowledge existed in both Britain and Kenya, and was a hinderance to the best exercise of trusteeship. In Britain there was little knowledge of the extent of liberal opinion in the European community in Kenya. During the War colonial affairs had been discussed in the British Parliament for the most part in a calm atmosphere free from party bitterness, but in the nineteen fifties party political tactics were apt to use colonial affairs for their own ends. Political tactics do not always have regard to impartial appraisal of facts and strict adherence to truth. Misunderstandings arising from lack of correct information were frequently accepted as truth and, because they were believed, had adverse effects on race relations.

Bi-Partisan Agreement in Britain

During the nineteen forties the Labour and Conservative parties in Britain managed to agree to a great extent on the details of colonial policy, but during most of the fifties agreement went little beyond the basic aim of arriving at ultimate self-government. Methods and timing were in dispute and pressure groups and societies outside Parliament aroused interest in colonial affairs along party lines.

The Fabian Colonial Bureau was founded in 1940 and had great influence in Labour circles. The Africa Bureau, the Movement for Colonial Freedom and the National Council for Civil Liberties were also on the Left. Labour courses and conferences also focused attention on colonial affairs. The joint East and Central Africa Board had a Conservative outlook and approached colonial issues from the standpoint of commerce and economic development. It proved impossible to keep colonial matters outside the orbit of party controversy in the fifties as had to a great extent been possible in the forties. Colonial affairs were apt to be used for party political purposes at Westminster and different communities in Kenya believed that their salvation lay in the successes of a particular party at the British elections.

In 1948, during the bi-partisan period, a farmer at Subukia, writing to the Chairman of the Rift Valley Electors' Organisation, referred to "the declared policy of the British Government, and one that has—most unfortunately—been subscribed to by Conservative, Liberal and Socialist, i.e. that we are only in administrative charge of a Territory until such time as the original native inhabitants are considered fit to take over the country's administration for themselves".[2] This was British policy for the future of Kenya although it was envisaged that the full benefits of citizenship would be respected and accorded to all citizens of whatever race they might be, and the writer of this letter realised that, although the different philosophies of the parties could be expected to produce differences in emphasis and timing, its ultimate implementation did not depend on party politics in Britain. In Kenya, however, some Europeans believed that the Labour Party was bent on their liquidation, e.g. "Africa's only hope is the defeat of the Socialists at the next General Election,"[3] and "It is not surprising that Mr. Gordon Walker, Secretary of State for Commonwealth Relations, sees communities such as ours destined to become protected minorities".[4]

In 1951 Oliver Lyttelton, the Secretary of State for the Colonies, said in the House of Commons that "certain broad lines of policy" were accepted by all sections of the House as being above party politics. They had been "clearly stated by former Secretaries of State "from both the main parties". "Two of them", he said "are fundamental. First, we all aim at helping the Colonial Territories to attain self-government within the British Commonwealth. To that end we are seeking as rapidly as possible to build up in each territory the institutions which its circumstances require. Second, we are all determined to pursue the economic and social development of the Colonial Territories so that it keeps pace with their political development".[5] The Conservative party had for a long time been especially concerned with the latter. Indeed, Kenneth Robinson believes that "In colonial affairs the party's main preoccupation was economic development"[6] in the period between the Wars. And an official Conservative statement in 1949, while accepting that self-government was the goal, maintained that "Progress towards self-government must also depend upon economic stability, since no country can be politically independent unless it is also financially independent".[7] The importance of European agriculture in the economy of Kenya made the Conservative Party particularly sympathetic to European settlement. The Labour Party's traditional concern with the condition of the British working class affected its approach to colonial problems, but it too appreciated the need to gear political advance in the colonies to economic progress.[8] Later on, the need for economic advance was appreciated equally fully by African politicians. In 1958, when the attainment of African political power seemed to be quickly coming closer, the African Elected Members of Legislative Council wrote in a document entitled *Our Pledge, Our Goal and Our Constitution*, "We realise that political freedom without economic well-being is like a car without petrol".[9]

The bi-partisan alliance was not easy to maintain. Colonel (later Sir Charles) Ponsonby, Conservative M.P. for Sevenoaks, was one of the Conservatives who backed Oliver Stanley, the Conservative Secretary of State for the Colonies in the National Government, in his attempt to support Creech Jones during Labour's period of office and "keep the Colonies out of party politics". Looking back in 1965 on the events of those years, he wrote that some of the Conservative "die-hards thought that Oliver Stanley went too far in doing this, but in the light of subsequent events I am sure he was right".[10] What J. M. Lee calls "the height of the mood of bi-partisanship"[11] was seen in 1947 when Sir Drummond Shiels, a Labour Party spokesman on colonial affairs, published a pamphlet on *The Colonies Today and To-morrow* and included in it a foreword by Oliver Stanley, the Conservative shadow minister, and Creech Jones, the Labour Secretary of State in office. But, as Creech Jones said ten years later, although the broad aims were shared by both the Labour and Conservative parties there were "differences in

long and short-term policies which cannot be reconciled", because,
as he explained, "each of the political parties has its distinctive
philosophy and they are concerned with its application in public
affairs".[12]

Break-up of the Bi-Partisan Alliance at Westminster

In the fifties party political tactics became more important at
Westminster than calmer methods of discussion on colonial problems
and "from the early fifties onward the element of partisan hostility
was seldom lacking". The Conservative Party had a long run of
office and the Labour Opposition "was glad to put a strain on a
Minister—especially Lyttleton—and used Questions for this purpose.
The Colonial Secretary had to answer as many as 1,000 Questions
a year in the nineteen fifties".[13]

As the bi-partisan alliance of the forties began to break up at
the beginning of the fifties, differences in aim with regard to political
development as well as of timing and method started to appear in a
more pronounced form than hitherto. The value of the larger firms
was appreciated by all parties and to a great extent the Labour
Party continued "to welcome the efforts of individual traders,
planters and farmer-settlers as well, as a means of economic development", as they had done during the bi-partisan period,[14] although
the exclusive "whiteness" of the White Highlands in Kenya aroused
increasing opposition from the Left Wing of the Party. Goldsworthy
concludes that with regard to the colonies in general "Labour
recurrently took the part of indigenous peoples against the Government, white settlers, or both. The arguments used were basically
moral".[15] In the fifties partisan tactics at Westminster found colonial
problems, above all Kenya problems, a useful weapon to use against
their opponents. In 1947 Creech Jones, when Colonial Secretary,
had written "Much of the land in European occupation to-day
was for all practical purposes vacant land when taken up. . . .
The African land problem is less one of the distribution of existing
land . . . than of the use to which the lands are being put. . . . It is
hardly the case that a solution to the Africans' large and complex
problems can be found by individual or communal settlement of
Africans in the highlands marked for European settlement".[16]
An example of the change to political partisan tactics was seen ten
years later when in a Parliamentary Question John Stonehouse asked
"to what extent the Kenya Government now propose to implement

the recommendation of the Royal Commission on Land in East Africa that the Highlands should no longer be subject to exclusive occupation by white settlers but should be available for African farming under proper safeguards"[17] This question had an anti-settler bias, which contrasted with the attitude earlier expressed by Creech Jones, because it omitted part of the Royal Commission's recommendation and gave a false impression of the conclusions reached by Sir Hugh Dow and his colleagues. The Commission recommended the removal of all land barriers and Lennox-Boyd, the Secretary of State, reminded Mr. Stonehouse that in November 1957 he had told the House that "the Royal Commission expressly linked the reservation of African land and the reservation of European land as being two aspects of the same problem of reservation".

Even before colonial affairs were used for party political purpose there had been lack of consistent policy. Mitchell had been alarmed by the recurrent theme appearing in official memoranda of "we cannot control" and "we cannot prevent: ergo", he wrote, "laissez faire. It is high time we injected some strength and decisiveness into our affairs".[18] The lack of firmly consistent policy continued and, looking back on the history of the colonies, he wrote in 1956, "There was no colonial policy, for Secretaries of State changed every eighteen months or so".[19] In Kenya the assertion that party politics in Britain produced lack of decision in the colonies was advanced to support the claim of those Europeans who demanded freedom from the control of the Colonial Office and a Rhodesian type of development. To Mitchell, eight months after his retirement, the solution seemed to lie in stopping "this change of Ministers every 14 months" and in getting "a really good one with ideas; then make up your mind what you want to do, take the initiative and do it".[20] In the year in which Mitchell wrote this the pattern changed. Lyttelton introduced a constitution which opened the door to African and Asian ministerial advance and his successor, Lennox-Boyd, kept Kenya's development on the same course and added a qualitative franchise in place of the nomination of African Members of Legislative Council.

Ignorance in Britain

In spite of the existence of political societies concerned with the colonies there was great ignorance in Britain, and there was no informed public opinion to which the Colonial Office had to answer. Even in such a society as the Royal Institute of International Affairs meetings on colonial subjects were poorly attended and colonial affairs received scant attention in the country as a whole. Some, but only some, appreciated that, as citizens of the trustee country, they had a duty to take an informed interest in the progress of their wards. J. H. Oldham's assertion that "Indifference, when the destinies of a continent are in the balance, is a dereliction of duty"[21] would not have had a wide appeal.

G. K. Evans in a survey written for the Colonial Office in 1948 talked about "the true state—not so much of public knowledge—as of public ignorance" about the colonies and discovered that "nearly three quarters of the population" were "unable to explain the distinction between a Dominion and a Colony". He did conclude, however, that 55 per cent of the British public felt that they had some "personal responsibility for Colonial government" and 62 per cent were "seen to be in favour of our spending money on Colonial development and welfare."[22] Unfortunately with regard to Kenya there was considerable ignorance among members of Parliament also. Even Lyttelton, after he had been Secretary of State for three years, wrote: "As far as we outsiders can judge we have always underrated the volume of decent liberal opinion amongst the Europeans".[23] In the previous year two Labour Members of Parliament, George Brown and Charles Hobson, visited Kenya and were surprised to see people of all races waiting in bus queues and to find that Africans were "conscious of trade union principles";[24] Labour and Conservative alike were ignorant of the increase of moderate and liberal opinion among the European community in Kenya in the middle fifties. This ignorance at Westminster deprived the progressive Europeans of a lead from the trustee and deprived the trustee of the knowledge of how far in a liberal direction initiative from London could go.

The ignorance in Britain of changing attitudes in Kenya might have been lessened if the liberal Europeans in Kenya had had more moral courage and had been willing to face unpopularity with their European neighbours. Some years before hotels were open to Asians and Africans, for instance, Colonel Butt of Ngobit wrote to the *East African Standard* to advocate their being opened and said that he knew that other Europeans felt as he did but would not sign their names on letters to the newspapers. "That is, as I see it," he wrote, "one of the big obstacles to leadership in Kenya. We are many of us frightened of what the other fellow will think or say if we have the courage to speak out what we believe to be right".[25] The less liberal element were less reticent and were more politically minded and happy to attend political meetings. Their letters to the Press and the reports of their utterances at political meetings gave an unbalanced picture of European opinion.

The Implications of Trusteeship

Even before the Second World War there were a few Europeans in Kenya who saw that *some* Africans would rise above the general level. In April 1939 Lord Francis Scott, the Leader of the European Elected Members of Legislative Council, deplored the lack of interest shown by his colleagues in African development. He wrote to S. V. Cooke, the recently elected Member for the Coast, that at a meeting of the Elected Members "no one seemed to want to discuss native affairs, except you, and no one had any constructive ideas to offer". Among other things, he wrote, he thought it was necessary to consider "the position of educated natives".[26] Scott was more liberal than the normal European politician of his day and he was unusual in recognising the emergence of educated Africans as early as 1939.[27] He sympathised with Cooke's liberal views and promised to force the Government "to make a statement of policy in Leg. Co., which", he wrote, "will give you an opportunity of making the points you want".[28] And, when Cooke spent a day with him at his farm at Rongai in July, 1939, they agreed that "a progressive native policy . . . should be a first concern of European Elected Members".[29] Soon afterwards the War broke out and Scott went into the Army and was out of politics till 1943 and then did not return as Leader. He kept his views on African educational development up to date and wrote in 1946, ". . . we must face the fact that as time goes on there will be an increasing number of completely detribalised Africans, who will include a high proportion of educated persons".[30]

Lord Francis Scott was not only a politician with more progressive views than those of most of his contemporaries. He was also a realist and immediately after the War he saw that the hope of perpetual European dominance was no longer tenable. Before the War it seemed to a well qualified observer that "difference in practice between South Africa, Rhodesia and Kenya" was "one of degree rather than of kind",[31] but immediately after the War Scott accepted the fact that a Rhodesian development was impossible for Kenya. "We were born too late", he wrote, "had Kenya been in her present state of development in 1914, undoubtedly we should have had self-government long ago. In the meantime the principle has grown up that subject races must be treated on the same lines as the ruling British race, and it is no good pretending that it is not so".[32]

Four years after the publication of the White Paper containing the Devonshire Declaration of the paramountcy of African interests the Secretary of State announced that the Imperial Government might "be prepared to associate with themselves in that trust the members of the resident immigrant communities", but that the Imperial Government was "still under an obligation to ensure that the principles of this trusteeship will be observed".[33] The European community read into this statement a devolution of authority to themselves and they still thought that they ought to be responsible for what was called "Native Policy" even after another Memorandum from the Secretary of State declared that His Majesty's Government "fully accept the principle that the relation of His Majesty's Government to the native populations in East Africa is one of trusteeship which cannot be devolved, and from which they cannot be relieved. The ultimate responsibility for the exercise of this trusteeship", the Secretary of State continued, "must accordingly rest with them alone".[34]

The presence of a resident, mainly British, European population was of value to the trustee, but any possibility of handing over to them the ultimate responsibility was negatived by the many European political speeches which showed that for most Europeans "trusteeship" meant "control". There was a constant clamour for "freedom" from the control of the Colonial Office and a desire to get rid of "the intervention of the Colonial Office over African problems",[35] but the idea of an ultimate African majority in Legislative Council, in however distant a future, had little or no place in any European political thought until the nineteen fifties. The offer of "sympathetic tutelage", leading eventually to "full participation in the government of this country",[36] did not rouse the hopes of Africans, who read at the same time that some Europeans believed that "the European community had never accepted"[37] the doctrine of the paramountcy of African interests as enunciated in the

Devonshire Declaration of 1923, which the right wing weekly paper, *Comment* described as "the blessed phrase of ambiguous mumbo-jumbo of the late and unlamented Duke of Devonshire".[38]

The exercise of full trusteeship by an advanced and privileged minority on behalf of a less developed majority demands an altruism which it is perhaps unrealistic to expect. It was not from altruistic motives that the European community in the nineteen forties hoped to attain power free from control from London and to declare themselves trustees for the African population. The dilemma attaching to these aims was not always understood, but at times it was admitted as when in a speech to the annual conference of the Electors' Union in 1948 a spokesman for the Rift Valley Electors Organisation made a revealing and astute statement on the responsibilities of trusteeship and their relation to European political aspirations.

"Why then, some of you may ask", he said, "do I not propose that we now demand full self-government in the sense of the right of the elected representatives of the European community to form a Government to rule all Kenya? I do not demand that for one good reason: it means, in practice, a demand for the transfer of the sole responsibility for the exercise of trusteeship. Apart from the fact that I do not believe that at this present time any British Government, of whatever party, would grant such a demand, it would mean that the European community of Kenya would be placed in a position whereby, the more successful the exercise of trusteeship, the sooner would every ethical argument, and all liberal opinion, impel them to hand over more and more power and responsibility to their wards. That is not an enviable lot".[39]

The dilemma became more obvious in subsequent years and at the end of the decade Sir Andrew Cohen, a man of great knowledge and acute observation, wrote that he thought there were "comparatively few Europeans" who "would actually have welcomed being entrusted with the government of the country".[40] The aim of perpetual power and the exercise of trusteeship were incompatible.

In 1947 E. A. (later Sir Ernest) Vasey, Member for Nairobi North in Legislative Council, a leader of liberal European opinion, told the Annual Conference of the Electors' Union that the European population had "only one reason for its presence in the Territories

and that was trusteeship for the African peoples and its determination
to lead . . . and to take the burden of the African and the burden of
trusteeship, which was their only justification for their existence in
this country".[41] Vasey avoided the use of the word "demand" when
he spoke about trusteeship. He said, instead, that trusteeship was
the Europeans' duty, and his political career won for him the trust
of both Africans and Asians.

By the early nineteen fifties many Europeans were beginning to
accept the fact that their hope of perpetual political dominance was
unrealistic, and by 1953 Mervyn Hill, the Editor of the *Kenya Weekly
News*, which was often regarded as the settlers' paper, admitted that a
Rhodesian form of the plural society was no longer possible and
was no longer a matter for practical politics. "The idea of European
self-government", he wrote, "—that is of a government elected by
Europeans but with control over all the country and its peoples—
has died hard in Kenya".[42] It had been replaced by a struggle to
maintain parity of Unofficial European Elected Members with
Unofficial representatives of all other races combined. Mitchell,
the Governor, could not understand why "the Elected Members
and most of their constituents had worked themselves into a passion
over it . . . nor what was achieved by parity".[43] The Electors' Union
stressed the "fundamental demand" of the European community
"to be associated in the trusteeship of the African" and it was
claimed that the "loss of parity would jeopardise their mission
of trusteeship".[44] They still found it hard to believe that assistance
to the Imperial trustee was all they could give. In East Africa
education was beginning to produce an African elite, small though it
was in the late nineteen forties, and in Kenya Mitchell was
a Governor with a knowledge of Africa and a prestige which the
British Government could not easily have disregarded, even if it
had wanted to do so. Creech Jones was Secretary of State, followed
by James Griffiths. Both recognised the contribution which the
resident Europeans could make towards the development of the
African population, but neither would think of relinquishing the
responsibility of trusteeship.

European Ignorance about Africans

The European demand to share in trusteeship was not backed by
knowledge of the Africans for whom the Europeans wished to be
trustee. They often said, "We know the African", but they came into

contact with few Africans except the farm labourers, domestic servants and office boys. A trustee needs knowledge of the thought and background of his ward and an ability to appreciate his aspirations and progress. In Kenya's plural society it was difficult for most Europeans to have any experience of the educational progress of the Africans. In 1945 there were only a handful of Africans with anything approaching the educational standards of the majority of the Europeans living in Kenya and even those few were economically so far below almost all members of the European community that social mixing on anything like equal terms was impossible. Most European farmers had no chance of meeting any Africans other than farm workers and junior clerks, while in the towns economic disparity was an insuperable barrier. The greatest need was for actual face to face meeting. During the years between the end of the War and Independence, behind the turbulence of politics and the violence of Mau Mau, institutions and individuals were working to make such meetings possible.

The fact that Europeans, other than members of Government services and missions, lived in the main only in the White Highlands and Nairobi or far away in Mombasa cut them off from contact with or knowledge of Nyanza where much educational and cultural progress was being made. The northern areas and the plains where the Masai wandered with their herds were hardly touched by education, but ignorance of Nyanza meant that the majority of Europeans were unaware of an important area of African development, while their traditional exclusiveness blinded them to the progress being made in Nairobi and the Central Province also. There were exceptions. Michael Blundell was a politician who knew Nyanza as well as the central area of Kenya and in fact was able to speak the Luo language. He saw that, as he wrote,

"the average European in Kenya considers that he is in a white country in which there are few Africans specially created by God for his own particular purpose. There are very few of them indeed who realise that they are in effect in an enormous African continent in which there are few Europeans who can only survive if they have something to give to the African rather than to take". And he went on to say that what he called the die-hards' "reactionary tramline outlook" would eliminate the European faster than anything else, just as the French aristocracy were eliminated because they would not realise that there was a mass of Frenchmen all around them who had nothing to do with the Almanach Gotha".[45]

It is possible that if an Institute of Race Relations had been established after the conference held in Nairobi in 1946, Government officers, politicians and the European public would have had the opportunity of reading accurate publications about the Africans and Arabs and about the contribution to the economic development of Kenya made by the other immigrant race, the Asians. As the years passed, they might have learned that as early as 1951 the three Rural Deans of the Anglican Church in Nyanza were Africans; they might have heard about the educational progress being made by the other races; they might have noticed that as early as 1952 many of the settlers at Londiani were glad to be treated by the Luo doctor, Dr. Arua, at the local hospital.[46] It would have been possible to show how unwise it was to adhere strictly without exception to the three-fifths rule even in the case of a man like Mbiyu Koinange on his return to Kenya after several years of study overseas. The desire of Africans to have more responsibility in local government could have been explained and suggestions made, such, for instance, as the appointment of African Chairman of Local Native Councils with an ultimate veto reserved to the District Commissioners. But an Institute of Race Relations, which could have undertaken the necessary research and published pamphlets and articles, would have cost money. There would have been little chance of this being raised by voluntary subscriptions and it is unlikely that the "small town politicians", as Mitchell described the European Elected Members,[47] would have voted the necessary money in the Budget. As in the case of the National Theatre the funds would have had to be given by the Imperial Government and there was little chance of that.

Neither the Imperial Government and its representatives, the Kenya Administration, nor the European politicians who claimed a share in trusteeship undertook serious research to understand and publicise the progress being made by Africans. The general mass of Africans were regarded by the resident Europeans primarily as a source of labour and the better educated were either ignored or looked upon as dangerous upstarts. Little contact was made with the Asian communities, even though economically and educationally some Asians were reaching high standards. The European community, though socially divided into many groups within itself, remained exclusively isolated from all others. Little was done to bridge "the gap of ignorance which separates non-white from white".[48]

Mental Isolation of Europeans

Laurence van der Post has pointed out that, although in South Africa the Afrikaners have had intimate contact with "the black and coloured man" for generations, yet in their literature they have not shown any "awareness of him as a human being". He goes on to say that "as a rounded human being in his own individual right" the black man in Afrikaner literature "is as absent as the English working-man from a tea party of Miss Austen's young ladies".[49] The economic and social class consciousness of Jane Austen's young ladies impersonalised the working classes and dismissed them from the thinking of the fortunate occupants of Kellynch Hall and Mansfield Park. It persisted for a century after Jane Austen's days. As late as 1922 Katherine Mansfield was writing of social conditions known to her readers when she published her brilliant short story, "The Garden Party", which shows how social and economic differences robbed the working classes of their humanity in upper class thinking and describes the insuperable difficulty which prevent- ed the child, who did appreciate their humanity, from communicating her understanding to her family. In Kenya in the first half of the 20th century the economic status of most Europeans was as far removed from that of almost all Africans as was the status of "Miss Austen's young ladies" from that of the working classes of her day; and in addition the world-wide feeling of white superiority added an emotional factor to intensify the sense of exclusiveness.

Again and again in Kenya what seemed to be racial discrimination or racial attitudes had social and economic parallels in the history of the western world a century or so earlier. Writing in 1936, Dr. Louis Leakey quoted a letter written by a European to the East African Standard in 1935. ". . . we are being taxed to the uttermost", said the writer, "without having any control whatever of the manner in which the taxes are imposed, this is obviously contrary to the basis of British liberty so firmly expressed in the phrase 'no taxation without representation." Dr. Leakey commented that at that time the European Community of about 16,000 persons was represented by 11 Elected Members in the Legislative Council, while 3,000,000 Africans had only 2 nominated Europeans to express their views.

The 3,000,000 Africans and Indians, wrote Dr. Leakey, "also pay taxes, both direct and indirect, and in proportion to their wealth are probably more heavily taxed than the Europeans".[50] In the circumstances the letter writer's claim that "Such conditions of slavery . . . are without parallel in all records of modern British history" sounds like an echo of Patrick Henry's outburst, "Give me liberty or give me death", to the Virginia Provincial Convention in 1775 when the majority of the inhabitants of that Colony were negro slaves and he and his colleagues were their owners.

The economic and social differences between the races were so great that the effect of race or colour on all thinking was unavoidable. More than ninety per cent of the Africans in the years immediately after the war did not have "the slightest smattering of education", as Mathu pointed out in Legislative Council,[51] and of the other ten per cent only a few acquired more than a primary or very junior secondary education. Few Europeans had a chance of meeting the few Africans who had become well educated and the African and European races were so far apart economically and culturally that a communal pattern of life was inevitable. Economically the Asians were at all levels, but their Asian cultural background set them apart as a community, however, various within itself. Their sub-communities looked after their own interests and as a whole they were "great segregationists".[52] To those in Kenya who were trying to improve race relations the chief task seemed to be to make it understood that some Asians were willing to co-operate with Europeans and that a few Africans were coming on the scene with hitherto unknown standards of education and behaviour, but with so little information to hand it was natural for many Europeans to class together as "the African" the nomads in the northern deserts, still barely touched by the modern world, and the few students who were reading for University degrees. And, on the other side, to most Africans, with the exception of those who were included in the feudal relationships on European farms, all Europeans were equally remote and all Asians were usually regarded as unscrupulous traders.

In 1950 Derek Erskine referred to a European who expressed a not uncommon view when he suggested that the solution to the problems of race relations lay in "humane, just, kindly yet firm treatment of African employees by European masters". At that time, wrote Erskine, only 196,000 African men, women and children were employed on European farms and 105,000 in European and Asian industry and commerce and in domestic service. "Most of the remaining 94 per cent of Kenya Africans", he wrote, "tend their own cattle, camels, sheep and goats, grow their own crops and run their own businesses and rarely make contact with Europeans other than Government servants and missionaries".[53] Smuts seemed to have had a similar thought twenty years earlier when he said in his Rhodes lectures at Oxford that "the easiest, most natural and obvious way to civilize the African native is to give him decent white employment".[54] Geography and racial numbers made it impracticable to base a policy on such a means of education anywhere in Africa. In Kenya, as Erskine showed, the European population was so small that, whether the ethics of such a policy were good or bad, it was entirely unrealistic.

As Erskine pointed out, the Africans had contact with missionaries and Government servants. Oldham had criticised Smuts for under-estimating the extent of the influence of the missionaries and had cited their educational work in South Africa. In Kenya their influence was no less great. Sir Andrew Cohen, with his wide knowledge and experience, recognised also the work of the administrative officers in the colonies and claimed that "British officials have been the spearheads of progress since British administration in Africa began".[55] In Kenya there was, however, a considerable lack of cordiality between the settlers and the officials, not as individuals but as officers who were carrying out the policy of the Colonial Office. From as early as 1903 "Hostility soon grew between the settlers and officials, who considered themselves as having a long-standing and prior duty to the natives."[56] The desire for self-governing power was in conflict with trusteeship.

Lack of Understanding of African Conditions

Lack of knowledge could only lead to ill-founded criticism and ill-conceived policies. Ignorance about the other races was prevalent in every community and was an obstacle to peaceful progress in inter-racial co-operation. It helped African racialist politicians to foster racial hatred and it prevented Europeans from seeing that prejudices and privileges of past years were no longer tenable in a new age.

Early in 1946 the Chief Native Commissioner felt it necessary to remind the members of Legislative Council that Africans were

"human beings and not robots" and to warn the European unofficials against "a tendency to consider the African more for the
particular purpose of labouring than anything else". One member
had deplored "the habit of Africans who work in Nairobi of retaining
their foothold in the reserves while at the same time", as she put it,
"drawing Nairobi wages". The Chief Native Commissioner had to
explain that wages in Nairobi were too low to make it possible for
African workers "to sustain and educate their families without
drawing on the reserves to supplement their incomes".[57] That it
should have been necessary to mention so fundamental a fact of
African life in Legislative Council supported the African contention
that African needs would only be adequately understood and met
if there were more African members of Legislative Council and
municipal bodies.

The unhappy conditions of Africans in the towns continued. In
1952 the Commissioner for Community Development wrote,
"Even now the minimum wages in the towns only provide for a
single man".[58] And in 1953 the Social Welfare Officer of the Nakuru
Municipal Council reported to the European Elected Member
for the Rift Valley, who was concerned about the poverty of
Africans in the town, that "There can be little doubt that all but a
handful of Africans are living at or below subsistence level". The
minimum wage, he pointed out, was 50/- a month and an African
"simply cannot live on 50/- a month".[59] What was properly an
employer/labour problem became a racial issue. In 1946 Beecher had
attacked the Report of the Development Commission because, he
said, "equality of opportunity is nowhere in that report applied to the
African people".[60] Again and again came "the recurring phrase:
'The utilization of African manpower' as if they were so many
checkers on a board. I hate the phrase", said Beecher, "and I know
my African friends hate it even more".[61]

Economic greed not a racial matter

But the tendency to regard the African workers as "so many
checkers on a board" and to pay as low a wage as the law allowed
was not a racial characteristic confined to Europeans. It was the
result of economic forces and of human failings. Many of the
characteristics of the Industrial Revolution in Britain and elsewhere
and many developments of the nineteenth century had their counterparts in Kenya in the twentieth. In the late nineteen forties there

was a wages Board.[62] On one occasion the African members of the Board signed a minority report demanding a minimum wage considerably higher than the figure agreed by the majority of the Board, who were all Europeans. The reports were published, the minimum wage was set at the figure advised by the majority and one of the African members paid his own domestic staff at that rate. When a European friend asked him how he could pay his labour at a rate which he had publicly said he considered to be below the adequate minimum, he replied, "Why should I pay more than the law compels me to?" This was not an isolated case. African employers were frequently less generous than the Europeans. In the case of this Wages Board's recommendation, however, the general mass of the African population would only know that the African members of the Board had demanded a higher minimum wage than the European majority had agreed to and the sad moral truth would be obscured by an unjust racialism. Not only did Africans often pay lower wages but they took less interest than Europeans did in the living conditions of their employees and in racially mixed administrative bodies it was not unusual for the European members to have to protect the interests of African workers against selfish suggestions made by the African councillors. "African employment of labour", wrote Carey Jones, "tends to be at a lower cost than European. Wages are lower."[63] Many of Kenya's problems were economic and social, but always they were aggravated by race, and considerations of race and colour often blinded people to the real facts of a situation.

Need for Personal Contact to overcome Prejudice

In the commercial field leading Asians and Europeans met as fellow employers and businessmen. The Nairobi Chamber of Commerce was not confined to Europeans and in 1947 the Association of Chambers of Commerce and Industry of Eastern Africa showed its recognition of the equality of the leading Asians by appointing George Tyson and Chunilal Kirparam to "constitute an interim executive to deal with outstanding matters",[64] Asian firms were drawn into the economic fraternity as they reached the required standards. In December 1950, for instance, Chandulal and Company were elected to membership of the Nairobi Chamber of Commerce.[65]

Inter-racial co-operation, however, would require something more than an appreciation of common economic interests. Some degree

of social intercourse would have to be achieved if racial prejudice
was to be overcome. Until the equalisation of salaries among the
races had time to affect African living standards it might have been
expected that social meeting between Europeans and leading Asians
would have been easier than between Europeans and Africans.
There were a few Asians of whom this was true. They were Asians
whose wives had learned how to mix with the Western world,
into the commercial and professional sides of which their husbands
had become integrated. They could be found in Nairobi and Kisumu
and, perhaps above all, in Mombasa, where, as Sir Philip Mitchell
noticed in 1947, "a very agreeable sundowner party given by Dr.
and Mrs. Rana on the flat roof of their home near the Treasury . . .
was the usual cheerful Mombasa party of all races."[66]

Many of the Asians, however, especially the Hindus, adhered so
closely to their traditional culture that their wives were unable to
enter into the social life of the European community. The wives of
some of the richest Indians never learned to speak English. African
women on the other hand, when the increase in the education of
girls began to take effect in the later nineteen fifties, were able to
accompany their husbands as guests and hostesses, and liberal-
minded Europeans and Africans were able to come closer together.
Colour bar, the greatest enemy of inter-racial co-operation, could
only be lessened by actual face to face meeting, which could help to
overcome prejudice and misconceptions and discrimination.

1. O. E. B. Hughes: Memorandum on *Nyeri District, 1949–1952*, (mimeo-graphed). A copy is in the Frost papers.
2. Blundell 3/1 contains a copy of this letter by T. P. Ward, 28 Sept. 1948.
3. *Comment*, No. 82, 5 April 1951, p. 20.
4. *Comment*, No. 80, 2 March 1951, p. 2.
5. H.C.D., Vol. 493, Col. 984, 14 Nov. 1951.
6. Kenneth Robinson: *The Dilemmas of Trusteeship*, p. 53.
7. *Imperial Policy: A Statement of Conservative Policy for the British Common-wealth and Empire*, p. 54.
8. e.g. *The Colonies: The Labour Party's Post-War Policy for the African and Pacific Colonies*, 1943.
9. Mimeographed. A copy is in Blundell 22/3.
10. Colonel Sir Charles Ponsonby, Bart, T.D., D.L.: *Ponsonby Remembers* pp. 116–7.
11. J. M. Lee: *Colonial Development and Good Government:* p. 15.
12. Letter: *The Times*, 17 April 1957.
13. David Goldsworthy: "Parliamentary Questions on Colonial Affairs: A Retrospective Analysis" in *Parliamentary Affairs*, Vol. XXIII, No. 2, Spring 1970.
14. David Goldsworthy: *Colonial Issues in British Politics* 1945-61, p. 176.

15. ibid., p. 247.
16. Colonial Secretary to Fabian Colonial Bureau, 22 July 1947 quoted in ibid.
17. H.C.D., Vol. 584, cols. 1403 and 1404 20 March 1958.
18. Sir Philip Mitchell's Diary, 9 Aug 1947.
19. ibid, 16 Jan 1956.
20. ibid, 12 Jan 1953. Conversation with Christopher Holland-Martin, M.P.
21. J. H. Oldham: *Black and White in Africa*, p. 5.
22. G. K. Evans: *Public Opinion on Colonial Affairs*, A survey made in May and June 1948 for the Colonial Office-N.S. 119 June 1948 (Mimeographed).
23. Oliver Lyttelton to Michael Blundell, December 1954, Blundell 5/2.
24. E.A.S. 16 Oct 1953.
25. ibid. 13 April 1951 (Colonel T. B. Butt).
26. Lord Francis Scott to S. V. Cooke, 8 April, 1939: Letter in possession of S. V. Cooke.
27. Sir Michael Blundell considers that Scott was well to the left of centre (interview with Sir Michael Blundell, 14 April 1970).
28. Lord Francis Scott, op. cit.
29. Note by S.V. Cooke in file in his possession.
30. *Draft Outline of Self-Government for Kenya*, undated, but seems to have been written in 1946: mimeographed. A copy is in Blundell 16/1.
31. L.P. Mair: *Native Policies in Africa*, p. 19.
32. Lt. Col. Lord Francis Scott, K.C.M.G., C.M.G.,. D.S.O.: Op. cit.
33. *Future Policy in regard to Eastern Africa, CMD 2904 (1927)*, p. 6.
34. *Memorandum on Native Policy in East Africa, CMD 3573 (1930)* p. 4.
35. The Electors' Union: *An Outline of Policy*, 1946, p. 9.
36. The Electors' Union, *Chairman's Annual Report, 1949-1950*. Kenya National Archives.
37. E.A.S., 21 Oct. 1949. Letter from C. E. Christopher of Thomsons Falls.
38. *Comment*, No. 97, 19 July 1951. p. 4.
39. *Electors' Union (1948 Conference and After)*: mimeographed pages in Havelock File on Electors' Union Conference, 1948, in Kenya National Archives.
40. Sir Andrew Cohen: *British Policy in Changing Africa*, p. 21.
41. The Electors' Union *Report of the Fourth Annual Conference, March 1947*.
42. K.W.N. 13 Nov 1953, p. 7.
43. Sir Philip Mitchell's Diary, 9 May 1951.
44. The Electors' Union: *Report of the Fifth Annual Conference, May 1949*.
45. Blundell to Kendall Ward, 14 April 1955. Ward Deposit, file The Voice of Kenya, Confidential Correspondence ex London 53/55 in the Kenya National Archives. The cabon of this letter is in Blundell 3/2.
46. Informaton supplied by Mr. L. Foot-Gaitskell of Londiani and confirmed in a letter on 7 April 1972.
47. Sir Philip' Mitchell's Diary, 16 July 1946.
48. Alan Paton: *Contact* 1 No. 6, 1 May 1958, quoted in *The Long View*, edited by Edward Callon, Pall Mall Press, London, 1968.
49. Laurence van der Post:*The Dark Eye in Africa*, pp. 17-18.
50. L.S.B. Leakey: *Kenya Contrasts and Problems*, p. 111.
51. L.C.D., 14 Nov 1945, Col. 153.
52. Interview with John Riddoch, 7 April 1970.
53. E.A.S., 1 July 1950.
54. General J. C. Smuts. *Africa and Some World Problems*, p. 48.
55. Sir Andrew Cohen: op. cit., p. viii.
56. cf. George Bennett: *History of East Africa*, vol. II ed. Vincent Harlow and E. M. Chilver, p. 268.
57. L.C.D., 11 Jan 1946, col. 8.
58. T. G. Askwith: *Some Observations on the Growth of Unrest in Kenya*, 24 Oct 1952 (mimeographed).
59. Letter to Blundell, 22 July, 1953, Blundell 16/3.
60. L.C.D., 20 Nov 1946, Col. 245.

61. ibid., 20 Nov 1946, Col. 244.
62. *The Central Minimum Wage Advisory Board* (*W. K. Horne, Chairman*).
63. E. Carey Jones, op. cit. p. 56.
64. Association of Chambers of Commerce and Industry of Eastern Africa:
    Minutes of Executive Meeting, 19 Sept. 1947, No. 2091.
65. Nairobi Chamber of Commerce: Minutes of Meeting, 19 Dec. 1950.
66. Sir Philip Mitchell's Diary, 21 April 1947.

5

DISCRIMINATION AND MISCONCEPTION

Colour Bar

During the late nineteen forties and early fifties there were two
contrary trends. Among a section of the Africans there was a growing
antagonism to Europeans, but at the same time there were many
Africans who believed that inter-racial co-operation held the greatest
promise of sound development for Kenya. There were Europeans
who remained arrogant and were intent on an *apartheid* way of life
and hoped for self-government under white domination, but the
liberal element was gradually increasing. Violence broke out in a
minor way in the Trans-Nzoia and in a major civil war in the Central
Province, but the growth of inter-racial goodwill continued and was
in fact strengthened by the violence of Mau Mau. The increase of
liberalism was scarcely noticed outside Kenya, largely because
the liberals, while still a minority, were apt to hide their progressive
thought for fear of ostracism by the majority. Mau Mau provided
the news which received attention overseas and the considerable
body of goodwill among Africans remained unnoticed.

There was great poverty among Africans, great urban overcrowding suffered by Africans and Asians, grievance over land and
frustration among the educated at not being given the responsibility
which they thought was their due, but two months after the
Declaration of a State of Emergency Sir Mitchell still thought that
"The most dangerous factor is colour bar, prejudice and rudeness".[1]
He saw in those days as a European what Abu Mayanja saw in
Uganda in 1959: "The economic argument loses sight of the basic
fact in contemporary Africa, namely the African's compelling need
for respect as a human being".[2] In May 1952 the Committee of the
Kenya African Union passed a document demanding agreement
to seventeen points, the first of which was the ending of racial
discrimination.[3] Land, education and the constitution were the
issues next in order of priority, but racial discrimination came first
of all. Racial discrimination affected salary scales, residential

restrictions and many other aspects of life, but it was social discrimination, like exclusion from hotels and restaurants, which hurt the
leading Africans and Asians most of all, because it offended their
human dignity and caused emotional wounds which possibly meant
more than any material considerations. President Kaunda of Zambia
once wrote that "Because Europeans had a monopoly of power and
skills it was inevitable that they should assume positions of leadership
and control, the original tribal societies being unable to withstand
the impact of their aggressive presence". "But", he continued, "all
too often this practical superiority was transformed into a philosophy
of racial dominance".[4] Technical pre-eminence gave the white
races mastery over the world in the 19th century and a feeling of
racial superiority was one result of this. It was not confined to Britain
but was found throughout Europe and the Americas. In a country
such as Kenya, where different races had to live side by side,
communal solidarity bred racial antagonism. Power and privilege
were not easily given up but were a source of envy and ill will. When
he left Kenya in 1946, General Anderson, the General Officer
Commanding, who had grown to admire the African troops under
his command, "stressed how great a blot racial antagonism was
in Kenya".[5]

The Word "Native"

The Africans who emerged after the Second World War with
standards of education which only a very small number had reached
before suffered from a sense of frustration and lack of acceptance
by being classed with the illiterate masses as "the natives". The
word "native" was heartily disliked. By that time there were
Europeans and Asians who were natives of Kenya, some of them
even of the third generation; but the word "native" was never used
of them and the leading Africans felt that it implied an attitude of
contempt which hurt their human dignity and disregarded their
educational advance. In 1951 there was a long correspondence in the
East African Standard about the use of this word. It was finally
brought to a close by a letter which asked for the word to be given
up and, after pointing out that "all Europeans whose homes are in
Kenya must claim that their children are natives", went on to say
that "no one who has anything like an appreciation of the feeling
of words can deny that the word has acquired a somewhat contemp-
tuous implication when applied to the inhabitants of countries less

developed than Britain" and cited the Concise Oxford Dictionary as
giving, among other meanings, a "member of a non-European or
uncivilised race".[6] The intense dislike of Africans for the word
"native" as a name for the Africans of Kenya showed how deeply
the emerging elite craved for recognition. At the same time they
were on their guard against being patronised. What they asked for
was sympathetic acceptance of their progress. Six years after
Independence the final letter in the correspondence in 1951 on the
word "native" was still remembered among the intelligentsia,
because it had shown a European sympathy with their hopes and
susceptibilities.[7]

"The Human Problem"

The African Members of Legislative Council agreed with Mitchell
when he stressed the importance of "the human problem". Two
months before the declaration of a State of Emergency they wrote,

"We agree with the statement made by His Excellency the
Governor recently that one of the qualities that people of all races
have to cultivate is Courtesy. We know that Africans are offended
in many places by the way they are unreasonably treated. This is
commonplace in their places of employment, in public places and
in any other place where they meet with non-Africans. It does not
cost any person anything to treat another human being as a
human being and to respect his human dignity. In fact it pays very
high dividends".[8]

The best of the European settlers often established a happy paternal
relationship with their employees and the farmer and his family were
often regarded with affection. They communicated in bad Swahili,
a language foreign to both sides, and a class distinction made
association easy. But only a few of such Europeans could happily
avercome the difficulty of getting onto an unselfconscious footing
with Africans who had had some Western education and spoke in
English. They had few opportunities of meeting the best educated.
When they did meet them, they were often astonished. The work
of improving race relations was much concerned with creating
more and more constructive opportunities for acquiring knowledge
of the progress of the other races.

Misconceptions about Land

While efforts were being made to improve relations between

Europeans and the better educated Africans, grievances over the
question of land were being fostered by African politicians and in
the Central Province especially they embittered relations between
the two races. The propaganda was based on inaccuracy and was not
countered by the dissemination of correct information. This
propaganda started in the early years and it was generally thought
overseas that nearly all the good agricultural land was reserved
for Europeans and included in the White Highlands.

The first sales of land in Kikuyu country near Nairobi were based
on a misunderstanding resulting from lack of knowledge by the
Europeans about tribal custom and lack of knowledge by the
Kikuyus about British interpretation of the meaning of sale. Rinder-
pest and drought had caused the area of Kiambu and Limuru to be
temporarily uninhabited. The Europeans who bought land there,
which they found unoccupied, believed that sale of land meant sale
of the freehold as it did in England; but the Kikuyus, who sold,
understood sale of land to mean sale of the use of it for a time,
because no-one could sell the freehold of the clan's inheritance.[9]
Modern capitalised agriculture requires long range security,
however. The area concerned was small, no more than 100 square
miles. Later transactions at Kiambu did not have the same excuse
and the eviction of Kikuyus from Tigoni in 1938 had no excuse
whatever. They were removed, as Dr. Leakey said, "because settlers
objected to having an island of Reserve among them."[10]

The cry of "Give us back our land" began in Kiambu and was the
result of these early transactions. Kikuyu tribal aspirations used it
as the starting point of a propaganda which went beyond any
claims based on fact. It was even asserted that the European estates
round Ol Doinyo Sabuk and the farms at Molo and other places
west of the Rift Valley had formerly been cultivated by Kikuyus.
In fact, however, the sisal and coffee estates at Ol Doinyo Sabuk
were too far down in the plains where the Masai held sway for them
ever to have been the scene of Kikuyu agriculture, while the Masai
grazing grounds of the Rift Valley prevented any possibility of
westward penetration by Kikuyus. The areas west of the Rift
Valley were heavily forested and inhabited only by a small number
of Dorobo forest dwellers until the Europeans turned them into
productive farms. But propaganda is easily believed unless there is
adequate knowledge to refute it, and by the time of Mau Mau
Kikuyus had spread all over the White Highlands as farm labourers

and many believed that the farms of Naivasha and Rongai had
once been their tribe's ancestral lands.

This propaganda was so successful that Kikuyus with education as
well as the illiterate believed it. They thought, moreover, that
Europeans had taken all the best land everywhere in Kenya and
left only inferior areas to be farmed by Africans. The fertility of the
European farms at Limuru and Kiambu, the area which caused so
much bitterness, was plain for all to see, but the fact that the rain-
carrying winds made the eastern slopes of the mountains fertile and
the western sides far less well watered and that in areas in and
near Kikuyuland the former were occupied by Africans and the
latter by Europeans was not pointed out by the Kikuyu politicians.
North of Nairobi the Kikuyu Reserve had a good rainfall and was
well watered by streams and rivers flowing from the Aberdare range,
whereas on the western side of these mountains were the European
farms in the Rift Valley with a much lower rainfall. Further north
still in the area of Mount Kenya, starting from the north east of the
mountain and going clockwise to the south west, were the Meru,
Embu and Kikuyu Reserves, which were perhaps the most well
watered and fertile lands in Kenya. The drier land from Nyeri in the
south-west through Nanyuki and Timau to the north-east was an
area of European settlement, much of which was so dry that, as
the farms stretched away to Thomsons Falls and Rumuruti, nothing
but ranching was possible and ten acres or more were needed to feed
a single head of cattle.

Even a scholar like Professor Rosberg seems to have been mistaken
about Kikuyu land. He wrote that they were "hemmed in between
the Aberdare Mountains and the areas of European settlement."[11]
The Kikuyu never went over the Aberdare range into the Rift
Valley: the Masai saw to that. And for the same reason in the east
Kikuyu land did not reach the border of Kamba country. "The
Masai of Hamitic origin had wedged themselves between the
two pacific pastoral tribes, domineering, raiding and destroying
anything that resisted their advance."[12] The name of the hill which
stands in the middle of this plain, Ol Doinyo Sabuk, is Masai, not
Bantu. If the Europeans had not gone to Kenya, this hemming-in
would still have been effected by the Masai. North of Fort Hall
there was no European settlement on the Kikuyus' eastern border,
which marched with the Embu tribe. Although south of Fort Hall,
and only there, Rosberg's remark is literally true, it gives a false

impression even of the situation there by ignoring the fact that the Europeans continued a hemming-in which the Masai had previously enforced. Later on Kikuyus were able to settle in parts of this Masai country and to cultivate the Mweia area. The establishment of European government in fact enabled the Kikuyus to advance into land from which the Masai had previously barred them. "Soon they had dispersed over a much greater area of land than they had occupied before the advent of British rule."[13] Donald N. Barnett in his introduction to Karari Njama's autobiography was mistaken about the size of the area of Kikuyu land alienated for European farming. "While most of the White Highlands was obtained by the British from the pastoral Masai," he writes, "large sections of Kikuyuland, particularly in the rich southern districts of Kiambu, were alienated for European use."[14] In fact in 1895 "unequivocal Kikuyu territory" amounted to 1,640 square miles. The total amount alienated was 120.64 square miles, of which 93.41 square miles were in the Kiambu district.[15] If this were in a single block, it would be 12 miles long and 10 miles wide, but Barnett's phrase gives the impression of a much larger area.

A large part of Kenya has too low a rainfall to make agriculture possible. The area which has a climate and soil suitable for agriculture lies mainly above 3,700 feet. In it lives about 90 per cent of the population and it contained the European farms. Below 3,725 feet are the Coastal strip and the northern areas like Turkana and the semi-desert districts north and east of Mount Kenya. Misconceptions about land have affected the writings of scholars and journalists on both sides of the Atlantic. In 1958, for example, Professor Gwendolen Carter and William O. Brown edited a book published by Boston University. In this it is said that, "The center of Kenya's agricultural development lies in the upland country, an area in which ninety per cent of the population lives, and the European has succeeded in legally reserving about one-third of this valuable land for his exclusive ownership and use."[16] Five years earlier in Britain the Movement for a Democracy of Content told the public that "the best land in Kenya, comprising 50 per cent of all land available, has come into the possession of some 3,000 European settlers, while 5,000,000 Africans are forced to share the rest."[17] A few years earlier George Padmore wrote, "The Kikuyus and other African tribes occupying the highlands were gradually squeezed out to make homes for the settlers. Today most of the best lands and fertile parts of Kenya are owned by white immigrants who are still pouring into the country."[18] In fact, however, after the Second World War there were not many new farming immigrants. Only some 160 had been settled by the time Padmore was writing and up to 1960, when the Lancaster House Conference put an end to all further thoughts of European settlement, the European Agricultural Settlement Board had placed on farms 504 persons as tenant farmers, assisted owners and individual purchasers.[19]

It was not only about land in the Central Province that inaccurate figures were given. "Shortly after the War,"—that is the First World War—George Padmore wrote, General Northey, the Governor, "confiscated about 2,000,000 acres belonging to the Nandi tribe which was divided up into small estates and given to demobilised British Army officers".[20] Ghai and McAuslan, referring to the Discharged Soldiers Settlement Ordinance of 1919, state that "Approximately 2,000,000 acres were earmarked for the scheme, a large part of it being excised from the Nandi Reserve without compensation."[21]

After the First World War land was taken from the Nandi at Kipkarren and at Kaimosi, where some farms had been surveyed for alienation in 1913, and was given out to soldier settlers. The alienation of land in these areas was a disgraceful breach of faith, because it was inside the boundary of the area which the Nandi had been promised would be "theirs for ever" when the Nandi Native Land Unit was defined in November 1907. Tindiret, the Nyando Valley and the Nandi Hills areas were outside the defined area, but Kipkarren and Kaimosi were certainly inside it. The amount of land concerned at Kipkarren and Kaimosi was sixty square miles, 38,400 acres, which is nowhere near 2,000,000 acres. At one time the Plateau had been an area of Masai migratory grazing, but the Nandi had defeated the Masai in battle towards the end of the 19th century and the "unoccupied Uasiu Gishu Plateau"[22] was a no-man's land, which the Nandi used for grazing and hunting more than any other tribe and through which they passed on raiding expeditions without fear of molestation. Early in the 20th century farmers arrived from South Africa and the Plateau became their main area of settlement and settlers arrived there from Britain also in the early days. The Plateau was never an area of Nandi settlement and Kipkarren and Kaimosi were the only areas "exised from the Nandi reserve"[23] for the soldier settler scheme.

About another part of Kenya Padmore wrote, "Three months
after the introduction of the 1939 Order in Council, officially
designating the Highlands 'White Man's Country', the Wataita
people were forcibly evicted from their land at Taita Hills."[24] The
Taita Hills, however, are 100 miles away from the nearest part of
the White Highlands. A certain Dr. Verby lived there and there were
a few Christian missions, but otherwise the Taita Hills have always
been entirely in African occupation.

False statements about land were sometimes used to give an
opposite impression. In a book written by a European in 1954,
under the map used as a frontispiece, it is stated that "The area
reserved for European settlement is about one-twentieth of the
Colony."[25] The author failed to mention the fact that of the whole
area of 225,000 square miles only 40,700 square miles were of
agricultural value and that the European farms covered one-
seventh of this agricultural land.

The correct figures were given by the Secretary of State in the
House of Commons in November 1960 in answer to a question put
by Mr. Stonehouse. The total area of "good mixed farming land"
was "a little under 37,000 square miles." Of this area Africans
occupied "32,000 sq. miles—corresponding closely with the areas
of settled population which the European explorers found seventy
or eighty years previously." "The balance of 4,700 sq. miles," the
Secretary of State explained, was "farmed by immigrant farmers,
mostly Europeans", and that area of one-seventh of the whole
yielded nearly one half of the agricultural production "measured
in terms of monetary value" and included "no less than four-fifths
of the exportable surplus."[26] If some 3,700 sq. miles "of poor quality
rough and steep land on European farms was included, the figure
was 8,459 sq. miles and the total was 40,700 sq. miles."[27]

In 1959 there were 3,540 European farms, made up of:

(a) Small holdings "whose occupants are not entirely
     dependant on their holdings for their livings"   600
(b) Plantations (coffee, tea, sisal, wattle)   780
(c) Mixed farms and ranches   2,160
                                                               ─────
                                                               3,540

When the white Highlands were opened to "other races," there
was not an immediate change of any great size. Absolutely accurate

figures cannot be obtained from the Kenya Agricultural Censuses, because before 1959 European and Asian farms were returned together and after 1959, when the White Highlands had been opened, the Census recorded farms in "Scheduled Areas and Coastal Strip". However, the number of Asian plantations on the Kano Plains and the Coast was very small and few European farms, except those affected by the settlement schemes on the Kinangop and other parts of the one million acre scheme, were occupied by Africans before Independence. The Census figures therefore give an almost, though not absolutely, accurate figure of European farms each year. The discrepancy can be seen in 1959 when the Census gives the number of farms in the Scheduled Areas and Coastal strip as 3,693 and the Chairman of the European Settlement Board returned the number of European farms as 3,540.[28] Thereafter the Census figures are as follows:

Scheduled Areas and Coastal Strip

1960	3,609
1961	3,624[29]
1962	3,606
1963	3,368[30]

The ill will and resentment felt by Africans about the White Highlands were in the main caused not by European farming but by the total exclusion from the area of African farmers, even as tenants. Commercial farming was an invaluable asset and until the later years very few Africans could have engaged in anything beyond subsistence agriculture. Subsistence farming could maintain a man and his family, but capital and agriculture knowledge and modern techniques were needed to produce foodstuffs to supply the urban markets and the export trade. Much of the milk consumed in Mombasa, for instance, came from the large F.O'B Wilson estate at Ulu near Machakos and most of the Nairobi demand was met from European farms at Limuru, Kiambu and Karen. The vegetables required by the Nairobi markets on the other hand were almost entirely produced by Kikuyu smallholders at Kabete, Kiambaa and other neighbouring areas. The production of vegetables does not require the capital and acreage needed by commercial dairy farming. As Africans acquired a taste for wheat flour bread, more and more flour was required and this intensified the need for large-scale commercial agriculture, which could supply crops which at that time were beyond the reach of co-operative farming. The difficulties attending large-scale co-operative farming were shown at Bukhura near Kakamega, where a carefully planned scheme failed because the idea of co-operation had not yet been sufficiently accepted by the peasantry. The exclusion of Africans and Asians from the White Highlands was racial discrimination, but there was a difficulty which was not understood by the Africans. If the White Highlands were to be opened to non-Europeans, the Africans would not benefit unless discrimination were applied against the Asians, who were in a far better economic position than the Africans to buy land from a European who might be willing to sell.

Administration of Justice

One result of the existence of the two views of colonialism was that there were different methods of trial for Europeans and others. British immigrants, who regarded themselves as colonists in the classical sense, wanted to live within a traditional framework and demanded trial by jury as a birthright: not merely trial by jury but trial by a jury composed of Europeans even when members of other races were concerned in the case. This seemed to them to be entirely logical, because the right of an Englishman to trial by jury meant trial by his peers and the European in Kenya did not regard Asians or Africans as his peers. In criminal cases, then, a European was tried by a European jury even when Africans or Asians were concerned, while Africans and Asians were tried by a judge with assessors. Ghai and McAuslan are highly critical of this practice and write, "Whatever the validity of the reasons given for the use of assessors, the assumptions behind the use of the jury for trials of Europeans in Kenya were always clearly erroneous, and the contrast between the two systems of trial as they operated in practice reveals the essentially discriminatory nature of jury trial".[31] It is true that the opinions of the African assessors did not bind the judge, but they did enable him to ascertain the African point of view and they were a compromise between the traditional African methods of trial and the more sophisticated system of an English Assize Court, for which Government had reasons for believing the general mass of Africans were not yet ready. It is not clear what Ghai and McAuslan mean by "the assumptions behind the use of the jury", but it certainly proved to be erroneous to assume that a European jury would give an impartial verdict in an inter-racial case. They forgot that impartial justice was an ideal which the British way of life demanded and that, although in Britain practice often fell short of the ideal, juries really did try to find verdicts based on the facts as presented to them. In Africa, however, the universal feeling of superiority held by the Europeans proved to be stronger than adherence to the truth, because Europeans and Africans were felt to be on different levels and therefore, if justice were administered on the assumption that they were equal, the verdict would in fact be false. "For all men cling to justice of some kind", wrote Aristotle," but their conceptions are imperfect and they do not express the whole idea. For example, justice is thought by them to be, and is, equality, not, however, for all, but only for equals. And inequality is thought to be, and is, justice; neither is this for all, but only for unequals".[32] The census of 309 B.C., a few years after the death of Aristotle, disclosed that there were 400,000 slaves in Attica. The idea of inequality as a natural order of society was fundamental in Greek thought. A paler reflection of this arose in Kenya from the superior and privileged position of the Europeans.

In Kenya juries so often perjured their honesty that no European suffered the death penalty on the conviction of a European jury till 1960. Then the case of *Poole v. R.* went to the Court of Appeal of East Africa, which upheld the conviction and a further appeal was dismissed by the Privy Council.[33] It was the jurors, not the system, who deserved condemnation. Historically, from the European point of view trial by jury seemed to be logical, but difficulties faced suggestions for its extension. When, for instance, Asians demanded that trial by jury should be extended to them, reflection showed an unsurmountable difficulty.

"On the question of trial by jury of Indians", wrote Sir Philip Mitchell, "Patel was asked to discuss with the Congress and to ask them to be more explicit; did they really mean that a Hindu, for instance, might be tried by a jury of Moslems—it would be a matter of chance if they were Moslems or not—a jury of Moslems for killing a Moslem?"[34]

The disgrace attaching to trial by jury lay in the inability of European juries to exercise honestly and impartially a privilege which they claimed by historical right. Time and time again in cases involving an African juries found verdicts in favour of the European in the teeth of apparently contrary evidence. One Attorney General even went so far as to consider asking for special legislation to enable the

Crown to appeal against the verdict of a jury.[35]

An Englishman who went to Kenya in 1947 was invited to a party soon after his arrival. He heard two Europeans talking about someone whom they had both known before the War. "I remember he killed a native", said one. "What happened to him? I don't think I ever heard". "Oh, he was put inside for a short time", the other replied, "and he did very well after he came out". "But", asked the newcomer in his ignorance, "if he murdered an African, why wasn't he hanged?" "Well, we don't look on African life in quite the same way as European life", was the reply.[36] It would be wrong to assume that many Europeans would have expressed this sentiment so blatantly, but it would be idle to pretend that some such feeling did not lurk deep down in many minds. In 1897, for instance, Joseph Chamberlain said that in the course of bringing order in the colonies there had been "loss of life among the native populations, loss of still more precious lives among those who had been sent out to bring these countries into some kind of disciplined order".[37] One sees the same attitude being condemned in America in 1969 by Eldridge Cleaver, the Black Panther leader. "America", he writes, "has never been truly outraged by the murder of a black man, woman or child".[38] It was an attitude compounded of racial prejudice and the possession of power, arising largely from economic and technical superiority. Although such racial attitudes in Kenya are not to be excused, it ought not to be forgotten that tribal and sectional behaviour in Africa and elsewhere has been, and still is, equally perverted and that the possession of power has led to perpetration of evil and disregard of the sanctity of human life among the coloured races also. A communal loyalty is a false loyalty if it offends general moral principles: it is perhaps a mark of high civilisation to accept the principle that "all power is a trust".[39]

Southern Rhodesia had the same experience as Kenya. The colonists claimed trial by jury as a British birthright, but in inter-racial cases it was abused as it was later in Kenya. In Southern Rhodesia the Attorney General suggested the introduction of "special juries", composed of five selected people, in cases where Africans and Europeans were involved. These juries, however, came from the roll of voters, all of whom were white. "It was not a very happy solution"; writes Philip Mason, "from the African point of view, the Court was still white; from the European, the idea of a jury

"specially selected" was unattractive; it sounded", continued
Mason, "very like a 'packed jury' ".[40] In fact, members of the legal
profession in Southern Rhodesia told Mason that they did not
find "the special juries to differ in any marked degree from ordinary
juries in respect of impartiality".[41] It was hoped to find jurors who
would put adherence to the truth above racial partiality. Such a
system was never tried in Kenya and it is doubtful whether a white
jury, however carefully selected, would have been able to overcome
African suspicion. As it was, a European privilege became a source
of unjust discrimination and added to the European feeling of
racial superiority.

When Colonel (later Sir Arthur) Young went to Kenya as Commissioner of Police in 1954, he was struck by what he called the
Europeans' "first-class citizenship", which "was manifestly a
selfcentred one". And it seemed to him that "so far as the police
were concerned, the African constable was, to the privileged class,
no symbol of law and order but a minor official of small account
who could be put in his place as the circumstances warranted".[42]
This had been strikingly shown in January 1953 when Europeans
marched to Government House after the murder of the Ruck family
by Mau Mau. Michael Blundell tried to prevent a racial confrontation by advising the Commissioner of Police to have no African
askaris, except Traffic Police, on duty at Government House when
the marchers arrived. His advice was ignored. The crowd forced
the askaris back and pressed so hard against the doors that they
began to give way and had to be reinforced by tables held against
them by African servants and Europeans inside the house. Then,
to avoid the dangers of further violence Blundell agreed to have the
askaris removed if the crowd would retire from the building.[43] The
racialism of the crowd had a profound effect on the African
community, who saw the askaris treated not as agents of the law
but as inferior beings, whose presence affronted the members of
the "master race". The incident also showed how difficult was the
position of a liberal European political leader in the early fifties.

Legal Discrimination
The privileged position occupied by the Europeans was a constant
irritant to the other races, especially to the leading Asians, who were
on the same economic level as the Europeans. A demand for an
enquiry into discriminatory legislation was made by an Indian

Member, Chanan Singh, in December 1953, and the Parliamentary
Delegation from Westminster in its report in January, 1954, advised
examination of the laws of Kenya "with a view to eliminating
discrimination".[44] Chanan Singh's resolution requested the Government to compile a list of laws and subsidiary legislation which
"discriminate between persons on the ground of race and to report
thereon".[45] Every Department of Government submitted reports
and on the 1st March, 1956, the Memorandum compiled by the Chief
Secretary was laid on the table of Legislative Council.[46]

The Memorandum showed that in fact there was hardly any
legislation which discriminated against Africans. Some regulations
had become racially discriminatory, though not seriously so,
because conditions had changed since their inception, and they
were easily altered; and some regulations discriminated in favour
of Africans, as for instance the Tea Ordinance (16/1950), Section 27,
which stated that the Ordinance did "not apply to the growing
of tea by Africans in the native areas", the reason being that "it
was undesirable that the Kenya Tea Board with a majority of
representatives of European Tea Estates, should be given power
to control large numbers of small African growers in widely
separated parts of the Colony". Ordinance 192 Sections 4 and 5
limited the granting of licences to tap palm trees to Africans and
Arabs, "except on the authority of the Governor in Council",
in order to keep the trade "as far as possible in the hands of the
local producer". Ordinance 104 of the Ministry for Legal Affairs
controlled "the granting of credit to Africans by non-Africans"
and was, said the Chief Secretary, "discriminatory in favour of
Africans and the main provisions of the Ordinance safeguarded
African interests". Section 82 of the Civil Procedure regulations in
the Ministry for Legal Affairs discriminated in favour of "women
who by the custom of their community should not be compelled
to appear in public", by exempting them "from personal appearance
in Court".

"But", said Chanan Singh, "racial discrimination in this country
is not so much in theory as it is in practice. It is in the day to day
administration of the country that discrimination exists, and it is
very real too". For example Europeans and Asians were able to use
their power on boards and committees to gain advantages for themselves at African expense. This evil was not new. In the early years
after the War, to take an example, when Africans were trying to get

into the transport business, Transport Licencing Board licences were
sometimes refused to Africans after they had been allowed to
purchase lorries because, as *Mwalimu* reported, there were many
roads on which transport facilities were monopolised by Asians or
Europeans.[47]

At the same time in those earlier years to discriminate in certain
economic fields and to maintain discrimination based on race was
felt by some to be necessary for the safeguarding of African, and
sometimes of Asian, interests. In 1948, for instance, the Financial
Secretary explained in Legislative Council that, if in matters of
payment there was to be no distinction between Europeans, Asians
and Africans, many African artisans would be unemployed or
soaring costs would curtail the amount of work offered by employers.
"I would suggest", he said, "that discrimination on racial grounds—
frankly racial grounds—is in the interests of all communities".[48]
It was the same in the case of Civil Service salaries until Africans
and Asians became able to fill posts with an efficiency and reliability
equal to that displayed by Europeans whose services in consequence
would not be so uniquely required as before. Then equal pay became
the just reward for equal work, but the abolition of the three-fifths
rule entailed the abrogation of what some Europeans had come to
regard as a European privilege; and privilege is seldom relinquished
without a struggle.

Chanan Singh also said that "the Government cannot find a single
Indian or African to be a Magistrate. The situation is aggravated
when one finds that many (or probably most) of the Magistrates of
the Colony haven't seen the inside of a Law School. There are
scores of Indian Barristers and Advocates who have higher qualifications to administer the office". Multi-racial societies need the
appointment of legally qualified stipendiary Magistrates, but
throughout the White Highlands there were also many European
Magistrates who carried on the traditions of the English Bench,
composed of men and women, not trained in the law but chosen for
their impartiality and honesty of judgement. In Kenya in the
fifties there was not the same confidence in Asian impartiality.

Admission to Hotels
One of the most harmful aspects of discrimination which had no
legal backing was the exclusion of Asians and Africans from hotels
and restaurants patronised by Europeans. Social discrimination

offended against human dignity and self-respect and caused deep emotional wounds and resentment.

In the nineteen-forties Africans were only able to go to public cinemas if they were "recommended by the Municipal Affairs Officer as being able to behave themselves".[49] This restriction was the result of instances of bad behaviour by some of the less advanced Africans and was imposed in order that decent standards might be preserved. The better educated, who had to get official recommendations, suffered because of the behaviour of others, but with such a recommendation they were admitted. Admittance to hotels posed a more difficult problem. Kenya was a British colony and the development of its social life was along western lines. In the nineteen-forties there were few Africans who could have paid the prices charged by the good hotels, and these few would have acquired in Britain or America the standards of behaviour required. But there were many Asians who could have paid the prices, but who were conversant with eastern rather than western manners, and the hotel proprietors were afraid of offending their European customers if they opened their doors to Asians; and so the 'westernized' Asians and the few eligible Africans suffered and European social exclusiveness was supported by discrimination against members of the other races in hotels and restaurants. However, change was beginning to appear. A few years after the end of the War, although the main hotels were ordinarily still open to Europeans only, several of them were willing to allow African and Asian guests to attend official functions in their reception rooms. This was a beginning of change, but although it was welcome in one respect, from another point of view it brought a sense of patronage to exacerbate the Africans' sense of grievance. In 1948 Ohanga told Legislative Council how deeply Africans could be wounded by the situation. "We consider," he said, "that European hotels, like European shops and garages, should be run on non-racial lines. Sometimes, on special occasions, my colleague and I are invited to parties or receptions in European hotels in the company of European officials or friends. These gestures are appreciated. But we are sometimes forced to wonder whether it is really genuine and proper when we realise that if one happened to forget his hat and had to return alone, a minute after the party had dispersed, he would not be accorded admission".[50]

The European outlook of exclusiveness and privilege was so complete that it did not differentiate between private and public places and institutions: the Muthaiga Club and the Norfolk Hotel were regarded equally as European preserves. Even when the Lake Hotel at Naivasha was being used by the Solent flying boat service as the starting point of the journey to Britain, African travellers were not served with breakfast in the dining room. In 1950, for instance, J. K. arap Chemallan, a Member of Legislative Council, flew from there on a visit to England sponsored by the British Council. Even though he was accompanied as far as the aircraft by a British Council officer, he was not allowed to go into the dining room but had to have his breakfast in the bar, which was still littered with the uncleaned ash trays and unwashed glasses of the previous evening. This discrimination was humiliating. It was also absurd, because his next meal would be served in the more congested conditions of an aeroplane with no racial segregation.

It was natural that Asians and Africans should have demanded legislation to end discrimination in hotels, but in the nineteen-forties almost all Europeans were opposed to any relaxation of the "Europeans only" rule. Legislation to force hotel proprietors to discard racial discrimination could only have been passed if the Government had overridden the European Elected Members. Most of the few Europeans who wanted to see an end to racial discrimination in hotels were opposed to its abolition by law because they thought that that would have created such ill will that the cause of inter-racial goodwill and tolerance would have been seriously harmed. In fact in the early fifties a sufficiently liberal change took place among some of the European Elected Members with the backing of some of their constituents that they themselves asked the Hotel Keepers' Association to bring an end to racial discrimination.

Few unofficial Europeans followed the lead given by the Governor in the matter of inter-racial entertainment. During Mitchell's Governorship there was no colour bar at Government House and he and Lady Mitchell regularly attended parties in Asian houses. Although the Governor was the Representative of the King, the leading settlers did not feel that this made him the social leader of the Colony. His entertainment of senior Africans and Asians was novel. His predecessor once said to Leonard Beecher, then Archdeacon, with reference to a leading African, educated in Britain, "Are you suggesting that I should have a black man at my table?"[51] Government House did not have this novel experience till Mitchell became Governor; but his policy did not influence the

European social hierarchy.

One evening in 1946, when the Governor was in conference at Government House with the General Officer Commanding in Chief, he was called out to the hall to see an indignant young African, who announced himself as the son of the Governor of Chad, who had kept the Allied flag flying in 1940. Young Eboué was on his way from Paris to Madagascar and on arrival in Nairobi found that no decent hotel would take him because of his colour. He had been directed to an hotel which he found "sale et impossible". Mitchell invited him to stay at Government House and found him "a very pleasant guest".[52] A few years later things were just as bad. In 1950 the Chief Justice of Kenya and Lady Nihill had a dinner party and took their guests on to a concert at Torrs Hotel, for which they had already bought tickets. Among their guests were Apa Pant, the Commissioner for the Government of India, and his wife. When the Chief Justice presented the tickets at the hotel entrance, he was told that, tickets or no tickets, the Pants could not be admitted because they were not Europeans. The hotel authorities were adamant and the fact that they were the Commissioner for the Government of India and his wife and the guests of the Chief Justice made no difference.[53]

In Nairobi the Avenue Hotel in Delamere Avenue (now Kenyatta Avenue) was owned by Asians, but only Europeans were allowed to use it. When Sir Dingle Foot went to Kenya for the Koinange trial in 1953 Wycliffe W. W. Awori, Member of Legislative Council, booked him a room at the Avenue Hotel. Awori took him there and went in with him into the hall but was rudely ejected.[54] The Queens Hotel (now called Brunner's Hotel), however, although owned by an Asian, had no colour bar after 1948 when Emile Brunner arrived as Manager. He opened it to suitably dressed Asians and Africans for meals and accommodation. A few Africans stayed there and many more, as well as Asians, had meals there.[55] Elsewhere discrimination lasted for some years, but as early as 1948 the British Council Representative was allowed to take Joseph Thuo and Laurence Kibui, journalists on the staff of *Baraza*, to have coffee *on the verandah* of the Norfolk Hotel.[56] At the New Stanley Hotel Africans and Asians were able to have meals towards the end of 1953, but it was not till later that Africans were allowed to stay there. In that year even the African Member of the Royal Commission was refused accommodation in the New Stanley. The change came about because in September 1953 the European Elected Members at Blundell's instigation, arranged two meetings with the Hotel Keepers' Association and the Association "agreed that access to hotels will not be prevented on grounds of colour".[57] Could the Nairobi Hotel Keepers be sincere? Africans wondered. In 1954 Wycliffe Awori went with two or three other Africans to have lunch at the New Stanley Grill, which was one of the smartest restaurants in Nairobi, in order to find out. To their astonishment none of the Europeans who were lunching there seemed to notice them and they subsequently commented on the courtesy of the staff and the excellence of the service. As the more progressive Europeans had foreseen, this resolution of the Hotel Keepers Association did not result in the immediate flooding of hotels by Asians and Africans. The type of food served did not appeal to many Asians at that time and prices were too high for almost all Africans.

Although African politicians very understandably inveighed against racial discrimination in social matters, the most bitter utterances against European exclusiveness came from Asian, not African, sources, because there were many Asians on the same economic level as Europeans. In his long Presidential Address to the East African Indian National Congress in 1950, J. M. Nazareth said that "the racial insult implied in the exclusion of non-Europeans otherwise unexceptionable, solely because they wore 'the livery of the burnished sun', is vicariously taken as an insult to the whole race, not readily forgotten for it is wholly gratuitous". "Tinkerings by means of palliatives, such as the United Kenya Club" he declared "will not do. Indeed they may be worse than useless", because "Small reforms are often the enemy of big ones". He told his audience that European officials and unofficials had banded together to resist any demands for legislation against racial discrimination and he maintained that legislation was necessary because "a few race-prejudiced, loud-mouthed European bigots can hold the fort of race prejudice against a whole army of better-disposed persons".[58]

The Society of Civil Liberties was showing at that time how possible it was for a group of determined racialists to overturn moderate, co-operative policies and, without breaking the law, to hamper the enactment of progressive legislation. They wanted to ensure the maintenance of European supremacy and the network of European privilege. But they were strongly opposed by many Europeans and similarly there were Asians who did not approve

Nazareth's outburst and saw that the social discrimination, which offended the humanity of leading Asians and Africans, could not be ended by legislation but only by a change of attitude. A more imaginative approach led one highly placed Asian to see that the Europeans were a self-contained society who did not need the company of the other races. "We were asking them", Dr. Hassan Nathoo said, "to give up their exclusive, privileged position. Let us be understanding and patient". As Lawrence Gandar, the Editor of *The Rand Daily Mail*, put it, "the history of multiracial communities is essentially the story of the reluctant accepting the unthinkable".[59]

Although in 1953 the European Elected Members had persuaded the Hotel Keepers Association to agree to abolish the colour bar, this agreement was disregarded in the White Highlands and on the Coast where Europeans spent their holidays; but during the mid-nineteen-fifties the progressive element among the Europeans had grown so considerably that it became possible for the European Elected Members to support legislation to enforce everywhere the assurance given by the Hotel Keepers Association in 1953. There was little need to expect much opposition when in June 1957 Masinde Muliro moved a Motion in Legislative Council urging Government "to take every necessary step towards the progressive elimination of all forms of discrimination in hotels, restaurants and public places". Arap Moi wisely said in the debate in Legislative Council that "one cannot force somebody to admit somebody of a lower standard who would be an embarrassment to other guests". Every year more Asians and Africans were coming on the scene with standards acceptable anywhere, but still in the White Highlands and on the Coast the doors of hotels were shut against them. Arap Moi justifiably said that "the situation as a whole in the Rift Valley is intolerable". And not only in the Rift Valley. Ronald Ngala mentioned an African doctor at Malindi who could not get "any sleeping accommodation or any eating facilities in any of the hotels" there, and that, said Ngala, "is a very shameful thing, because as an officer serving in that District he should be given some respect in the place where he is serving". In Mombasa Makerere graduates working with the Shell Company suffered discrimination in hotels and Ngala himself, when he gave two English soldiers a lift on the road from Mombasa to Nairobi, was unable to have lunch with them at Mac's Inn at Mtito Andei but had to go for his food to an Indian eating house nearby. The fact that Ngala was a Legislative Councillor did not affect the issue and Arap Moi experienced the same discrimination in Eldoret, Kitale and Nakuru. In Nyanza, however, as Mrs. Shaw told the Council, there was no discrimination in hotels by the middle of the fifties. The hotel at Kisumu had been enlarged in the late nineteen forties when Kisumu seemed likely to be the site of an intercontinental airport and had been open to all for many years, and the excellent Tea Hotel at Kericho was also by then free from racial prejudice. It was widely recognised in Legislative Council that discrimination in hotels and restaurants could no longer be tolerated and the question was put and carried. J. R. Maxwell sounded a discordant note. The cynical attitude, which for so long had embittered race relations, was heard when he said, "I cannot treat this Motion with the seriousness which it possibly deserves".[60] In the Legislative Council of 1957 such an attitude was out of date. This debate provided an instance of the inter-racial co-operation which had been achieved in many ways behind the public arena of Legislative Council. In May 1957 Ngala and Oguda had supper with Blundell in his flat in Nairobi. Both told him of discrimination which they had suffered, including the episode at Mac's Inn. Blundell took the matter up with the Council of Ministers and the debate was preceded by inter-racial agreement at the highest level. It is interesting to notice that only four years earlier Blundell and Havelock, Awori and Gichuru had to have lunch together almost in secret.

But, even later, racial prejudice was not entirely ended. In 1959 a group of back benchers in Legislative Council toured the Central Province. They included Bernard Mate, Dr. Kiano, Jeremiah Nyagah and Tom Mboya, an Asian, K. D. Travadi, and Humphrey Slade, who acted as Secretary. At Nyeri Nyagah arranged for Travadi, Slade and Mboya to stay at the Outspan Hotel, while the other members of the party stayed with friends. In the morning all four tyres of Mboya's car were found slashed. The Hotel Management were greatly distressed and immediately provided new tyres. It was later found that the slashing was the work of a European police officer, who objected to an African staying at the Outspan.[61] In 1959, however, such behaviour was only an echo from a dead past. Opinion had widely changed and legislation, which would have aroused European opposition in 1947, was almost universally accepted ten years later.

Inadequate Information Service

Racial discrimination became increasingly harmful to race relations as education increased among Africans. One by one discriminatory practices were abolished and the work of promoting inter-racial co-operation was patiently pursued by organisations and individuals. There was, however, a lack in Government circles of aplpreciation of the post-War spirit of the senior Africans and their feeing of frustration at being given so little responsibility in the spheres of government and administration. There was also an inadequate information service to combat the propaganda resulting from this sense of frustration.

Explanation of policies was especially necessary in a period of new ideas and social changes like the late nineteen forties, but understanding and explanation were inadequate. The Government did little to find out the opinions of leading Africans when new policies were being advocated and to use them to explain new policies to the people. Academically in the late nineteen forties there were few highly educated Africans, but there was not a lack of men whose experience and social position in the Districts made them leaders among both the peasantry and the growing "white collar" class. The Government showed a lack of imagination in ignoring them. The Report of the Committee on African education under the chairmanship of Archdeacon Beecher published in 1949,[62] illustrates this point. It was a sincere attempt to lay sound foundations for future advance, bearing in mind the inadequate funds made available; but Africans thought it was an attempt to keep back African progress in order that Africans might remain servants of the Europeans. The Administration had made the mistake of including only one African in the Committee and Africans felt that their opinions, expressed through Local Native Councils, had received scant attention.[63]

In the same way the reasons for a lower price paid for African-grown than for European-grown maize were not adequately explained. Europeans had to transport their maize themselves and pay for their own capital development, but the African Land Utilisation and Settlement Board and the later African Land Development Board existed to help the African growers, who had no transport problems and received help of various kinds from the Board.[64] In this matter explanation could have helped to a considerable extent, but, as S. V. Cooke showed in Legislative Council when he attacked Major

Keyser, who was a principal grower of maize in the Trans Nzoia, the difference in price was such that it could be claimed that discrimination as well as the provision of benefits for Africans entered into the calculations.[65]

Importance of Human Relations

It was a confused period. The growth of liberalism among Europeans was gaining momentum, but the effect of this change was often marred by some political speech or some action springing from the diminishing "master race" outlook. Many Africans were anxious to achieve inter-racial co-operation, but an African nationalism was gaining in strength as a sense of frustration increased. The extremists of every race might become more extreme as the fear of losing a position of dominance made the die-hard Europeans more adamant and the indications of unexpectedly quick success made the African nationalists more uncompromising. The promotion of inter-racial harmony required an enlargement of the moderate, co-operative centre, because, as Sir Andrew Cohen wrote out of his great experience at the Colonial Office and as Governor of Uganda and British representative on the Trusteeship Council of the United Nations, "However important policy and policy-making may be, human relations are still more important in successful government and development".[66]

In South Africa in 1955 the frustration and wounded self-respect of Africans had found expression in the Freedom Charter adopted by the African National Congress in Johannesburg. "All national groups", one clause declared, "shall be protected by law against insults to their race and national pride".[67] Legislation can prevent discrimination, but it cannot provide goodwill, although it may sometimes be a step towards the provision of goodwill. It is the last resort, a negative sanction, to be employed when positive human understanding and appreciation of standards have failed, but legislation is only possible when the legislators are willing to agree to it. In South Africa in 1955 the Freedom Charter was an unattainable dream, because the legislators were in the main opposed to its principles and elected by voters equally opposed. In Kenya in 1957 the legislators were able to condemn discrimination because the opinions of the majority of the electorate had undergone profound changes during the previous few years.

Tribal Rivalry

Discrimination and prejudice were not vices confined to Europeans. Tribalism was, and is, a strong force in Kenya and what was regarded as loyalty could become discrimination in inter-tribal relations. Local African politics and tribal rivalry could on occasion even use racialism as a weapon with which to discredit their opponents, if it seemed opportune to do so. The most astonishing case of smear which could not fail to harm racial goodwill, occurred in a quarter where inter-racial harmony was at its richest.

In a book called *A Place To Feel At Home* Professor B. A. Ogot of the University of Nairobi wrote that soon after the appointment in 1955 of the present Archbishop of Kenya, the Most Reverend Festo Olang', as Assistant Bishop, working in Nyanza, the Venerable K. E. Stovold then Archdeacon of Nyanza, went to England "on furlough". Ogot continued, "Unfortunately, it was widely believed by many Christians in Nyanza that he had resigned from his post because he was opposed to working under an African bishop. And in the racial atmosphere then prevailing in Kenya the story sounded quite plausible. . . . Whether or not the accusation against Stovold was true, it was believed in London as well as in Kenya".[68]

Stovold was in fact convinced that the Church in Kenya would not advance in any significant way unless African leaders were trained and established in office. He appreciated that lack of background and experience would make it necessary for Europeans to help and advise them and his policy, ever since he went to Nyanza as a Rural Dean in 1947, was to produce African leaders and himself to serve under them and continue to train them by helping them with advice and whatever practical assistance they needed. When in 1950 the British Council Representative invited the Anglican Bishop to suggest an African clergyman to be the recipient of a British Council scholarship, it was Stovold who recommended Festo Olang' who then spent a year at Wycliffe Hall, Oxford, and some months as a curate in Bristol. It was Stovold who arranged for his Rural Deanery to be Africanised and who served under Olang', who became Rural Dean at Maseno. And, when a new Assistant Bishop had to be appointed to replace Leonard Beecher who succeeded Bishop Reginald Crabb, Stovold did all he could to secure the appointment of an African. Bishop Beecher chose Festo Olang', who was consecrated by the Archbishop of Canterbury in Namirembe Cathedral, Kampala, in May 1955.

Then Stovold felt free to agree to the request of the Church Missionary Society that he should be appointed Metropolitan Secretary for London and the South of England, an appointment which enabled him to be in England for a few of the years during which his children were at school there.[69] J.M. Lonsdale has pointed out that in Nyanza Province the attitude of the Church Missionary Society was very different from that of the Roman Catholics and the American missions. "The C.M.S.", he writes, "evangelized the area from Uganda, which had a very long tradition of African responsibility in church affairs".[70]

Ogot's assertion that "the accusation against Stovold . . . was believed in London as well as in Kenya" is strange, because the Church Missionary Society had wanted him for some time to work in London, but he had insisted on staying in Kenya until an African Assistant Bishop had been installed. The explanation of the affair may perhaps lie in tribalism.

All the land round Maseno was originally held by Luyias. In or about 1900 some Luos, who had conquered the flat lakeside area from the Luyias, advanced up into the hills and acquired land round Maseno by force. The majority of the congregation in the church at Maseno have consistently been Luyias,[71] but many Luos believe that Maseno was formerly an entirely Luo area, into which Luyias infiltrated. The appointment of the Luyia Olang' was resented by the Luos, who wanted the Assistant Bishop to be a Luo and resented the presence of a Luyia Assistant Bishop at Maseno, which they erroneously regarded as a traditional Luo Centre.

Luo objection to Bantu authority was of long standing. For instance, in 1920 the Chief Native Commissioner wrote that the Paramountcy of the famous Mumia as Chief, which he held by hereditary right, was something which should not be allowed to pass to his successor because "the Nilotic section of North Kavirondo have always viewed with disfavour any active interference in their affairs by Mumia because he is a Bantu". Indeed, he continued, "the original request by the Nilotic section to be brought into the Kisumu District was actuated by their desire to be free of Bantu Paramountcy".[72] Rivalry between the Luos and the Luyias, the Nilotics and Bantus, of the Western part of Kenya, continued to be a strong emotional force and it could easily show itself at the appointment of a Luyia Bishop in an area where many of the clergy were Luos. Soon after Olang's consecration tribal enmity was

further shown when Olang' was "accused of discrimination against
the Luo".[73]

Towards the end of the colonial period inter-tribal discrimination
received some of the odium which had previously been reserved for
inter-racial favouritism. Throughout the fifties Africans in the civil
service felt that they were always discriminated against by the
Asians who occupied positions in the hierarchy between them and the
Europeans at the top; and they believed that in commercial concerns
also Asians discriminated in favour of their fellow Asians. But
when Africans reached responsible positions in commercial firms,
it was no longer only the Asians and Europeans who discriminated
in favour of their own kind. "When there is an African Personnel
Officer of a particular tribe", an African complained, "instead of
employing people on their merits, he goes to employ people of his
own tribe".[74] Discrimination in favour of one's own community
was not a phenomenon confined to the immigrant races of Kenya
before Independence. What is discrimination to those who suffer
is sometimes regarded as group loyalty by those who discriminate.
It is not impossible that in 1955 tribal jealousy and resentment
wanted to discredit the appointment of Olang' and tried to do so by
casting aspersions on the European who had lived for so long
at Maseno and worked so closely with him. The incident showed the
danger of ethnic disunity and discrimination taking the place of
inter-racial tensions, when the causes of these had been removed.

The White Highlands

A curious example of discrimination arose after the publication
and consideration of the report of the Royal Commission on Land
and Population. The Commission concluded that land in East
Africa should be used to the best advantage and should not be
subject to racial or tribal restrictions. In 1959 the Kenya Government
issued a Sessional Paper and the Chief Secretary told Legislative
Council that "Government policy is to aim at the progressive
elimination of racial and tribal land barriers".[75] The "declared
policy of the Government" as set out in the Sessional Paper was
"to ensure that the basis of tenure and management of agricultural
land will be similar throughout Kenya, regardless of race or tribe,
as far as local economic and agronomic factors will permit".[76]
That policy, which was in keeping with the recommendations of
the Royal Commission, was not implemented, however. The

Highlands Order in Council was to be altered to enable any one of any race with the necessary knowledge and finance to acquire land in the hitherto *White* Highlands, but the boundaries of the African Reserves were still to remain inviolate. It was a novel situation. The Europeans became the victims of racial discrimination when the White Highlands were opened to other races but the African Reserves remained closed to them. One of the causes of African grievance was removed, but the geographical basis of tribalism remained untouched.

1. Sir Philip Mitchell's Diary, 17 Dec. 1952.
2. Quoted in Corfield Report. *Cmnd. 1030, 1960*, p. 26.
3. A mimeographed copy is among the Miller papers.
4. *A Humanist in Africa. Letters to Colin Morris from Kenneth Kaunda*, p. 50.
5. Sir Philip Mitchell's Diary, 11 Oct. 1946.
6. E.A.S. 13 April 1951.
7. Interview with Joseph Thuo, 21 Feb. 1970.
8. *A Statement by the African Members of Legislative Council*, 15 Aug. 1952. A copy is in Kendall Ward Deposit (V.O.K. Box) in the Kenya National Archives.
9. "Absolute ownership of land is an idea foreign to all the tribes in Kenya". (Norman Leys: *Kenya*, p. 35).
10. L. S. B. Leakey to S. V. Cooke, 16 March, 1939, in file belonging to S. V. Cooke.
11. Carl J. Rosberg: "Political Conflict and Change in Kenya" in *Transition in Africa*, ed. Gwendolen M. Carter and William O. Brown, p. 115.
12. Fr. C. Cangolo, I.M.C.: *The Akikuyu*, p. 17.
13. Elspeth Huxley: *White Man's Country*, Vol. I, p. 111.
14. Donald L. Barnett and Karari Njama: *Mau Mau from Within*, p. 33.
15. Cmd. 4556, p. 74.
16. Carl J. Rosberg: *Transition in Africa*, op. cit., p. 105.
17. Movement for a Democracy of Content: *Kenya under the Iron Heel*, p. 2.
18. George Padmore: *Africa: Britain's Third Empire*, p. 59.
19. European Agricultural Settlement Board: Report 1960.
20. George Padmore: *How Britain Rules Africa*, p. 104.
21. Y. R. Ghai and J. P. W. B. McAuslan: op. cit., p. 81.
22. A. J. Matson: *Nandi Resistance to British Rule*, p. 145.
23. Ghai and McAuslan: op., cit. p. 81.
24. George Padmore: *Africa: Britain's Third Empire*, p. 61.
25. Ione Leigh: *In the Shadow of Mau Mau*.
26. H.C.D., vol. 631, cols. 16–17, 25 Nov. 1960.
27. Telegram from Governor to Secretary of State, 24 Nov. 1960, File Court 2/2 1957/61, in Kenya National Archives.
28. Chairman of European Land Settlement Board to Minister of Agriculture, 10 April 1959. Blundell 5/4.
29. *Kenya Agricultural Census 1962. Scheduled Areas and Coastal Strip: A Statistical Analysis Prepared by the Economic and Statistics Division, Ministry of Finance and Economic Planning 1963*, para. 5.
30. *Kenya Agricultural Census 1964. Large Farm Areas, Statistics Division' Ministry of Economic Planning and Development*, Table 2.
31. Y. R. Ghai and J. P. W. B. McAuslan, op. cit., p. 42.
32. Aristotle: *Politics* (Jowett's translation), Book III, section 9, sub-section 1.
33. *East African Law Reports*, 1960, pp. 62ff and 644ff respectively.

34. Sir Philip Mitchell's Diary, 16 July 1948.
35. Sir John Whyatt to R. A. Frost, 1953.
36. Personal experience of R. A. Frost, July, 1947.
37. Speech at Royal Colonial Institute quoted in Rita Hinden: *Empire and After*, p. 74.
38. Eldridge Cleaver: *Soul on Ice*, p. 73.
39. Benjamin Disraeli: *Vivian Grey*.
40. Philip Mason: *The Birth of a Dilemma*, p. 307.
41. ibid., p. 308.
42. Memorandum, pp. 3–4 in Sir Arthur Young's papers.
43. Note by Blundell: Blundell 12/4.
44. Cmd. 9081, para. 61.
45. L.C.D., 3 Dec. 1953, Col. 739.
46. There is a copy of this document in *Papers Laid, Vol. VI* 1955/56 in the Library of the National Assembly. Another copy is in the Library of the Kenya National Archives. The Departmental Memoranda from which the Review was compiled are in the Office of the Chief Secretary, Deposit No. 8/1400 II, in the Kenya National Archives.
47. L.C.D., 4 Dec. 1946, Col. 580.
48. L.C.D. 27 Aug. 1948, Col. 575.
49. L.C.D. 26 Jan. 1949, Col. 1353.
50. ibid., 8 March 1948. Col. 169.
51. Interview with Dr. Beecher, 15 March 1971.
52. Sir Philip Mitchell's Diary, 3 April 1946.
53. Interview with Sir Barclay Nihill, 21 May 1969.
54. Interview with W. W. W. Awori, 10 Feb. 1970.
55. Interview with Emile Brunner, 12 March 1970.
56. Incident recalled by Joseph Thuo in interview on 21 Feb. 1970.
57. Blundell to Joelson, 10 Sept. 1953, Blundell 12/4.
58. The East Indian National Congress, 20th Session, Eldoret, August 1950.
59. Quoted in Julius Lewin: *The Struggle for Racial Equality*, p. 70.
60. The debate is reported in L.C.D. 13 June 1957. Cols. 1289–1331.
61. Interview with Hon. Jeremiah Nyagah, M.P., 10 Feb. 1970.
62. *African Education in Kenya. Report of a Committee Appointed to Enquire into the Scope, Content and Methods of African Education, its Administration and Finance and to Make Recommendations.* (Ven. Archdeacon L. Beecher, Chairman).
63. This point was made for instance by Philip Ngutia, Secretary of the Local Native Council at Kakamega. Interview in August 1950, Frost papers.
64. D. P. Ghai and J. P. W. B. McAuslan: op. cit. p. 110.
65. L.C.D., 14 April 1947, Col. 50.
66. Sir Andrew Cohen, op. cit., p. 64.
67. Quoted in Julius Lewin, op. cit. p. 55.
68. F. B. Welbourn and B. A. Ogot: *A Place to Feel At Home*, p. 41.
69. Archbishop Olang' regards the "accusation" against Archdeacon Stovold as utterly false. Interview with Archishop Olang', 14 March 1971.
70. J. M. Lonsdale: "European Attitudes and African Pressures: Missions and Government in Kenya between the Wars", *Race*, Vol. X, No. 2, October 1968.
71. Interview with Archdeacon Stovold, 4 March 1970.
72. *Native Tribes and Their Customs:* Vol. IV, Par.1.10. "Some People of Nyanza Province", Addendum to Memo on *Mumia and the Position of Paramount Chief*, paragraph 6, in the Kenya National Archives.
73. Welbourne and Ogot: op. cit. p. 140.
74. E.A.S., 16 March 1962 (letter).
75. L.C.D., 22 April 1959, Col. 92.
76. *Land Tenure and Central Outside the Native Lands: Sessional Paper No. 10* of 1958/9.

6

RESORT TO VIOLENCE

A failure in Trusteeship

Tribalism was a fundamental fact in Kenya. Colonial government had stopped tribal warfare but had not put an end to inter-tribal animosity, although education was beginning to lessen tribal feeling among those who went to secondary schools. One of the greatest achievements of the Alliance High School, whose pupils came from all over Kenya, was the substitution of a common loyalty for tribal rivalry, but in general tribal feelings and rivalries remained strong. An Institute of Race Relations might have helped to make known the various differences in tribal custom which existed throughout, Kenya but the Colonial Office did not support the proposal to found one.

The Colonial Office probably had two reasons for its objection to the formation of an Institute of Race Relations. Premises and a staff competent to engage in research and write reports on African conditions and inter-racial problems would have cost money. There would have been little hope of raising the necessary funds by voluntary subscription in Kenya and the majority of the European Elected Members would undoubtedly have opposed a proposal to provide the funds from the Kenya budget. The money would have had to be supplied by the British Government.

The Colonial Office may also have feared that an Institute working on the lines of the South African Institute, whose activities had been explained to the Nairobi conference by Dr. Rheinhallt-Jones, might have stirred up trouble in a situation which was more complicated than anything known in Kenya before the War. Its surveys into African conditions inevitably caused the South African Institute to be in opposition to the policies of the South African Government even without engaging in political activities, and the publication of surveys into the bases of Kenya society, the poverty of Africans and the discrimination which maintained European privileges, might have given support to the discontent, which was growing among the nationalist politicians and the disappointed soldiers and the unemployed.

It was an unfortunate decision. What was most needed was knowledge. The Europeans were ignorant of African progress and were apt to think that there were no Africans different from the farm labourers and the manual workers with whom they came into contact in the towns; and the Africans had little understanding of the managerial work and the various skills needed in farming and commerce. As it was, there was no organisation to provide scientific and impartial information about any race. The right wing element was still preponderant among Europeans and might have been critical of an Institute which threw light into dark corners. The Governor himself was willing to support the proposal, but the Colonial Office seems to have been less willing to follow bold, though perhaps risky, policies.

Mau Mau was evidence of a failure of trusteeship. A trustee ought to have knowledge of his ward's hopes and desires. It may not be possible to grant all that he wants, but without adequate information and understanding there is likely to be conflict. The Government's information services were inadequate. For this the European Elected Members were largely to blame. Their budgetary cheese-paring seriously restricted the social welfare and community development services, which were an important link between the Administration and the peasants. Officialdom also was to blame. The effects of the World War do not seem to have been recognised. Contact with the outside world made African politicians impatient for greater responsibilities at all levels. Even Sir Philip Mitchell did not appreciate the need for bold, and perhaps dangerous, innovation when he said that Kenyatta, who had just returned from Europe as the acknowledged leader of the Kikuyus, would have to serve an apprenticeship in local government before he could be nominated to Legislative Council.[1] Lack of imagination caused strict adherence to three-fifths salary scales for Africans and prevented Africans from holding the chairmanships of Local Native Councils, even with ultimate safeguards remaining with District Commissioners. The more senior members of the Administration seemed to wish to deceive themselves into thinking that all was well and to prevent any reports of disaffection from reaching the Governor. Few of them could speak Kikuyu, and indeed, as one District Commissioner reported, "they were not encouraged to sit down

and learn Kikuyu."[2] One Provincial Commissioner even said that
he thought it was wise not to be able to speak the vernacular.
District Officers were frequently moved: eighteen months was a long
period for a single posting. "Had some of us stayed longer in the
Reserve," Hughes wrote, "and had been freed by the acquisition of
adequate staff at Headquarters to get out and live in the Reserve,
our tocsins would have been sounded earlier and with far greater
clarity."[3] Such warning reports as were sent to the Secretariat in
Nairobi were often unacknowledged. The administrative dislike of
criticism made some senior officers turn a deaf ear to the warnings
of unrest which the missionaries, who could speak Kikuyu, tried to
give them. Even Leonard Beecher, who had served for many years
in Legislative and Executive Councils, was not allowed to suggest
that all was not well. Once when he was Assistant Bishop in Western
Kenya, he went to dedicate a church in the Fort Hall Reserve.
The District Officer who attended the service asked him how he
liked being back in an area which he had formerly known intimately.
The Bishop replied that he was disturbed by the disaffection which
he knew to be strong among the Kikuyus. That evening the District
Commissioner telephoned to him to ask him what he had been telling
the District Officer. Beecher said that such things could not be
discussed on the telephone and suggested a meeting. This the District
Commissioner refused to agree to, because he said that everything
was well in the District, and he asked the Bishop never to speak to
his District Officers in such terms again.[4]

The warnings given by the missionaries in the Districts were no
more listened to than was the warning given by Mathu in Legislative
Council in 1948 when he described the clandestine meetings held in
banana groves and caves.[5] The Kenya African Union also warned
the Government about what was going on, but they too were
ignored. The Attorney General mentioned Mau Mau by name in
Legislative Council in November 1950 and its existence among
squatters and in the Reserves was known among Government
circles two years before a State of Emergency was declared.[6] Africans
believed that M. E. W. North, who was District Commissioner at
Thika, was removed because he knew too much and might embarrass
the Administration.[7] However much the Administration was to
blame for allowing Mau Mau to grow like a plant in the darkness
until it burst out into the light, the European politicians also were
not free from blame and their protestations that their warnings had

not been heeded were deprived of their validity because, as the
Governor wrote a year after the declaration of a State of Emergency,
"If the Elected Members really thought that Mau Mau was about to
come why did they cut out the Information Offices and the
Community Development Officers from the Budget?"[8]

North at Thika was not alone in his knowledge of unrest and
subversion among the Kikuyus. R. E. Wainwright, who subsequently
became Provincial Commissioner, Rift Valley, wrote at the beginning
of the Emergency from Kisumu, where he was then District
Commissioner, that when he was a District Officer at Nyeri during
the War, the District Commissioner and the District Officers there
realised that, "although 90 per cent of the Kikuyu were decent
citizens, there was a small hard core of really bad thugs". The
District Commissioner begged for more and better trained police,
but after the War, when Wainwright was District Commissioner at
Embu, he "was still screaming for the police". He was always
promised them, "but each year they were cut out of the Estimates".
"Time and time again", he wrote, "we warned Government of the
dangers arising. . . . The trouble largely seems to be that Nairobi—
and I include European Members in that term as well as Government
Officials—become more and more isolated from the reserves and
the mass of African people as each year passes".[9] The Higher Administration seemed to turn a blind eye to possible trouble and to prevent information from reaching the Governor, and those European
Elected Members whose Constituencies bordered the reserves showed little eagerness for co-operation with their African neighbours.

European politicians had for many years asserted that they ought
to have a large part to play in the administration of trusteeship for
the Africans, but the majority of the European community showed a
racial attitude which contributed to the frustration and ill will which
led to the outbreak of Mau Mau and which was at odds with the
principles of trusteeship. Until a colony became independent
Britain's responsibilities remained. "Even though there were
African Members in Executive and Legislative Council", Mitchell
wrote, the position remained that "Africans were still wards in
trust".[10] European attempts to entrench themselves in power in
Kenya were not compatible with that trusteeship.

The Kikuyu Tribe and Mau Mau

African tribal life was minutely regulated by custom and every

action was based on a code, learned and practised during the months
of preparation for circumcision or other initiation to adult status.
Group outlooks as well as individual actions were regulated by
tradition. The breakdown of tribal custom, which resulted from the
advent of the Europeans, produced a moral vacuum in which
perverted values could grow.[11] The Kikuyu tribe was more open than
any others to disruption as a result of the arrival and settlement of
Europeans. The capital of the colony was established at Nairobi on
the southern edge of Kikuyu country and the disruptive influence
of urban life naturally had the strongest impact on the nearest
tribe. The first European farms were developed from Kikuyu land
and employed Kikuyu labour. Detribalising influences were less
keenly felt in the early years in Nyanza and on the coast and these
areas suffered less from the void left by the breakdown of tribal
sanctions and tribal customs. The intelligence of the Kikuyus, which
was apparent to many of the immigrants, made the situation all the
more dangerous and in the late nineteen forties the Administration
was worried by the standard of behaviour of sections of the tribe. One
District Commissioner wrote in 1950, "An effort to concentrate
public opinion in the distressing state of Kikuyu morals was made
in 1946, when a large conference was held . . . here in Nyeri the
position still leaves much room for improvement".[12] A similar
anxiety was felt by the District Commissioner at Fort Hall, who,
when commenting on the vital need for better farming methods,
wrote, "it is of course intimately connected with the human problem
of reintroducing Tribal Integrity".[13] Colonel Meinertzhagen had
noted at the beginning of the century that the Kikuyus were the most
intelligent tribe he had met and therefore would be the most
progressive under European leadership and "the most susceptible
to subversive activities".[14]

Writers like Donald L. Barnett and Karari Njama in *Mau Mau
from Within* and Ruth First in *The Barrel of a Gun* seem to disregard
the fact that Mau Mau was a Kikuyu uprising and not a general
African national struggle, although all over Kenya the more
advanced Africans wanted to have more responsibility in public
affairs and to see the end of racial discrimination. The majority,
however, did not accept the philosophy or the methods of Mau Mau.
"The revolt lasted for more than three years", writes Ruth First,
"and was defeated by a combination of overkill and terror against
the Land and Freedom Army and the civilian population at large".[15]

She continues by stating that the years between the end of the fighting and the granting of independence were "a most as important as the years of armed conflict in breaking the back of African resistance and grooming a tame and emasculated generation of politicians for the independence era. For by the time that independence constitution-making for Kenya was begun, less than a decade later, the peasant revolt was defeated, and its aims were all but obliterated".[16]

It may, however, be claimed that although there were great overcrowding in the Kikuyu Reserves and inadequate food, resulting to some extent from bad agriculture, and grievances arising from the squatter system, Mau Mau was not a peasant revolt in its inspiration and leadership, but was an attempt by a section of the Kikuyu politicians to seize power, for which they needed the militant help of the peasants. Even within the Kikuyu tribe itself there were some politicians and peasants who were not willing supporters of the revolt.

Neither the Luo in KANU nor the other tribes who formed themselves into KADU[17] had fought in the forests of Mount Kenya and the Aberdares. Tom Mboya rose to national leadership and international status through his creation of the Trades Union Movement. Ronald Ngala, Masinde Muliro and others were acclaimed as leaders by the Coastal tribes, the Kalenjin and the Western Bantu. Kenyatta, when still in detention, was unique in being acclaimed by all as the leader of all the Africans of Kenya. "The generation of militant fighters was dead", writes Ruth First, "imprisoned or black-listed. In its place was a generation that, for the most part, was ready to accept independence as a gentleman's agreement, with the political process as a prerogative of a privileged elite".[18] The militant fighters had been members of the Kikuyu, Embu, and Meru tribes; the Mau Mau rising was a civil war; and the politicians of the later fifties were not a replacement of the "generation of militant fighters" but a generation who had existed during the Emergency and who profited in their negotiations with the British Government by the shock which Mau Mau gave to the slow complacency of the past and to the European community in Kenya.

Mau Mau was a political creation. Its organisers used the hardships arising from overcrowding in the Kikuyu Reserves, the discontent and poverty due to unemployment in Nairobi, the

grievances of squatters on European farms and the ill feelings so
often deriving from European and Asian racial attitudes to forge a
weapon to be used for the attainment of their political purposes.
Sir Andrew Cohen, writing in the late fifties, saw the dangers
inherent in the urban situation at that time. "The mass of Africans,"
he wrote, "is still not modernised, and urban leaders can only
gain support by appealing to the suspicions of the illiterate as well as
the aspirations of the educated".[19]

Remembrance of former wrongs

Alienation of land and fears for the future security of Kikuyu
land were the base on which the organisers decided to build hatred
of Europeans, but there were other causes of discontent which
were to be used by the politicians to feed the fire. The compulsory
carrying of the *Kipande*, unemployment and the terrible conditions
of housing in Nairobi, the recollection of earlier labour regulations
and the behaviour of some of the early settlers all supplied tinder
to augment the flames. In former days, when Sir Edward Northey
was Governor, the settlers' demands for labour were often suppoited
by the Governor's regulations.[20] After the Second World War
Sir Philip Mitchell became Governor and his standards of
impartiality were strict. The settlers' earlier demands for labour
and the methods which some of them advocated for securing it had
left no doubt that, however useful the resident Europeans might be
for the economic development of the Colony, the British Government
could not devolve upon them the responsibility of trusteeship for the
Africans. As the country became more developed, however, and the
number of Europeans increased after the First World War, unofficial European co-operation with Government in the Settled
Areas became increasingly useful and after the Second World War
Creech Jones, when Assistant Secretary of State for the Colonies,
told the House of Commons in London "that the Kenya Government's efforts to develop African land units and raise the living
standards of the African population needed not only the assistance
of the Africans themselves but also of the European Settler community".[21] At that time the Government policy showed no signs
of earlier policies of coercion. In 1949 the Government's Public
Relations Officer told the Editor of the *East African Standard* that
"while Government would accept the principle that Africans should
pay for increased social services and for law and order, they would

not accept the principle that they should be taxed in order to make them come out to work".[22] Liberalism increased among Europeans after the War, but the remembrance of former policies and practices remained and hindered the progress of inter-racial co-operation and harmony.

Although the *Kipande* was a useful document in some respects, bitter remembrance of it remained after it had been abolished in 1947. The obligation to carry it at all times had been felt by the educated to be not only a burden but a humiliation. It was hated by them as a document which discriminated against Africans because they were Africans and it humiliated them as the Jews in Nazi Germany were humiliated by being forced to wear the Star of David as a mark of their inferiority to the master race. The makers of revolutions are not the illiterate and, as the seventeen points proclaimed by the Kenya African Union in 1951 showed, discrimination against the human personality caused greater resentment than was provided by material injustice.

Discriminatory regulations were imposed in order to maintain European privileges. The ban which prevented Africans from growing coffee was an example of this. It was particularly harmful to race relations because it was imposed among other areas on land adjacent to the European estates at Kiambu and Limuru, which the Kikuyu regarded as having been stolen from them by trickery. The capital and skill which had turned them into prosperous coffee estates made the moral position all the more difficult. Whatever might be the truth about the circumstances in which these lands were originally acquired by Europeans, there could be no doubt at all about the fact that it was European capital, skill and effort which had turned them into productive and valuable estates which contributed much to the revenue and reputation of Kenya; but nostalgia for the past and envy of the present caused a problem which the Carter Commission, which Sir Philip Mitchell thought was "a bad and wrong settlement",[23] had been unable to solve. The situation was made more inflammatory by the ban imposed on the cultivation of coffee by Africans. The Europeans at first showed willingness to help their African neighbours to share their prosperity, but selfish greed later caused them to use their power to secure a monopoly for themselves. Looking generally at policy in Africa, Dr. L. P. Mair concludes that European opposition to the growing of coffee by Africans "is actuated primarily by a genuine fear that native plantations will spread disease, and that the native owner will steal his European neighbour's produce and pass it off as his own".[24]

Adjoining a section of the alienated land between the township of Kiambu and the farms at Limuru was the home of Senior Chief Koinange, the leading African in that part of the Reserve. He and his family had offered friendship to the Europeans in former days and their position in the society of the tribe made them a family whose goodwill was of special importance to the Government. Although to begin with his European neighbours showed a spirit of neighbourliness, economic selfishness subsequently displayed itself in blatant form. Ralph J. Bunche was told by Chief Koinange the story of his coffee trees at Kiambu. Canon Leakey gave him some coffee bushes after the District Commissioner had given him permission to plant coffee. He bought other plants from European farmers at Kiambu and also made his own nursery. Later on, however, European coffee planters at Kiambu raised a protest and, as Canon Leakey told the Chief, they said that, if he planted coffee, "all the Kikuyu would follow his example and the white farmers would lose money". Moreover, Canon Leakey said that the Europeans expected "the natives" to steal their coffee and, as they would have coffee of their own, it would be impossible to check theft. Koinange was forced to uproot all his coffee bushes, being paid a small sum in compensation. His nursery was bought cheaply by an Italian, and, said Koinange, "was planted right on my boundary. . . . I've never planted any coffee since".[25] No Government should have been surprised if the Koinanges' home at Kiambu became a centre of disaffection.

Although the Government and the European coffee growers said that the European coffee crop was so valuable for Kenya that a ban had to be placed on the growing of coffee by Africans for fear that their coffee might be diseased and infect the European estates, Africans who wanted to grow coffee, but were forbidden to do so, felt certain that the ban was imposed because, if Africans had grown coffee, they would have been busy on their own holdings, making a small income, and so would have been unwilling to work on the European estates. If they were forbidden to grow coffee, however, they would have to work on the European estates in order to earn the money they needed for their Hut Tax. When, as a result of the insistence of the Rev. Dr. Clive Irvine at Chogoria, the Meru were allowed to grow coffee in 1934 and, when the Kisii also were soon afterwards released from the ban, the Kikuyu were all the more certain that the real reason for the ban was to ensure a supply of labour for the Europeans. Meru and Kisii were far from European farms and so the labour market did not depend on them, but the African Reserve at Kiambu was an essential source of labour for the European estates nearby.[26] Later on, the coffee crop did present difficulties and school children were needed to supplement adult labour. A letter in 1946 from J. S. G. Kanyua, a political figure of some standing in Nakuru, showed the African suspicions that the Government was in league with the settlers and expressed the resentment aroused by racial discrimination. "I have known African school children in the Kiambu Reserve", he wrote, "being ordered against their wish by the local Chief (acting upon instructions from the D.C.) to help with coffee picking whenever the labour position became serious. What about the European and Indian children in Nairobi and district receiving similar instructions and helping with this important crop?"[27] But Africans were not altogether impotent in such matters and, when it was suggested in Nyeri that the date of African school holidays should be changed to coincide with the coffee picking season in order that the children might pick coffee on European farms, a proposal to that effect was rejected by the South Nyeri Local Native Council.[28] The Africans also believed that the Europeans objected to their growing coffee because, if they were allowed to engage in this side of agriculture which had been started and developed by Europeans, they might think of themselves as equal to Europeans and demand social recognition.

Such a fear was seen in the insistence by many Europeans on African use of Swahili. A similar phenomenon was seen in Poland after the German conquest in 1939. The Poles were to be hewers of wood and drawers of water and they were not allowed to speak the language of the "Herrenvolk", the German Master Race. Similarly many Europeans in Kenya considered it right that Africans should not be allowed to speak English. If they conversed with Europeans in English, they might be tempted to suppose they could become the equals of the Europeans. Africans who had a little education and felt that ability to speak a little English was a mark of progress, were saddened by this European rejection, and the better educated were wounded by the humiliation which it brought on them. The master race mentality seemed particularly strange to such Africans as the non-commissioned officers of the Army Education Corps,

who during the War met some Europeans whose education was far
below theirs. At an Anti-Aircraft battery at Embakasi, for instance,
some of the European soldiers asked an African member of the
Army Education Corps to write letters to their wives and families
in Britain because they could not write themselves.

Mau Mau—a Civil War

Professor Sorrenson in his valuable book on Kikuyu land says,
"The conflict over land lay at the bottom of much of the unrest
in the Kikuyu reserve during the post-war years and which was to
develop into the Mau Mau revolt—as much a civil war between the
Kikuyu as a revolt against the colonial government".[29] Litigation
was a great pastime among the Kikuyus. Disputes over land were
frequent and caused frictions and antagonisms within the Reserves.
Among the better educated were some who thought that they could
achieve their aims by violence, but there were others who hoped
to be able to raise African educational and economic standards and
to gain recognition and their rightful place in the life of the country
through co-operation with the Government. "It became", said
Kingsley Martin, "a civil war, mainly fought between the
modernisers, Western-minded, and those who were determined to
maintain the ancient religion of Mount Kenya".[30] To the adherents of
the movement all Kikuyus who were friends of Europeans or
acquiesced in government by Europeans were traitors to the cause
and any who gave evidence against Mau Mau had to be destroyed.
The Lari massacre on 24th March 1953 stemmed from the acceptance
by Chief Luka Wakahangara of the removal of ten *mbari* from
Tigoni to Lari. This move, brought about by the dislike of European
farmers to having a group of Kikuyus living in the otherwise
European area of Limuru, not only meant the expulsion of Kikuyus
from their traditional lands at Tigoni, but their being settled on land
at Lari to which other Kikuyus had claims.[31] The massacre was a
frightful settlement of an old feud within the Kikuyu tribe. Mau Mau
was a civil war, because fundamentally it was not only against
Europeans and the Government but also against anyone including
Kikuyus, who stood between the Kikuyu politicians and power.

Representation in local government

The breakdown of the regulated, customary pattern of tribal life,
the remembrance of former wrongs and the pressure of present

poverty caused great discontent. This however was not itself the
motive force of insurrection. It was a weapon ready to be sharpened
and used by frustrated politicians aiming at the attainment of power.
Power in local government was the first prize to be won, but this
was denied to them. Trustee and ward disagreed over the lengths
to which the devolution of authority could go in the years after the
end of the War. In 1946 James Gichuru, Dedan Mugo, Solomon
Memia and other Africans were elected to membership of the
Kiambu Local Native Council. Some of them believed that it was
time for Africans to be appointed to positions of responsibility
and the first motion, proposed by Solomon Memia, was that an
African should become Chairman of the Local Native Council in
place of the District Commissioner. At the same time the Kamba
Chiefs and Councillors had a similar wish for greater African
responsibility and they presented a memorandum to Creech Jones,
the Assistant Secretary of State, expressing the hope that Presidents
of District Councils would in future be Africans with the District
Commissioner as adviser.[32] The Administration did not agree that
Africans were yet sufficiently experienced to hold such offices and
a few of the most politically minded Kikuyus planned to weld the
Kikuyu people together to demand and secure leading positions,
first in local administration and later at a national level. Ten years
later and after three years of Emergency the African leaders were
still unable to secure the position they wanted in local government
in the African Reserves. In February 1956, Legislative Council
rejected a proposal put forward by the African Members that an
African should be elected as President of the North Nyanza District
Council in place of the District Commissioner. Awori supported
Mathu in saying that only by making mistakes could Africans
learn to carry out various jobs satisfactorily,[33] and Mathu asked in
1954 for opportunities for helping to run the country "for all
communities together".[34] It was not in fact till 1959 that an African
became Chairman of an African District Council. In March of that
year Joseph Pascal Nabwana of South Bukusu became Chairman
of the African District Council in Elgon Nyanza.[35]

The Administration failed to understand the new spirit which
resulted from the experiences of the War. Young men were acquiring
influence and chafed at the lack of political opportunity offered to
them. The paternalistic and too static attitude of the Administration
denied them a share in government, because the implications of the

increase in education were not recognised. Many young men had a certain amount of education. "A little learning is a dangerous thing",[36] and practical experience was all the more necessary. Instead of taking the younger, better educated Africans into the administrative fold the Government left them outside, where, feeling that they could not express their views and make any mark in local government, they turned to anti-Government activities and spent much time in the political world and underworld of Nairobi, where such people as the unemployed ex-soldiers who made up the Forty (1940) Group, who were circumcised together, were stirring up anti-Government and anti-European feeling. Oswald Hughes, District Commissioner at Nyeri, reflecting on the events of those years, acknowledged the mistake when he wrote, "The progressive young Kikuyu, both farmers and traders in the Reserve spent a great deal of their time in K.A.U.[37] Headquarters in Nairobi, while others had become K.A.U. barrack room lawyers. K.A.U. gave them an opportunity, largely denied to them in their locations by chiefs and elders who were out of sympathy with their aspirations. It was our fault—while we wasted our time trying to resuscitate the indigenous authorities, we should instead have been leavening the Chiefs' Advisory Councils with this class and reorientating the chiefs themselves to cater more for the educated young man".[38] These younger men felt frustrated because in local as well as in national government they had no real responsibility.

In Nairobi and other towns the European hold on government was overwhelming and in the White Highlands, where thousands of Africans lived and worked, European councils were in complete control, although to some extent the Administration had a position as guardian for African interests. County Councils were not allowed to levy rates in the African locations, where the standard of living was very low. A few Africans lived at a higher level, but in the early years after the War rating them would probably have required so great a staff to collect so little money that the exercise would have been uneconomic. Similarly, although Europeans often said that the richer Africans ought to pay Income Tax, their number was at first too small to justify the administrative expense required to tax them. "I agree", wrote Blundell in 1948, "the rich African is not deliberately avoiding taxation; the point is no one is making any attempt to get it from him. This applies equally to the highly paid Indian artisan",[39] but six years later it was noted in Legislative

Council that more and more Africans were paying Income Tax.[40]

Over the whole field of taxation experts agreed that in proportion to their capacity to pay, Africans were quite as heavily taxed as Europeans,[41] but the European communal attitude, which was sometimes seen with regard to the financing of education, affected the whole subject of taxation. In Nakuru in 1957 the District Commissioner reported that the County Council system was tending to flounder through lack of funds, and he cited the very low rate imposed on the settlers as the prime cause of this lack. "A further difficulty", he continued, "lies in the fact that the services the Council can provide will mainly help the poorer members of the community, the Africans, and Councillors seem unwilling or unable to face up to the [European's] criticism that they get nothing from the rates themselves".[42]

Colour frequently blinded Europeans to the principle, which they would have accepted in Britain, that taxation was provided to meet national needs. Chanan Singh made the point clearly in a Note of disagreement with the 1948 Report on educational expenditure. "The recommendation of the Majority Report", he wrote, "for the division of expenditure on racial basis is tantamount to the repudiation of the basic principle of public finance, namely that all persons should contribute to the pool of state revenue in proportion to their ability to pay and that expenditure from the pool should benefit all in proportion to their respective needs".[43]

Local rates were not the only taxes levied in the White Highlands. There were also indirect taxes, such as profits from the sale of beer, which were paid by Africans, but it was the Councils, mainly composed of Europeans, which decided how they were to be used. "I think", wrote a District Commissioner in Nakuru in 1959, "an African Advisory Council should be formed so that the Africans can have some say in how the money derived from beer profits is to be used".[44] Immediately after the First Lancaster House Conference in 1960 there was an advance and it was announced in April that in October Africans and Asians were to have elected instead of nominated representatives on the Nakuru Municipal Council.[45] The Europeans had always been averse to any representation by other races in the settled areas. In 1952, for instance, the Trans-Nzoia Association opposed a suggestion that Asians and Africans should serve on the County Council. They said that they "disliked the principle that other races should be represented on councils in the White Highlands",[46] and in 1956 the Naivasha County Council refused to permit African representation on Rural Councils".[47] Although more Africans than Europeans lived in the White Highlands, many of the settlers saw no need to allow them a say in the management of the area.

European predominance in municipal as well as county councils extended beyond the settled areas and it was to be expected that Asians as well as Africans should feel that European power would always be used to European advantage. Asians felt that their economic contribution was not fairly rewarded. At Kericho, for instance, they complained in 1957 that, although they were the "main contributers of township rates", they got the least service from the Urban Council.[48] In Nairobi with its large African population there was scant African representation throughout the nineteen fifties. In 1945 there were 13 European members of the Nairobi Municipal Council and 7 Asians but no Africans. In 1946 European representation was raised to 18, 2 Asian Aldermen were added to the 7 Asian Councillors, and 2 Africans were nominated as Councillors. African membership was raised to 3 in 1953 and remained so till 1960 when there were 5 African Councillors and 1 Alderman. The posts of both Mayor and Deputy Mayor were held by Europeans till 1960 when an Asian became Deputy Mayor. The wind of change blew hard after Lancaster House and in 1962 both the Mayor and Deputy Mayor were Africans. Then in October 1963 the Mayor, Deputy Mayor, 5 Aldermen, and 23 Councillors were Africans, while European representation had fallen to 2 Aldermen and the Asians had 1 Alderman and 7 Councillors.[49]

The following figures for 1959 show how predominantly European local councils remained until the wind of change blew the past away and the First Lancaster House Conference in 1960 marked the beginning of a new age:—

Municipalities	Total	European	Asian	African	Arab
Nairobi	24	14	7	3	
Nakuru	18	11	4	3	
Kisumu	15	8	5	2	
Kitale	15	10	3	2	

	Total	European	Asian	African	Arab
Eldoret	18	10	5	3	
Mombasa	25	13	7	2	3

	Total	European	Asian	African	Arab
Counties					
Nyanza	20	14	5	1	
Kitale	17	16	2	1	
Uasin Gishu	24	20	3	1	
Naivasha	30	24	2	4*	
Aberdare	26	22	3	1	
Nakuru	25	22	2	1	
Nairobi	39	36	2	1	
Townships					
Machakos	11	4	4	3	
Kakamega	10	4	4	2	
Kiambu	11	5	5	1	
Meru	9	2	4	3	

* Including 1 Somali

Source   Note by Acting Deputy Commissioner for Local Governments to Permanent Secretary, 25 June 1959. Havelock File, Constitution and Franchise, H.3/4 11 folio 42, in Kenya National Archives.

The Kikuyu politicians who concluded that they would never achieve the results they desired unless they drew the people together as an active force used the traditional method of an oath to create solidarity, first among the Kikuyus of the Kiambu District and then, by the use of secret agents, throughout the Central Province. With the exception of Senior Chief Koinange the chiefs were excluded from this campaign of secret oathing. The "oath of unity and freedom", which began to be administered in 1946, was intended to highlight oppression and was an essential part of the campaign of preaching hatred of Europeans, without which the organisers believed they would never weld the tribe together, drive the Europeans out of Kenya and secure the Chairmanship of Local Native Councils and other responsible positions in the Reserves. Only when they had got rid of the Europeans could they seize power, and so, although they knew that there were many Europeans who were good employers and who were working for the progress of

Africans, they felt it necessary to preach that all Europeans were bad and should be hated by any patriotic Kikuyu. Violence resulting from such propaganda was seen before the campaign of hatred reached the stage of a State of Emergency. In 1948, for instance a European named Pittock was assaulted by two Kikuyus on his farm at Karen near Nairobi and sustained lasting injuries. As they attacked him they said, "We must kill all the Asians and Europeans, they are stealing our country, all the Fort Hall boys say so".[50] And in 1951 the District Officer at Naivasha reported that "A disturbing feature shows itself in the number of unprovoked assaults by Africans on Europeans recorded during the year".[51] The Asians would have to go too, but, because they did not have political power, they were not such objects of hatred as were the Europeans.

A great many Kikuyus lived as squatters on European farms in the Rift Valley. It was among them in fact that the police first heard the name Mau Mau. They heard it used when they were investigating a case of intimidation among squatters at Naivasha.[52] A large proportion of the normal labourers on the farms were also Kikuyus and the ill will which was growing among the squatters affected some of them also. When the Emergency was declared in 1952 Naivasha and other parts of the European farming area were as deeply affected as the Kikuyu Reserves themselves. The problem of squatters had been a thorny question for many years. In 1945 Mathu had told Legislative Council that he thought nothing in the whole country caused "more discord" than the question of resident labourers.[53] Squatters, or resident labourers, were Africans who lived on European farms and had to work for the farmer for a given number of days each year but who, in return, had land on which to grow their own crops. Lack of security for permanent residence was the factor which produced fear for the future and consequent ill will.

Resentment arising from the early alienation of land in the Kiambu District, frustration at being prevented from growing the crop which brought prosperity to Europeans, a sense of humiliation due to the *Kipande* and other causes provided a fertile soil in which politicians could sow the seeds of militant discontent. The demand for independence was made because it was believed that, unless the Europeans were driven out, the campaign to secure political power and to get back the alienated land was doomed to failure.

But the desire to get rid of all Europeans was not universal and

violence was not advocated by all members of the Kikuyu, Embu and
Meru tribes. Professor Ogot of the University of Nairobi has paid
some attention to the loyalists and has pointed out that from early
days there had been wide support for the hope that African
aspirations could be satisfied by constitutional means. In 1920,
for instance, "Chief Koinange formed the Kikuyu Association
which in 1931 changed its name to the Kikuyu Loyal Patriots in
order to stress its loyalty to the Government and to avoid confusion
with the Kikuyu Central Association". Settler pressure to prevent
Africans from growing coffee and other discriminatory practices
turned the influential Chief Koinange from being a supporter into
an opponent of the hope that the wisest policy for Africans was
co-operation with the Government. But there were other influential
Kikuyus who, although they were frustrated by official inability to
appreciate the strength of African nationalist feeling, continued to
hope that co-operation with the Government would be the best
way of creating a nation in which the Africans would occupy the
position to which the ideals of British democracy entitled them.
Prominent among them was Senior Chief Waruhiu, whose murder
in 1952 precipitated the declaration of a State of Emergency. Chief
Waruhiu was not only an advocate of constitutional progress
towards the attainment of African aims—and there were many
who saw in that policy the surest way to success—but he was a
devout Christian. He and his family were on excellent terms with
their European neighbours; he would have opposed violence; and
Mau Mau oaths would have been abhorrent to him. His Christian
faith was the dominant factor in his life and there were great numbers
of Kikuyu peasants who were no less devout and loyal to the
precepts of their religion. They faced a cruel dilemma when the Mau
Mau oath administrator demanded an answer to the question,
"Are you a true Kikuyu and so one of us or are you a European
in a black skin?" Those who replied that, although they were true
Kikuyus, they were Christians first were martyred in their hundreds
or even thousands—martyred often with ghastly cruelty—because
their faith meant more to them than life. Professor Ogot has aptly
compared them with the famous Uganda martyrs, the court pages
and others "who willingly embraced death at the hands of Kabaka
Mwanga rather than give up their newly acquired faith."[54]
    There are also leading Kikuyus of the older generation, such as
Chiefs like Muhoya of Nyeri and Njiiri and Ignatio of Fort Hall,

and many others among the Kikuyu elders who keenly opposed Mau Mau because its methods and its oaths, which were perversions of the traditional Kikuyu oaths, violated Kikuyu traditions and background. The Kikuyu Home guard contained many, both older and younger, who opposed Mau Mau for this reason, but it also contained men who used the opportunity to pay off old scores against fellow Kikuyus. They were loyalists because they felt that co-operation with the Government paid a good dividend. The make-up of the loyalist elements needs much further study and research, but one thing is certain. Mau Mau did not secure the willing allegiance of the whole tribe and many of its supporters were forced to take the first oath, which then propelled them through fear of the oath itself further and further into the oath-dominated movement.

Dini ya Msambwa

At the extreme northwest of the settled areas the Dini ya Msambwa among the Bukusu people showed features similar to the anti-European movement which was growing in the Central Province. Elijah Masinde, the prophet of the Dini ya Msambwa, had spent some time in Nairobi where he was able to learn something from Kikuyu discontent. Like Mau Mau the Dini ya Msambwa was fundamentally very anti-European and like Mau Mau it found in European farms a fundamental cause of grievance; but unlike Mau Mau it could not claim that the farms round Kitale had been 'stolen' from the Bukusu tribe. The Trans Nzoia had never been occupied by the Bukusu. It was an area of Masai migratory grazing. When it was developed by Europeans, the Bukusu to the west of it cast envious eyes at the rich farmland which was producing 20 bags of maize to the acre and feeding herds of dairy cows which contrasted dramatically with the cattle in the Reserve. The members of the Dini ya Msambwa wanted to get rid of all the European farmers, but the religious aspect of the movement forbade violence and the Bukusu hoped that the Europeans could be expelled as a result of prayer to the old Gods. The word 'Msambwa' is a Bukusu word and means 'any act intended to appease the spirits of departed ancestors'.[55] Sacrificial rites showed the anti-European aims of the movement. The most common of all the Dini ya Msambwa's rites was the sacrifice of a white fowl. Sometimes the stomach was cut open "across a stream, the result being that the entrails fall on either bank signifying the Division of Africans from Europeans" and,

when a black fowl was sacrificed, the entrails of the bird were
"thrown into the stream to signify the return of the European to
his own country across the water".[56] Many Bukusu wanted to get rid
of all Government Officers, because they supported the Trans Nzoia
farmers. The Dini ya Msambwa and Mau Mau both wanted to turn
all Europeans out of Kenya, and, like the Kikuyu, the adherents of
the Dini hated Asians also.[57] Like the Kikuyu they were a politically
minded people and, if Mau Mau had not come into the open in
1952 it is possible that the politicians might have overcome the anti-
violence precepts of the Dini ya Msambwa and the Government
would have been faced with insurrection in the west at the same
time as in the Central Province.

G. S. Were, himself an African from what used to be called North
Nyanza, maintains that "it would be naive to suggest that the
D.Y.M. was a purely, or even largely, religious movement".[58] It was
undoubtedly highly political and highly racial. Gangs patrolled
Kimilili township in 1947 "demanding that the Indians reduce
prices and, furthermore, that they give invoices for all goods purchas-
ed", and they later stole from Indian shops.[59] This bitter feeling
against the Asian shop keepers, however, was not confined to the
Kitale District or the Bukusu. In November 1948, the Kikuyus
living at Molo, Maji Mazuri, Gilgil, Njoro, Elburgon and Naivasha
boycotted Indian shops. The movement started when the price of
potatoes was decontrolled and the Indians offered the growers 4/-
a bag instead of the previous 12/-. The Indian shops were hard-hit
by the boycott and much of the retail trade passed to the European
stores and African 'dukas'.[60] It was, however, on a religious basis
that the Dini ya Msambwa was founded and religion, or what went
for religion, was used by the politicians for political and racial
purposes.

Among the Luo the Kikuyu organisers of Mau Mau had made
some headway with the educated and a prominent Luo, Achieng
Oneko, a journalist, was drawn into the innermost ranks of the
movement. Desire for a greater share of political power was felt
by educated Africans throughout Kenya but, although there was
agreement with the aims of Mau Mau, the methods were not
generally accepted. The masses outside the Central Province, with
the exception of the Bukusu, had not been subjected to the politicans'
preaching that "All Europeans must go" and had not been taught
to hate the White man. Oginga Odinga was in a minority among the

Luos when he was President of the Luo Union and said, two years after the declaration of a State of Emergency, that he favoured "a purely nationalistic movement that will aim at eliminating the immigrants in the shortest possible time".[61] Indeed the campaign of hatred of Europeans affected only part of the Kikuyu tribe itself. It was a secret movement and every effort was made to keep it so. Therefore any Kikuyu who was suspected of being an informer had to be eliminated and the 'simi' and the strangler's cord came into use as early as 1950.

Campaign of Hatred

In North Nyanza adherents of the Dini ya Msambwa were singing hymns corrupted from Christian hymns[62] just as adherents of Mau Mau were doing in the Kikuyu Reserves, and hatred of Europeans was being fomented among members of that sect as in a more militant way it was being preached among the Kikuyu. The Dini ya Msambwa, however, was a small and mild organisation of disaffection compared with Mau Mau, whose chief leaders, it has been said, employed the tactics of Machiavelli to deceive those Europeans who were the most liberal in outlook and fervent in their attempts to promote inter-racial goodwill. Such Europeans were a hindrance to a campaign designed to create hatred. This explains why the few Europeans who were murdered by Mau Mau were people who had shown particular care for their African neighbours and employees. This was not a new phenomenon. The same things had happened in Ireland. J. A. Froude wrote about a Protestant clergyman there, with whom he stayed in 1842, a man who was as kind to Catholics as to Protestants. At that time such men lived, as it were, on a volcano, this clergyman said. "His outdoor servants were Catholics, and they seemed attached to him; but he knew that they belonged to secret societies, and that if they were ordered to kill him they would do it".[63]

The early leaders of Kikuyu militancy maintain that they had no intention of doing anything to improve race relations and that in fact they were bent on preventing co-operation with the Government and the European community. Some say that Kikuyu advocacy of the Kenya Citizens' Association was intended to throw dust into European eyes while the campaign of hatred was gaining ground in Nairobi and the Reserves. The leaders of Mau Mau, they say, were 'tacticians'. In meetings of the Kenya African Union they said that their campaign for Africans must be conducted on legal lines, but at night in secret meetings they agreed that only illegal methods could achieve the results they desired. When he was Acting President of the Kenya African Union in 1952 and 1953, Wycliffe Awori found that most of the Kikuyu members of the committee were professing a desire for inter-racial co-operation in committee meetings but were organising Mau Mau outside.[64]

Perhaps the most effective lesson to be learned from Mau Mau was that the Europeans of Kenya could not govern the country unaided, and, as the Emergency wore on, it became more and more clear that Britain would not continue to pour in troops and money. *The Economist* put the matter plainly when it said that it was clear that Britain would have "to shoulder the military costs of the Mau Mau campaign and contribute largely to the cost of rehabilitation and development" and that "in return Kenyans have a plain duty to listen to reason and the British Taxpayer".[65] They had to accept the fact that the European community could not by itself hold back the rising tide of African nationalism and that Great Britain would not support future European dominance. It was a major force in the pressure which led to colonial independence in general, but it was only one among many factors. In East Africa the African state of Uganda became independent a year before Kenya achieved that status; and to the Trust Territory of Tanganyika, of which the Governor, Sir Edward Twining, said during the time of the ill-advised groundnuts scheme at Kongwa, "There are two things we do not have in Tanganyika: groundnuts and Mau Mau", Independence was granted in 1961. Pressures and influences outside East Africa affected all three territories. Margery Perham saw in 1951 that the Gold Coast elections of that year had "sent a shock right through Africa", because they showed that Britain was "committed in act as well as in word to the speedy promotion of self-government in her African colonies".[66]

But not even Margery Perham with her wide and detailed knowledge had any idea of the speed with which the colonies would rush towards independence. ". . . it is not a very bold speculation", she wrote, "to believe that they may become fully self-governing nation-states by the end of the century".[67] The speed of political development in West Africa, the rising tide of anti-colonial opinion in the United Nations and the United States, the disastrous Suez venture and a growing sense of dissatisfaction in Britain with colonial responsi-

bilities suggested possibilities which the African politicians in East
Africa were not slow to recognise.

1. Sir Philip Mitchell: *African Afterthoughts*, p. 259.
2. O. E. B. Hughes: Memorandum on *Nyeri District, 1949–1952*.
3. ibid.
4. Interview with Archbishop Beecher, 20th March 1970.
5. L.C.D., 9th January, 1948, Col. 761.
6. ibid., 22nd November, 1950, Cols. 289–290.
7. Interview with J. D. Otiende, 12th April 1970. Otiende was General Secretary of the Kenya Africa Union in 1951.
8. Governor to Blundell, 22nd November 1953, Blundell 5/1.
9. R. E. Wainwright to M. R. Hill, 21st November 1952, Blundell 12/7.
10. Sir Philip Mitchell's Diary, 28 August 1946.
11. L. S. B. Leakey: *Mau Mau and the Kikuyu* has a particularly good analysis of the Kikuyu customs and the impact of the West.
12. Nyeri District: Handing over Notes, P. S. Osborne to A. C. C. Swann, 13 September 1950. File DC/NY1/2/1 in Kenya National Archives.
13. Fort Hall: Handing over Report, April 1945, P. S. Osborne to D. O'Hagan DC/FH2/1 (b) in Kenya National Archives.
14. Colonel R. Meinertzhagen, *African Diary* 1902–1906, p. 152.
15. Ruth First: *The Barrel of a Gun*, p. 46.
16. ibid., p. 46.
17. Kenya African National Union and Kenya African Democratic Union.
18. Ruth First, op. cit., p. 46.
19. Sir Andrew Cohen, op. cit., p. 105.
20. Cf. W. McGregor Ross: *Kenya from Within*, Chapter 6 on labour.
21. H.C.D., Vol. 420. Col. 130. 7th March 1946.
22. European Elected Members Organisation. Minutes of Meeting, 25th November, 1949. Blundell, 14/1.
23. Diary, 14th December 1952.
24. L. P. Mair: *Native Policies in Africa*, p. 91.
25. Ralph J. Bunche, "The Land Equation in Kenya Colony": *The Journal of Negro History*, Vol. XXIV, January 1939, pp. 41/42.
26. Interview with Joseph Thuo of Kiambaa, 21st February 1970. Before and during the Emergency he was on the staff of *Baraza* and fulfilled a journalist's task of acquiring information.
27. E.A.S., 25th January 1946.
28. ibid, 7th June 1946.
29. M. P. K. Sorrenson: *Land Reform in Kikuyu Country*, p. 80.
30. Kingsley Martin: *Editor*, p. 163.
31. An *mbari* is the family, made up of husband, wives, children, living in a group of huts, the *mucii*.
32. E.A.S., 23rd August, 1946.
33. L.C.D., 16th February, 1956, Col. 94.
34. ibid., 15th December 1954, Col. 1154.
35. E.A.S., 6th March 1959.
36. Alexander Pope: *Essay on Criticism*.
37. The Kenya African Union.
38. O. E. B. Hughes: *Memorandum on Nyeri District, 1949-52*, p. 9.
39. Blundell to R. Hoddinot of Elburgon, 20th July 1948, Blundell 10/1.
40. L.C.D., 18th May 1954, Col. 81.
41. e.g. Woods Report: *A Report on a Fiscal Survey of Kenya, Uganda and Tanganyika, 1946, by Sir Wilfred Woods, K.C.M.G., K.B.E.*
42. Handing over Report, G. C. M. Dowson to F. A. Peet, 26th July 1957: DC/NKU/2/4 in Kenya National Archives.
43. *Report of the Committee on Educational Expenditure (European and Asian) 1948.*

44. Handing over Report, F. A. Peet to H. De Warenne Waller, 28th July, 1959. DC/NKU/2/4 in Kenya National Archives.
45. E.A.S., 28th April 1960.
46. ibid. 7th March 1952.
47. Annual Report for 1956, N. G. Hardy, District Commissioner, Naivasha, ADM/15/1, in Kenya National Archives.
48. E.A.S., 2 August 1957.
49. The sets of Nairobi Municipal, and, later, City Council minutes and lists of members of the Council kept in the Information Department in the City Hall and in the McMillan Library are incomplete. There is a complete set in the office of the Chief Committee Clerk in the City Hall.
50. John L. Pittock to Governor, 17 Feb. 1953, Blundell 5/1.
51. Annual Report 1951 Naivasha Division—Nakuru District written by E. E. G. Russell, D. O., Naivasha: File ADM/15/1 in Kenya National Archives.
52. Cmd. 1030, p. 77.
53. L.C.D. 26.7 .45, Col. 262.
54. Bethwell A. Ogot: "Revolt of the Elders: An Anatomy of the Loyalist Crowd in the Mau Mau Uprising 1952-1956" in *Politics and Nationalism in Colonial Kenya*, ed. Bethwell A. Ogot.
55. DC/GN/3/1. Folio 2A in Kenya National Archives.
56. ibid. Folio 1.
57. This paragraph is based on information given by Jonathan Baraza, Senior Chief of the Bugusu, on 23 Feb. 1970.
58. G. S. Were: "Dini ya Msambwa: A Re-Assessment", *Makerere Institute of Social Research, Conference Papers* 1967, p. 2.
59. ibid., p. 3.
60. Report by R. A. Frost: Frost Papers.
61. K.W.N., 21 Oct. 1955, p. 1.
62. Special Branch RVP Report Appendix A. 1955 p.a. in DC/TN/3/1, folio 13 in Kenya National Archives.
63. J. A. Froude: *Short Studies on Great Subjects*, Vol. IV, "The Oxford Counter Reformation, Letter V".
64. Information given by Awori to R. A. Frost in 1953.
65. *The Economist*, 10 July 1954.
66. Margery Perham: "The British Problem in Africa", *Foreign Affairs*, Vol. 29, No. 4 July 1951, p. 637.
67. ibid.

7

THE CIVIL SERVICE AND THE POLICE

While Mau Mau with its racial hatred was being fostered in the Central Province a remarkable degree of inter-racial co-operation and Service loyalty and solidarity was being created in the Civil Service. In the struggle to overcome racial prejudice and selfishness and to promote inter-racial co-operation, understanding and good-will the work of individual people often had great influence: and not only their actual work but the influence of their personalities, which acted as catalysts or like stones thrown into a pond and producing a series of widening circles over the surface. Africans like Musa Amalemba and John Muchura, Asians like A. B. Patel and John Karmali, Europeans like T. G. Askwith, at different times Municipal Affairs Officer in Nairobi and Commissioner for Local Government, and W. Kirkaldy-Willis, an orthopaedic surgeon, inspired confidence in the many friends whom they had among the other races and were allies in the campaign for co-operation. Many such names could be chosen in all walks of life. The inter-racial co-operation achieved in the Civil Service in the early nineteen fifties owed much to the inspiration of the European Chairman.

The Holmes Commission

In 1948 the Holmes Commission on the Civil Service expressed their admiration of the remarkable advance made by Africans in fifty years from a "society in which" in their own view, "the only rule was the rule of the spear and the sorcerer".[1] The Commission saw that Government was not free to fix salary scales without reference to other employers. Banks and commercial concerns were employing Asians and Africans, and businesses are not philanthropic institutions. The structure of personnel existing in the commercial section of Kenya could reasonably be taken to represent what was found to produce the most efficient and economic results. In 1948 it was found that in the business firms "the most highly paid posts, usually calling for professional or technical qualifications are filled

by Europeans, the less well paid posts by Asians, and the least well
paid by Africans".[2] The difficulty which faced employers was that
"equal pay for equal work" had to mean equal pay for "work of
equal quality".[3] In assessing quality the employer was almost
certain to differ from the employee and unfair treatment could be
alleged when unequal quality was not admitted. It was found
that in general Africans were inferior "in such matters as sense of
responsibility, judgement, application to duty and output of work"
to Asians of the same educational qualifications,[4] and therefore
commercial employers only employed them if they paid them lower
salaries than those paid to Asians. Salary scales were accordingly
determined by race and the individual African, who was an exception
to the rule, suffered from a racial discrimination, which was in
fact an economic pattern into which he did not fit. Commercial
concerns are guided by the profit motive and, in the case of public
companies, by their responsibility to their shareholders; and
Governments "are bound, in the interests of the general taxpayer,
to have regard to the law of supply and demand in determining"
the salaries and wages they pay.[5] The Commission recommended
that there should be "a single service with differential rates of salary
for officers of the three races".[6] The Government rejected this
recommendation and preferred the idea of A, B and C scales with a
provision that "exceptionally able and useful individuals should be
advanced from scale to scale according to their merits";[7] but they
did accept the Commission's recommendation that "the salary paid
to a non-European should be three fifths of" the salary paid to an
"officer recruited from the United Kingdom or the Dominions".[8]
As Africans and Asians advanced in education and experience the
three fifths rule caused increasing bitterness. It was abolished on the
recommendation of the Commission presided over by Sir David
Lidbury in 1954.[9] In the meantime within the Civil Service itself
remarkable advances in inter-racial co-operation and harmony
were achieved.

Unprecedented Co-operation

George Bennett wrote that "The European Civil Service
Association was working for a unified and non-racial Civil Service
under the leadership of a remarkable man: Lt.-Commander John
Miller, G.C.". And he went on to say, "Carey Jones indicates his
good relations with African civil servants. There are also letters in

the Fabian Commonwealth Bureau files", he continued, "which reveal that he was asked early in 1952 to assist, though a European civil servant, in a reorganisation of the badly running KAU[10] machine and did conduct for a while 'a study circle' for some KAU leaders, a fact which throws a strange new light on the situation so shortly before the Mau Mau Emergency".[11] According to Miller himself this participation in KAU was due above all to the backing of Sir Henry Potter.[12]

A Whitley Council for the European Civil Service had been formed in 1950 and, when Commander Miller was on leave in England in 1951, he discussed with the Colonial Office the enlargement of the Council to include all races, with four members each from the European, Asian and African sections of the Service. There was so little sense of corporate unity in the Civil Service as a whole that the first thing the European Committee had to do was to find out who were the Chairmen of the Asian and African Associations. The next problem was to find a place where a meeting which might lead to the formation of an inter-racial Staff Side could be held. Buildings used by the Europeans were 'out of bounds' to Africans and Asians and the African locations were unsuitable. Some Asian buildings were situated between the two and a room in the Cutchi Gujerati Hindu Temple of the Patel Brotherhood in Duke Street, Nairobi, was chosen. At 6 o'clock in the evening this unusual meeting assembled in an air heavy with incense and loud with the ringing of the temple bells. The proceedings were conducted in English and without question the Chairman of the European Association was elected to the Chair of the new inter-racial Staff Side, and he opened the meeting by saying that he assumed that all three sections agreed "to roll each other's logs".[13]

Such a suggestion for mutual support was novel, but the Africans could not understand how the Europeans, who seemed to them to be "rich beyond the dreams of avarice", could possibly have any problems. The Chairman pointed out that at all levels problems arose and he instanced the case of a few European women telephonists whose terms of service might at any moment leave them unpensioned and destitute. The Chairman of the African Association then cited the case of something like a hundred African technicians who had been on temporary terms for twenty years or more in spite of efforts to have them put on a permanent basis. It was astonishing for the Africans to find that the Europeans also had cases which might involve great hardship and perhaps even more astonishing to see a spirit of Service unity cutting across racial divisions. Within twenty-four hours, simply by using the telephone without having to arrange a meeting with the Official Side, the European representatives managed to have the case of the African technicians investigated and to get the best of them put on permanent terms. This episode showed how far communal solidarity gave Europeans opportunities which were denied to the other races. It also demonstrated an established British tradition: loyalty to colleagues was fundamental and, though there were three racial sections, they were all parts of one Civil Service. "From that moment on confidence between the African and European sections was monolithic and never faltered".[14]

The Asians did not seem to feel completely confident of the support of the representatives of the other two races, even though the African and European representatives all assured them that the Staff Side would stand together and "roll each other's logs". The meeting was a gathering of three separate racial Associations, open to all members of the Civil Service. The three Associations agreed that the Government was the common target and they subsequently met regularly for consultation among themselves and for meetings with the Financial Officers of the Government.[15] The Africans wanted to elect Commander Miller as one of their representatives, but, partly to reassure the Asians, it was arranged that he should be one of the four Asian representatives.[16] The result of this arrangement was that the Staff Side was composed of four Africans, three Asians and five Europeans. This arrangement was made with the unqualified agreement of the Africans, who is the Civil Service had confidence in the fairness and impartiality of the Europeans and appreciated their superior ability in negotiation and the value of their contacts with the Official Side. The significance of all this, however, did not seem to be fully appreciated by the most senior civil servants with the exception of Sir Henry Potter, the Chief Secretary, who later became British Resident in Zanzibar.[17]

COLA—Cost of Living Allowance

After the War the cost of living steadily increased and in the early nineteen fifties a galloping inflation caused hardship among all races. The plight of the poorest Africans was grievous indeed. Salaried workers, though not faced by such desperate conditions, found that it was difficult to maintain their customary standards and in the Civil Service COLA (Cost of Living Allowance) was a burning issue, because inevitably prices rose before allowances were increased and the danger of a continuous upward spiral could never be ignored. Africans in the Civil Service suffered more than others because, as in the case of the low-paid African wage-earners, as an African member said in Legislative Council, the African "was always regarded as single and no account was taken at all relating his cost of living allowance to his family commitments".[18] Moreover, as Colin Thornley, the Acting Chief Secretary, felt it necessary to point out in Legislative Council, "the lowest paid workers have no margin within which they really can manipulate their own domestic budgets in order to make possible the finding of the extra money required to meet their rising costs".[19]

A Select Committee on cost of living allowances for Government servants reported early in 1951. The Chairman was the Director of Establishments, but, when the Report was presented for debate in Legislative Council, the Government proposed that Paragraph 12 should be omitted. In that paragraph the Committee recommended that COLA should be 20 per cent on a first segment of salary, 10 per cent on a second segment and 5 per cent on the remainder, limited to £150 per annum. But, said the Financial Secretary in opening the debate, "the segments on which the different percentages are to apply differ in the three racial groups. For instance, the first 20 per cent is to apply up to £72 in the case of the African Government servant, up to £210 in the case of the Asian civil servant and up to £300 in the case of the European Government servant", and he told the Council that the Government did "not find it possible to agree" with that differentiation. "It is the Government's view", he continued, "that the *formula* governing the grants of relief should be the same for all".[20]

The debate which followed showed the usual racial approach or basis of thinking and what Dr. Rana, the Asian Elected Member for the Eastern Area, called "the racial bickering which is prevalent in this country".[21] As so often, impartial proposals submitted by the Government were attacked on racial grounds by the European Elected Members, who in this case would not allow the segments to be lowered for European civil servants and so, if the segments were to be the same for all races, COLA of 20 per cent up to £300 of salary would be paid to Africans and that would mean in effect that almost every African Government servant would receive an

increase of 20 per cent on the whole of his salary, whereas, said
Gerald Hopkins, European Elected Member for Aberdare, "only
the very lowest paid European would receive such generous treatment".[22] Other Europeans also objected to the Government's
amendment to the Report because it did not differentiate between
Europeans and members of the other races.[23] S. V. Cooke was, as so
often, out of step with his European colleagues. He refused to agree
that after perhaps twenty years' work, which brought his salary up
to £300 a year, an Indian's or African's standard of living, which,
as Cooke explained, meant "the expenditure to which he is bound,
is less than that of a young European schoolboy who enters perhaps
from one of the schools in Kenya on the lowest scale of £300 a year".[24]
This comparison between the European schoolboy and the
experienced Asian or African was to come up again after the Police
Commission had submitted its report in 1953. The cost of living
had risen for all; the three fifths rule kept the standard of living of
Asians and Africans lower than that of Europeans; and the argument
of most of the European Elected Members was that their COLA
should be racially depressed also. Chunilal Madan, an Asian
Elected Member for the Central Area, suggested that the standard
of living of Asians and Africans was kept low, not only by the three
fifths rule, but also by "the limited scope for Asians and Africans
in matters of commerce and industry",[25] that kept the standard
of living for Africans and Asians lower than the European standard.
Europeans might have claimed that Asians did well in commerce and
Africans that it was above all Asian commercial networks that
limited the Africans' scope, and Europeans might have given
instances of African inefficiency and naivety in business practices;
but, whatever the cause may have been for general discrepancies in
standards the fact was that the standard of living of African civil
servants was lower than that of the Asian civil servants and the
standard of living of Asian civil servants was lower than that of the
Europeans and would remain so as long as A., B. and C. scales of
salaries were in operation. The Government had accepted the
differential scales of salaries, but now maintained that it could not
possibly agree to differentiation in COLA, although the Director
of Establishments had been Chairman of the Select Committee which
recommended it. How could this change of policy be explained?

Within twenty-four hours of the first joint meeting at which an
inter-racial Staff Side of the Whitley Council was formed the

European Chairman managed to get Government agreement to a solution of a grievance which had worried the African Civil Servants' Association for many years, and then the representatives of the three racial Associations together set out to force the Government to change its policy on COLA. They demanded that there should be no racial discrimination such as was proposed in paragraph 12 of the Report of the Select Committee, over which the Director of Establishments had presided, but they appreciated that the Government budget was limited and, to the amazement of the Africans and of the Government, the European and Asian members agreed that, in order that COLA should be the same for all, they would, if necessary, agree to a reduction in the payments applicable to themselves. Such an example of inter-racial solidarity and Service loyalty was unprecedented in Kenya's history. The Government had to give way and withdraw a White Paper which had already been printed.[26] The Financial Secretary proposed that paragraph 12 of the Select Committee's Report should be struck out. The wishes of the combined Staff Side were known to members of Legislative Council. An Asian member welcomed the Government's proposal "to bring allowances for the cost of living in line with the wishes of the European, African and Asian Civil Service Associations, who", he said, "have expressed in no uncertain terms that they cannot accept the proposal that a particular salary should attract a different percentage of relief according to the race of the recipient".[27] The European Elected Member for Mombasa, Usher, however, referred with great disapproval to a Memorandum submitted by the interracial Staff Side and then quoted with horror a passage from the speech of the Chairman of the inter-racial meeting held at the Patel Brotherhood. "It is my duty to-night", Commander Miller had said, "as Chairman of this unprecedented meeting, emphatically to warn Members of the Legislative Council that proposals of the type we are considering now are likely to drive large sections of the Civil Service of this country, of all races, in the direction of indifference and, what is worse, in the direction of bribery and corruption". "I hope", said Usher, "that such a meeting will never be held again".[28] Such was not the view of the African and Asian Civil Service Associations. Nor was it the view of A. B. Patel, who welcomed the fact that representatives of the three racial Civil Service Associations were meeting together "for the first time in the history of this colony" and considered that "to treat them with contempt" was "retrograde and very reactionary".[29]

On March 1st the Governor saw the leader of the European Elected Members, who was "very het up" and said that the country was "in a turmoil and the Electors' Union spoiling for trouble".[30] The Finger-Print controversy was in full swing at the time and Major Keyser told the Governor that he resented the course of events over the Glancy Report and "made a plea for government by agreement with the Elected Members". The Governor concluded that the Elected Members were frightened and that there was little understanding that "there is another side to the picture".[31] Perhaps the European Elected Members thought that ideas of racial equality were becoming dangerous when equal treatment in national registration and in cost of living allowances for civil servants was being advocated at one and the same time.

Although the omission of clause 12 would mean an additional expenditure of £830,000, the Government did not accept the offer of the European and Asian Associations to carry that burden themselves by a reduction in the allowances paid to them. How then, asked the Financial Secretary, was this additional expenditure to be financed? Three suggestions were made in Legislative Council:

"Mr. Cooke: Company tax!

Mr. Blundell: Poll tax!

The Financial Secretary: And why not income tax?"[32]

Suggestions for imposing an increase in income tax were always violently opposed by the Europeans. During the course of the COLA debate these various methods of raising the necessary finance were argued and it was agreed that it should be found by savings, which were "effected by vacant posts not being filled". That, said the Leader of the European Elected Members during the Budget session in November was an expedient which could not be continued indefinitely and "for 1952", he said in a bitterly hostile speech, "Cost of Living Allowances are being paid for chiefly by increased revenue". The European Elected Members were no more sympathetic of the COLA formula than they had been when they debated it at the beginning of the year and their Leader maintained that "the introduction in 1951 of the Cost of Living Allowances very greatly emphasized the costs of these swollen services".[33]

Service Loyalty

The civil servants had shown that loyalty to a Service could be stronger than racial self-interest and the European and Asian representatives on the Whitley Council had made an unselfish offer which showed a spirit which the politicians would have been wise to emulate. Havelock, the European Elected Member for Kiambu did ask whether there were sufficient opportunities in Government service for Africans who had obtained British qualifications. "Is the door sufficiently open?" he asked. Or were they faced by "disappointing opportunities"?[34] But, whatever posts might have been available for them, in spite of their British qualifications the three fifths rule would have operated and opportunities for appointments would not have been accompanied by equality of salary with Europeans.

It did not seem that the removal of racial discrimination would come from Legislative Council and in 1952 the three sections of the Staff Side agreed to recommend that racial distinctions in the Civil Service should be abolished. Promotion should depend on merit alone without regard to race and every post should carry its appropriate rate of salary and conditions of service, which should apply to whoever was appointed to fill it. Moreover, just as in Britain young men were appointed straight from the universities to the bottom of the long administrative scale in the Civil Service, they wanted young Asian and African graduates to be appointed to the Civil Service in Kenya to be trained on the job, as was the case in the British Civil Service, and so to acquire the experience and expertise which would enable them to rise in the Service and eventually fill the higher posts.[35] It is true that there were a few Africans in the officer grades of the Administration, but the European representatives on the Staff Side of the Whitley Council advocated an increase in their numbers as young Africans returned from university study overseas. Their efforts to bring this about were remarkably altruistic, because any increase in the number of African officers could only be made at the expense of Europeans. The European civil servants offered to give them all possible help in their training. With this recommendation went the corollary that Asians and Africans should be appointed in increasing numbers to the executive grades of the Civil Service. As the majority of the European civil servants were in the executive grades or, as one might say, the warrant officer ranks, they were deliberately offering to sacrifice privileges which had always been confined to Europeans and to share opportunities on a basis of merit with the other races and to give up what was almost a European monopoly in the interests of non-racial development. This second unselfish proposal of the European section of the Staff Side was viewed by the Government with amazement and consternation. The European Chairman of the combined Staff Side of the inter-racial Whitley Council was summoned by the Labour Commissioner and was requested to arrange that the proposal should be withdrawn. He refused.[36] The Government, anxious to keep the administration of Kenya in European hands, turned down the suggestion, which had unanimous African support, that African and Asian graduates should enter the Civil Service on the bottom rung of the administrative ladder and work their way upwards, learning from the experienced Europeans, profiting from the knowledge and technique of the expatriates, whom they would eventually replace. The Government's policy, the Director of Establishments told Miller, was to keep the administration of Kenya in European hands as long as possible. The next step was the Report of the Lidbury Commission in 1954, and, although in a somewhat different form, the racial structure of the Civil Service was preserved.

The leaders of the civil servants' Staff Side looked on the Government as "the common target". Miller was removed from Nairobi before any other awkward instances of inter-racial co-operation could disturb the Establishment and the European Elected Members. At the beginning of July 1952 he was, as he put it, "promoted and restricted and uprooted in one move"[37] by being appointed Provincial Education Officer for the Coast. Mombasa saw the arrival of another far-sighted and liberal officer when O. E. B. Hughes was posted there from Nyeri in 1954.

Police Commission

Before the Lidbury Commission visited East Africa to enquire into the problems of Civil Service salaries another Commission went to Kenya to study the Police. The Commission was composed of Mr. S. J. Barker, Receiver in the Metropolitan Police of London, and Mr. W. A. Muller, Inspector General of the Colonial Police. On the 17th August, 1953, they submitted an interim report on salaries, which was accepted by the Government.[38] The Mau Mau Emergency was in full swing. The Police were facing great difficulties. Rapid expansion was needed to meet the demands of the Emergency, but the salary scales offered no inducement to the better educated

Africans and recruitment had to be largely from the backward areas
in the northern parts of the country. It was a time when the Security
Forces as a whole suffered from the results of the excesses of certain
sections such as the Kenya Police Reserve, which contained many
untrained, often extremely racially minded, young Kenya Europeans,
who made it all the more difficult for the regular Police to live down
their long history of unpopularity. If a police force is to be the friend
and protector of the public, the ordinary members of the public
must be co-operative as well as law-abiding. Over the years in Kenya
a hectoring attitude on the part of some of the European officers of
the Police and a sense of power on the part of illiterate askaris had
made it impossible to foster a co-operative attitude on the part of
the African public. This reacted on the Police and there was little
goodwill on either side. Such circumstances provided the answer to
a group of English-speaking Africans at Kitale who, on seeing a
film about the Police in Britain, said, "We hate our askaris. Why
can't they be like that?"[39]

During the Emergency a great many more askaris had to be
recruited. Many, completely illiterate, came from the Northern
Frontier. They were so unused to the ways of the world that, after
being shown films at the Police Training School at Kiganjo, they
rushed behind the screen to see where the actors had gone to. This
influx of primitive recruits joined a force with a fairly low standard
of education. The Police Force had never been able to offer good
pay and so had always had to recruit illiterate or at best slightly
educated Africans. In the Kenya Police Review, December 1950,
the Deputy Commissioner wrote that "without a single exception
every one of the Police Stations in the Colony has its complement of
African policemen who are able to record simple statements and
maintain records".[40] This was an achievement of which he had reason
to be proud and by that time there were some police stations "in the
sole charge of African Inspectors". The senior members of the
Force had had a difficult task and their work was often noted with
praise by Africans as well as Europeans.[41]

A few years before the Emergency an attempt was made to attract
boys from secondary schools, but the pay offered was quite inadequate and the attempt failed. Legislative Council was largely to
blame and the responsibility of the European Elected Members for
cheese-paring the social service votes was shown particularly in the
Budget session in 1951. When the Motion to adopt the Report of

the Committee of Supply was put to Legislative Council, Major Keyser, the leader of the European Elected Members, led European opposition "because of the unwilling attitude of the Government towards giving effect to the desire for economy".[42] The Financial Secretary declared that "opposition to the Motion in that manner . . . is in the annals and constitution of this country, unprecedented. And let me tell you this, Sir", he continued, "that if the Hon. Member succeeded in his expressed intention of opposing this Motion so that the Motion failed, he would in effect deny this country the supply necessary to carry on the vital services of this country in 1952". This warning only produced an interjection from Major Keyser: "We mean what we say".[43]

The better educated Africans were not recruited, because salaries were on racial scales, but the pay offered to European officers was not altogether inadequate. Many local Europeans, however, felt that police service was a profession to be entered only if a young man could not get another job, and for that reason the kind of young European in Kenya who became a police officer was apt to have a particularly bigoted racial outlook. Police officers recruited from the United Kingdom were sometimes amazed at and shocked by the outlook of some of their colleagues. There were, however, many good police officers, but the general image of the Police Force was badly affected by the behaviour of the least desirable.

It was in an atmosphere of racial tension and bitterness that the Commission set to work to examine the Kenya Police and make what recommendations they might think desirable about terms of service. They submitted an interim report in August 1953, but their full report was not published till 5th February, 1954, and it was debated in Legislative Council on 2nd March. Time and again in Legislative Council comment had been made about the bad relations existing between the Police and the public and European as well as African members had spoken of the need for police training in courtesy.[44] It came as no surprise that the Commission reported that relations between the Police and the public must be improved and "based on respect and mutual trust".[45] There was need for strict discipline, "which will not tolerate corruption or the abuse of office, and for training designed to impress on every member of the Force from the day he joins that he is the servant and not the master of the public".[46] In Legislative Council Chanan Singh thanked the Government for accepting the Commission's Report, which, he believed was "the first official document in which the abolition of racial discrimination in rates of pay has been recommended."[47] Moreover the Report, which the Government accepted, recommended that merit alone should in future determine an officer's rank. In the past, said the Report, race had been the determining factor: in the future merit alone should be the guide. "We found it difficult to understand", wrote the Commission about the racial structure of the Police Force, "how a system of this nature could ever have been expected to work satisfactorily in a disciplined service like the Police".[48] They then suggested a table of ranks "based purely and simply on functions, on the understanding that all ranks will be open to men of any race, the only test being that of ability".[49] Official Members announced the Government's acceptance of the Report during the debate in Legislative Council. Africans thought that at last in an important service racial equality had been established. At the end of April they were disillusioned when it was learned that the rank of Inspector Grade 1 was to be the lowest rank which a European could hold and when it was learned that African Inspectors were to be downgraded. "I want to ask Council to tell me", said James Jeremiah at the beginning of May, "whether people who were fit to be Chief Inspectors when their salaries were low—when the salaries were increased they became unfit".[50] David McDowell Wilson, the Editor of *Baraza*, the Swahili newspaper published by the *East African Standard*, was an outspoken champion of justice and of the interests of Africans. In a leading article, headed "Rank and Race in the Police", in English and Swahili on 15th May, he wrote:

"When the new badges of rank for officers were announced recently, it was stated that no European is to serve below the rank of Inspector, Grade 1. Moreover in some instances junior European officers have been placed over African officers nominally holding a higher rank.

Despite the fact that there are some Africans holding the rank of Inspector, Grade 1—and drawing the same pay for it as Europeans—there is a feeling that once again race has been a determining factor in allocating rank.

That is an understandable feeling. Africans are in effect being told that the youngest and least experienced European recruit is at once a better policeman than African officers of several years service.

They can be forgiven for doubting that this is necessarily the case, even if it is true of everyone now serving in the force".[51] "How can we be expected to go on being loyal to the Government", asked a leading African who stood out against Mau Mau at considerable personal risk, "when European influence can nullify even the recommendations of a Commission sent from England to investigate so important a service as the Police?"

Disillusion

The loyalty of such Africans was often sorely tried. During the period of the Mau Mau Emergency the African Civil Service received little encouragement and the official slighting of its President at its annual meeting was on a par with official disregard of African opinion elsewhere. The lead given by Sir Philip Mitchell was not followed in subsequent years.

In April, 1952, during his last year of office Mitchell attended the Annual General Meeting of the African Civil Service Association in the Kaloleni Hall, Nairobi, and in his Diary recorded that "Muchura, the President, made an absolutely first class speech".[52] Indeed he was so much impressed by the speech that he told Sir Andew Cohen, the Governor of Uganda, about it.[53] Muchura expressed gratitude for the many benefits brought to the Africans of Kenya by the British administration. African civil servants, he said, served the Government of their own free will, learning while they served. "We realise", he continued, "that it is because of English ideals of freedom and justice that we are able to stand up and speak to you as we do to-day". And then he went on to say, "But we think many of the British settlers here, and even some Government servants, hardly understand our attitude, or even the actual facts of the case". European farming and trade could not be carried on without African labour and the Africans had worked willingly to create the wealth without which schools, hospitals and other services could not be provided. "But the English settler and businessman seem to think that the Africans are going to be content for a long time with their present very small share in the life and wealth of the country." Nor would African civil servants be willing to wait any longer for acceptance into what was "called in the Army 'commissioned rank' ". They would make mistakes. They were like a motorist learning to drive with 'L' plates on his vehicle. "If he is not allowed to drive until he is efficient, he will never learn at all." And for clerical grades they asked for a common scale for Europeans, Asians and Africans, as, indeed, had been recommended by the Special Commissioner, Mr. L. C. Hill.[54] "Everyone in Kenya talks about co-operation", Muchura said, but nothing was put into practice. "The Government has everything down on paper, but in practice nothing of significance is done." His speech he said, was full of "difficult matters". All the points were put with restraint and courtesy and Muchura said to the Governor, "on such an important occasion to us we think that we must speak and that you will not resent it."[55]

When the next Annual General Conference was to be held in 1953 Muchura wrote to the new Governor, Sir Evelyn Baring, to ask him to attend it. The Governor did attend the opening of the Conference, which was held in the Desai Memorial Hall, but he thought that Muchura was too outspoken. In 1954 the Conference was held in less pleasant surroundings in the Akamba Hall at Starehe, one of the African 'locations' in Nairobi. Muchura sent the draft of his speech to Government House and was then told that it must be toned down. He refused to do this and was told that the Governor would not attend the meeting. Muchura, with the backing of his Committee, replied that the speech would be delivered whether the Governor attended or not. In the end the Chief Secretary, R.C. (later Sir Richard) Turnbull, attended and in his reply castigated all African civil servants so violently that several of the leading members of the Association, including Dr. Likimani and Duncan Ndegwa, who became head of the Civil Service at the time of Independence, walked out during his speech. In 1955 the Governor himself once more attended the opening session of the Conference. Muchura had been warned that, if his speech were to be as outspoken as the speech he delivered in 1954, the Governor would have to refuse the invitation, because he would be embarrassed and could not afford to be present when such an address was given in public. Muchura felt that he was "stifled".[56] The Governor did attend the Conference and rebuked Muchura for his speech. All this was reported in the Press and the loyalty of the African civil servants to the Government which they served was yet more sorely tried.[57]

In 1953 the Conference was held in the Desai Memorial Hall, but in 1954 and again in 1955 the far less pleasant hall at Starehe was all that the Association could get. In that year the City Council did not even have the hall cleaned for the occasion. The British Council

Representative was on the eve of leaving East Africa to take up a posting in England and decided to present a cup to the African Civil Service for inter-Departmental football. He went with Muchura to see that all was in order in the hall and they found that nothing had been done to it that morning. The floor and tables were littered with bottle tops and cigarette stubs and the place was extremely dirty. They found a broom and some cleaning rags and managed to make the hall somewhat cleaner before the delegates arrived; but the episode did not inspire the African civil servants with a feeling that their loyalty and service were appreciated by the Government or the City Council, which they regarded with justification as a European Government and a European City Council.

As a result of the Report of the Lidbury Commission the three fifths rule was cancelled and was replaced by 'B' and 'C' scales. For a long time African civil servants had felt that their chances of promotion were nullified because an Asian stood between them and the European at the top and that the Asian would always recommend a fellow Asian. Mathu made this same point in Legislative Council and went so far as to say that the Government had "given the Asian complete control of the African civil servant".[58] "The Asian stranglehold", wrote the President of the African Civil Servants' Association in 1954, "is very great".[59] There was nothing in the Lidbury Report that would alter that. A few Africans were moved from the 'C' to the 'B' salary scales, but they did not receive benefits such as were enjoyed by Europeans. Among them were John Muchura, James Otieno, Joseph Jairo, Justus Oluoch and Luke Musiga.[60]

The Staff Side of the Whitley Council had tried to create a really united Kenya Civil Service. For its failure the European settler community and some of the European Elected Members whom they influenced were much to blame. They had always been unfriendly to the Civil Service, however friendly some of them had been with senior individual Government servants. Moreover the official policy was to keep the Administration in European hands. Financial lapses were all too common among Africans in public life. To give Africans more responsibility would have implied risks and the Administration was unwilling to take them and to experience probable inefficiency; but without responsibility there could be no training. Among Asians commercial and financial standards often left much to be desired and, as an Asian Member of Legislative Council picturesquely said, policeman caused great fear among the Indian community and the askari was looked on as "black doom in a blue jersey". "For most people", he said, "the policeman is the ghost of their own guilty consciences".[61]

Conflict was perhaps inevitable in a country inhabited by several races and the implementation of trusteeship was complicated by racial interests. One of the most remarkable factors in the story was the unity achieved on the Staff Side of the Whitley Council which showed how loyalty to a service or a cause could transcend racial considerations. Although it did not permeate all levels of the Civil Service in Kenya nor triumph over the less generous policies which faced it, this unity, which was attained in the early nineteen fifties, showed how much could be achieved by personality and sincerity of purpose.

1. *Report of the Commission on the Civil Services of Kenya, Tanganyika and Uganda & Zanzibar, 1947-48, Col. No. 223, (1948):* (The Holmes Commission Report). para. 82.
2. ibid, para. 73.
3. ibid, para. 79.
4. ibid, para. 79.
5. ibid, para. 78.
6. ibid, para. 95.
7. Sessional Paper No. 2 of 1948, para. 6.
8. Holmes Commission Report, para. 92.
9. *Report on the Civil Services of the East African Territories and the East African High Commission 1953-1954.*
10. Kenya African Union.
11. George Bennett: "Revolutionary Kenya: The Fifties, A Review'. *Race*, Vol. VII, No. 4, Apr. 1967.
12. Miller was in the Education Department and was Chairman of the General Council of the European Civil Service Association.
13. Letter from Lt.-Commander Miller to R. A. Frost, 10 Sept. 1969, Frost papers.
14. ibid.
15. Interview with John Muchura, 16 Apr. 1970. Muchura was President of the African Civil Servants Association at that earlier time.
16. Letter from Lt.-Commander Miller to R. A. Frost, 10 Sept. 1969.
17. ibid.
18. J. Jeremiah in L.C.D., 17 Aug. 1948, col. 258.
19. L.C.D., 29 Aug. 1950, col. 305.
20. ibid, 23 Feb. 1951, col. 335.
21. ibid, 27 Feb. 1951, col. 384.
22. ibid, 27 Feb. 1951, col. 383.
23. e.g. Havelock, ibid, 23 Mar. 1951, col. 342.
24. ibid, 23 Mar. 1951, col. 353.
25. ibid, 23 Mar. 1951, col. 388.
26. Letter from Lt.-Commander Miller to R. A. Frost, 10 Sept. 1969: Frost papers. Muchura confirmed this in an interview on 16 Apr. 1970.
27. L.C.D. 27 Feb. 1951, col. 353.
28. ibid, 27 Feb. 1951, col. 368.

29. ibid, 27 Feb. 1951, col. 379.
30. Sir Philip Mitchell's Diary, 1 Mar. 1951.
31. ibid, 1 Mar. 1951.
32. L.C.D. 23 Feb. 1951, col. 337.
33. ibid, 13 Dec. 1951, col. 1058.
34. L.C.D. 16 Nov. 1950, col. 209.
35. Details in this paragraph come from Miller's letter of 10 Sept. 1969 and were confirmed in April 1970 by Muchura who consulted other former leading African Civil Servants for corroboration.
36. Letter from Lt.-Commander Miller to R. A. Frost, 10 Sept. 1969, Frost papers.
37. ibid.
38. *Report of the Kenya Police Commission, 1953.*
39. A British Council film showing in 1950.
40. Quoted in W. Robert Foran: *The Kenya Police, 1887–1960*, p. 151.
41. e.g. N. S. Mangat, Sir Charles Markham and Tom Mboya in Legislative Council, 12 June 1957.
42. L.C.D. 12 Dec. 1951, col. 1058.
43. ibid, 12 Dec. 1951, cols. 1069-78.
44. e.g. Debate in Legislative Council, 11 Jan. 1949.
45. *Report of the Kenya Police Commission 1953*, para. 487.
46. ibid, para. 487.
47. L.C.D. 2 Mar. 1954, col. 388.
48. *Report of the Kenya Police Commission 1953*, para. 55.
49. ibid, para. 56.
50. L.C.D. 20 May 1954, col. 218.
51. *Baraza*, 15 May 1954.
52. Sir Philip Mitchell's Diary, 13 Apr. 1952.
53. R. A. Frost was staying with Sir Andrew Cohen soon afterwards and Sir Andrew told him this.
54. *Report of the Civil Service Commission*, 1945.
55. A mimeographed copy of the speech is among the Frost papers.
56. Letter from Muchura to John Miller, 14 Mar. 1955, Miller papers.
57. Muchura gave the information contained in this paragraph in an interview on 16 Apr. 1970.
58. L.C.D. 15 Dec. 1954, col. 1147.
59. John Muchura to Lt.-Commander Miller, 27 May 1954, Miller papers.
60. Interview with John Muchura, 16 Apr. 1970.
61. L.C.D. 12 June 1957, col. 1239.

8

THE INFLUENCE OF CHURCHES, SCHOOLS AND VARIOUS ORGANISATIONS

The United Kenya Club, the British Council and the Civil Service Associations were not alone in working for inter-racial co-operation. The churches had great influence, and in educational and cultural fields much was done to overcome racial prejudice. This effort in human relations owed much to individual people, whose careful work and inspiration provided inter-racial leadership.

From the earliest years the missionaries exerted great influence. They were pioneers in medical services and education and, although they could sometimes be criticised for undue narrowness of view, they set standards which were vitally needed in a period of change from the ordered life of the tribe to the less regulated morality of the modern world. Sir Andrew Cohen wrote of them, "The contribution of missionaries to the progress of Africa cannot, I think, be fully grasped unless one has lived there, seen what they have built, and realised the leadership they have provided, the ideas and the moral values they have implanted and cultivated in these countries".[1]

The Africans' debt to the missionaries was generously acknowledged on the eve of Independence. At midnight of the 11th December, 1963 the Union Jack was lowered in the Uhuru Stadium and, as the last stroke of twelve ushered in the new day, the flag of the new nation of Kenya was seen flying from the flagstaff. On the morning of the 11th James Gichuru, the Minister of Finance, gave a talk in the hall of All Saints' Cathedral in Nairobi. He praised the work of the missions and generously acknowledged the great contribution which they made to the development of Kenya. His praise was a sincere and generous tribute from a leader of the new Kenya on the eve of Independence. In Nairobi the churches had been steadily overcoming social separation and within the Christian brotherhood had brought Europeans and Africans with education into touch with each other. As a European politician remarked in 1955, "Where else, if not in the Church, should one expect to meet an African at the same level?"[2]

The Anglican Church

Improvement in inter-racial understanding and co-operation depended above all on a change of heart in the European community. The majority of settlers were members of the Anglican Church. It was therefore the Anglican Church which could have exerted the greatest influence in the White Highlands, but in fact it was not until the fifties that any significant inter-racial meetings arose from membership of the same Church. In earlier days the idea of two separate churches existing within the Anglican communion was accepted as reasonable. When R. S. Heywood became Bishop of Mombasa (the Bishopric of Kenya bore the title of Mombasa) in 1918, his Registrar, Edward Figgis, a leading lawyer in Nairobi, told him that he was Bishop of two churches: he was Bishop of the Church of England in Kenya and he was Bishop of the missionary congregations.[3] Until 1955 throughout the settled areas European chaplains were appointed to minister to the Europeans alone, while African pastors held services for the farm workers and other Africans in the neighbourhood. Co-operation was born during the stress of war, when Christian principles were at stake. The Mau Mau civil war had been raging for three years. The Aberdare range of mountains was one of the main centres of Mau Mau activity, but on the 4th December, 1955, the European Chaplaincy and the African Pastorate of the Western Aberdares, centred on Ol'Kalou, were amalgamated into one as the Parish of the Western Aberdares at a service conducted by the Bishop of Mombasa, with the Rev. Donald Howes, the Chaplain, and the Rev. Obadiah Mwangi, the Pastor, a Kikuyu, as Vicar and Curate. The amalgamation had been preceded in June by a visit by the Rt. Rev. Obadiah Kariuki, who had recently been consecrated as Assistant Bishop. Meetings were held of Europeans and Africans and the proposal for amalgamation was endorsed everywhere.[4] It was, as the future Vicar wrote in November, 1955, "an experiment which is both visionary and bold, for the whole plan has been born in a very much troubled area". After the success of this experiment had been proved, similar amalgamations were made throughout Kenya.

Bishop Heywood's successor, Reginald Crabbe, who became Bishop of Mombasa in 1937, succeeded in establishing an inter-racial synod, but he had two church councils, an African council and a European council. When Leonard Beecher became Bishop of Mombasa in 1953, his amalgamation of the two councils into one aroused considerable antagonism among the more racially prejudiced Europeans, some of whom even expressed hostility to the Church in general because the new Bishop had sullied its racial purity.[5] By amalgamating the two councils he had attacked European exclusiveness and privilege. The die-hards were not surprised, because they remembered that from 1943 to 1947 he had been Representative of African Interests in Legislative Council, where he had aimed at the fulfilment of trusteeship and impartial justice. Impartiality, however, is the enemy of privilege and, in an atmosphere like that which prevailed on the right wing of Kenya European politics, it aroused accusations of partisanship. By those for whom "justice" meant the maintenance of European domination, a Church which gave practical effect to the Christian doctrine of the worth of the individual soul was accused of being partisan.

The influence of the Anglican Church in the promotion of inter-racial co-operation owed much to the Chaplains Department of the British Army which, during the Second World War, opened its ranks to African priests, the first of whom was a Luyia, the Rev. Esau Oywaya. His ordination and the fact that he was given the resulting responsibilities made a great impact, which was further increased when other Africans were ordained as priests in the Chaplains Department and were treated in the same way.[6] This, together with the establishment of an inter-racial synod and the amalgamation of the two racial councils inevitably affected the thinking of sincere church people and, as the moderate and liberal sections of the European community grew in size and strength, Christianity became increasingly a source of inspiration in the struggle for inter-racial co-operation.

Prejudice, however, died slowly in the White Highlands. At Limuru a European new-comer caused offence late in 1947 when he took an African friend to matins, and in the following year a protest was made which came from the spirit of the past, which lingered on into a changing present. The Rev. William Owen was at that time Principal of the Divinity School at Limuru. A member of his staff, the Rev. Desmond Givan, preached one Sunday in the Limuru church. He took with him the Principal and two of the African padres who were attending a course at the School. Several European eyebrows were raised and one old lady, who had spent many years of her life in Kenya walked out. She waited outside till the service was over in order to vent her sense of outrage to her friends, who had remained inside, and expressed her opinion by saying, "I don't mind employing Africans or even shaking hands with them, but pray with them I will not".[7] By that date such an uncompromising attitude had become rare, but mixed congregations in the White Highlands were still almost unknown. Prejudice, however, was not the only cause.

The violent and vivid manifestations of racialism in Kenya in the first half of the century sometimes hid the fact that the fundamentals of many situations were not purely racial. Worship in church was a case in point. In an English village, if the upper and middle classes spoke modern English and the farm workers and craftsmen spoke Anglo Saxon, would they worship together? In the late nineteen forties few of the African wage earners spoke English. Anglican services in the heart of the Reserves were in the local vernacular and in the African locations in Nairobi and other towns in Swahili. In the small townships in the 'White Highlands' few Africans would have understood services conducted in English. Unfortunately the difficulty of language gave a cover of respectability to racial prejudice and the state of cleanliness and hygiene, resulting from great poverty, still further led to the separation of Africans and Europeans and to European objections to the use of the same building by different races.

Excuses relying on hygiene were not always valid. The element of prejudice had been clearly seen for instance in the early nineteen forties when the European residents who went to morning services at St. Mark's, Parklands, in Nairobi, objected to the provision of Swahili services for their African servants on Sunday afternoons, because they would have to sit in the same seats on the following Sunday morning.[8] Prejudice alone can account for so great a lack of logic as an objection to sit in a pew where the man who cooks one's food or cleans one's house has sat seven days earlier. But change in European attitudes was growing in the fifties. Some congregations remained exclusively white for many years, but in others Christianity overcame colour and, when Bishop Beecher dedicated a church at Kipkarren in the mid-fifties, there were at least as many Africans as Europeans at the service of dedication and the European Church Warden gave a set of keys to the African catechist "because",

as he said, "you'll be using the church more often than we shall".[9]
Opinion began to change everywhere and at Molo in the nineteen
fifties some leading settlers of liberal outlook were sorry that an
African and a European church had been built almost side by side
and had come to regret that there was not one church where services
could be held at different times in English or Swahili.[10]

Another difficulty which faced the Church was the educational
standard of the African priests, which put them at a disadvantage
with both the Europeans and the new African elite, the products of
Makerere and overseas education. As Professor Roland Oliver saw
in 1952, there was a danger that the Churches might be led by
"peasant priests" and be "spurned and ignored" by the educated
Africans in whose hands political power would lie,[11] while contact
between them and the Europeans would be only on a "social service"
plane. The better educated Africans went into government service
and, later on, into business. The Rev. John Mbiti from Kitui was a
unique exception. From Makerere he went to America and subsequently to England, where he gained a Ph.D. at Cambridge. On his
return to Africa in 1957, however, instead of entering the ranks of
the pastoral clergy, he taught at a teacher training college in Kenya
and later became Head of the Department of Religious Studies at
Makerere. The first two African bishops of the Anglican Church,
Bishop Obadiah Kariuki of Fort Hall and Bishop Festo Olang' of
Maseno, were both educated at the Alliance High School but did not
have university or other overseas education, with the exception of
a year's training at Wycliffe Hall, Oxford, which Olang' attended on
a British Council scholarship. Both men, however, became bishops
displaying pastoral qualities of high distinction, and Bishop Olang'
was enthroned as Archbishop of Kenya in August, 1970.

By the later nineteen fifties religious *apartheid* was almost dead,
but as late as 1957 Bishop Kariuki noticed that, when he went one
Sunday with a friend to a service in All Saints Cathedral, Nairobi,
two European women, beside whom they sat, got up and moved to
another pew, and the Bishop felt that "Africans saw themselves
despised by the Europeans—even their fellow Christians".[12] In the
same year, however, although he did not know it, Bishop Kariuki
was the cause of a vivid confrontation of the then more general
attitude and the unreasoning racialism of former days. When
he was going to preach at a church in the White Highlands the
President of the local club announced that he would be entertained

at lunch at the club after the service. One member, however, said that, Bishop or no Bishop, he would see to it that no "damned nigger" had lunch at that European Club. The President happened to be a man of decision and action and promptly hit the die-hard member on the chin with such force that he laid him out on the floor.[13]

The structure of the Anglican Church made Africanisation possible at an early date, and the Church had African Assistant Bishops before the Government had African District Officers and African Bishops before the Government had African Provincial or even District Commissioners. Anglican dioceses were running their own affairs before Independence. Money for the salaries of Bishops, secretaries of Bishops, Diocesan clerks and clergy was contributed locally. Finance from overseas was used for the cost of missionaries and for capital expenditure.

The Church of Scotland and the Presbyterian Church

The Church of Scotland was organised from Scotland and all its services were in English. Outside Nairobi and other towns were Church of Scotland *missions*, which constituted the Presbyterian Church of East Africa, but they were only in Kikuyu country and their services were all conducted in Kikuyu. In Nairobi itself services in Kikuyu were conducted, first at St. John's Pumwani, and from 1954 at the Bahati Martyrs Church at Bahati. As the African congregations were composed only of Kikuyus, there was no need for Swahili. In 1948 the Rev. David Steel arrived as Minister of St. Andrew's Church, Nairobi, and in 1950 he preached a sermon which challenged the Church of Scotland and the Presbyterian Church to come together. His sermons acquired a great reputation and during the Mau Mau Emergency English-speaking Africans, who were no longer able to go to their homes in the Reserves at weekends, attended services at St. Andrew's where they found themselves at that time in a predominantly European congregation. In February 1956, the General Assembly of the Presbyterian Church of East Africa was formed and St. Andrew's became part of this unified Church and was no longer controlled from Scotland.[14]

The Roman Catholic Church

In structure and practice the Roman Catholic Church was very different from any of the Protestant churches. A long course of training, much longer than in the Protestant churches, lay behind the ordination of a priest. This, together with the authoritarian and hierarchical structure of the Roman Catholic Church endowed the priest with an authority which was not enjoyed by the pastor. Objection to inter-racial attendance in church could not draw support from the plea of separate languages, because the Mass, being in Latin, was in a language foreign to European and African alike and the sermon, if there was one, was much shorter than the sermons delivered at Anglican matins and other Protestant services.

In 1957, when the Rev. Maurice Otunga was ordained as Auxiliary Bishop in a service at Kakamega, the first African to become a Bishop of the Roman Catholic Church in Kenya, a visiting priest wrote, "Here was an African Bishop who was going to exercise authority, not only over the overwhelmingly African laity but also over priests and nuns who were primarily Europeans".[15] The authority of the priest, however, did not have to wait for his ordination as a bishop. All members of the Church, European and African alike, knew that a priest from the moment of ordination had full powers and that race could be no impediment to their exercise.

The career of Cardinal Otunga shows clearly the strength of priestly authority to overcome racial considerations in the fulfilment of priestly duties. He was ordained priest in Rome in 1950 and, as a priest, heard confessions there. Those who went to him for confession were not merely Africans, who were studying in Rome, but Italians and other Europeans. In 1951 he returned to Kenya and was confessor to European religious fathers and sisters and to such lay people, including Europeans, as resided in the western areas of Kenya where he worked.[16] Perhaps, if a European priest had been available, they would have gone to him, but as there was not one, they went to Otunga as priest, a man endowed with the full authority of the Church.

At the same time, although the authority of the priesthood was a bar to religious racialism, the long period of training before ordination delayed the Africanisation of the priesthood. In 1939 an African was ordained priest at Nyeri and in 1940 another was ordained in the Kisumu Diocese, but it was not till 1961 that there was an African priest in the Nairobi Diocese, and eight years after Independence, although the Archbishop was an African, of the thirteen Bishops eight were Europeans. Certainly the long period of training prevented the Roman Catholic Church from being led by "peasant priests", which Professor Oliver saw as a danger facing the Protestant churches, but it severely limited the number of priests whose educational qualities and authority might have contributed much to the inter-racial cause.

The Church in Public Life

In his sermons at St. Andrew's the Rev. David Steel frequently attacked racial intolerance and he was prominent in inter-racial activities. He defended the claim, which politicians were apt to dispute, that the Church should concern itself "with how men live together and behave towards each other", which, he maintained, "is what politics are".[17] They Very Rev. Hugh Evan Hopkins, the Provost of the Anglican Cathedral, held the same view of the position of the Church, which, he declared, "must maintain its independence at all costs" and that, he added "includes the liberty to criticise Government policy if it is considered to overstep the bounds of justice".[18]

Both David Steel and Hugh Evan Hopkins were able to exert great influence because they held important positions in Nairobi. It was there that the largest concentration of English-speaking Africans was to be found and it was therefore in Nairobi that it was most possible to bring Africans and Europeans together through common worship in church. In 1945 few Africans would have wished to worship in All Saints Cathedral, because only a few would have been able to understand a service and sermon in English. One or two could be seen on Sunday mornings sitting in the side aisles. Gradually, as more Africans became able to speak English, more attended Sunday services in the Cathedral. In 1953 the Provost took a revolutionary step. An African from Taita, the Rev. Alan Madoka, was appointed curate in the Cathedral, which served also as parish church for that part of Nairobi, and it soon became normal for Europeans and Africans to kneel side by side at the communion rails to receive the sacraments from the Provost or the Bishop and the African curate. Both the Provost and David Steel were ardent fighters for justice and for the abolition of racial discrimination and both were able to use the prominence which their ministries gave them to stir up men's consciences to active effort in the task of promoting co-operation and harmony between the races.

The Christian Council of Kenya was active in scrutinising political measures and proposals and did not hesitate to make known what it considered to be in keeping with or contrary to the Christian ethic. The War was scarcely over when the leaders of all the Protestant Churches through the Christian Council of Kenya issued a statement in which they said, "We believe that if these post-war problems are regarded as only political, economic or agrarian, we shall fail to solve them. They must be approached as matters which depend primarily on the relations of persons to one another" and they believed that Christian principles must be the foundation of these relations.[19] S. A. Morrison, Secretary of the Christian Council, exercised constant vigilance and was an inspiration to all who were concerned with inter-racial justice. He fought tirelessly for the Christian approach towards social and economic problems: he was the principal leader in the attack against the *apartheid* policy in housing, which tried to hide itself under the idea of "an African Mayfair". His zeal was of infinite value. He died in 1956 from overwork.

Such people as he had to work to the uttermost to bring Christian principles to bear on public life, because, as a group of men and women convened by the Provost in 1953 to discuss inter-racial problems reported, there was reluctance among lay people from Christian congregations to take part in politics and public service. The strength of Christianity was being shown at that time by the innumerable Kikuyus who suffered martyrdom for their refusal to take Mau Mau oaths. All over Kenya Christianity was regarded by many Africans as the greatest gift brought to Africa by the Europeans and many would have agreed with Ohanga when he told Legislative Council that, much as they desired education, they did not look on it as the greatest gift brought by the Europeans to Kenya but regarded it as the most "valuable asset" which western civilisation had taken to Africa "next to Christianity".[20] The Provost's group, however, found that the sacrifice of the Kikuyu martyrs was not matched by active public work by their fellow Christians elsewhere, and "this lack of Christian leadership of moderate opinion" seemed to them to be one of Kenya's greatest weaknesses and they found it most of all among Africans.[21]

The Danger of Apartheid in Housing

Among the social problems which perturbed the Christian Council of Kenya was the danger of racial *apartheid* gaining strength through efforts to provide better housing for the better educated

Africans. The Council and a few individual Europeans and Africans believed that the fundamental need was for housing to be thought of on economic, rather than on racial, grounds. Actually it was "settled policy that there should be no racial segregation in towns". Of course Mitchell himself upheld this policy. A case occurred in his first year as Governor. In 1945 a certain Mr. Fox sold a plot in the Ngong Road to an Indian. The Governor was asked by Europeans to exercise his power of veto, but had to refuse because of this "settled policy".[22] In practice everywhere the best areas were reserved for Europeans and in Nairobi Africans of all classes had to live on the treeless plains on the east side of the city. All urban Africans continued to be segregated in "locations" and be classed together as Africans, even when a few had become office workers and Civil Service executives. In the fifties the problem became acute. "Locations" had become the established pattern of urban housing for Africans, but a pattern which had met the needs of a purely working-class society was inadequate to satisfy the requirements of the nineteen fifties. In 1954 a Working Party of the Church Missionary Society went so far as to say that "Housing probably constitutes the most urgent of all social current problems".[23] Government servants and certain unofficials, such as G. A. Tyson, a leading member of the commercial community, Municipal Councillor, Alderman and former Mayor of Nairobi, were deeply concerned about the shortage of housing for Africans and the appalling conditions in which urban workers had to live. But it was the danger of complete urban *apartheid* among the educated which caused the greatest alarm to the Christian Council and others who foresaw the emergence before long of Africans who would economically be on a level with Europeans and the better-off Asians.

In the early nineteen fifties the Carpenter Report on African wages concluded that "the family minimum should be at least three times that proper for a single man" and that "for the great majority of the urban African labour force married life is at present only attainable at a sacrifice of health and decency".[24] George Tyson was particularly alive to this problem and felt, as he told the young Europeans who were members of the Young Kenya Association in 1951, that the population figures give "some idea of the tremendous responsibility which the European community has towards the African population of these three East African Territories".[25] He concerned himself deeply with the problem of housing and by his publications made the needs plain for all to see. New "locations" were planned and built, but the influx of Africans into the city caused the shortage of housing to be always greater than the efforts which were made to remedy it. "The City Council", said an article in the Geographical Magazine in 1950, "is certainly not blind to the situation, but building costs money and uses materials, both of which are limited".[26] But the greatest cause of tension was not due to lack of building materials after the War but to the persistence of classification by race rather than by economic or social distinctions. "The Africans with secondary school education", said the same article, "even those who have won distinction in the School Certificate, have to live in the same locations as the office-boys and even the illiterate manual workers with their shoeless feet and ragged shirts. Accommodation varies from part of a room to a four roomed house, but they are all situated together, and the Library Club has its meetings in a room attached to the Welfare Hall round which the illiterate gather in noisy groups".

The housing of the better educated Africans, many of whom were in the Civil Service, caused concern to the City Council, the Administration and the African Civil Servants Association. Their very concern to see the better educated more suitably housed nearly played into the hands of racialism. A principle, not apparent at all, was involved. The actual provision of good houses might increase the danger of segregation unless it could be accompanied by a penetration of non-African areas and a departure from the practice of classing all Africans together for administrative purposes. A suggestion was put to the Deputy, at the time Acting, Governor that an estate of good, but not expensive, houses should be built leading off the Ngong Road.[27] The better educated Africans could have been given priority as applicants for them. The estate would have been attached to the European Ngong Road area and the two could gradually have been merged together into an erea where racial considerations did not apply; but nothing came from this suggestion.

In 1953 the President of the African Civil Servants Association brought to the notice of the Government the difficulties of the Africans, of whom there were about seventy, who, in the opinion of the Association, should be housed in better accommodation than was available to any African in Nairobi. The three fifths rule, whereby an African received three fifths of the salary which would be paid to a European, was still in operation and the low rate of

African salaries would have made it impossible for African civil
servants to pay the rents charged in other areas, even if residential
discrimination had been abolished. At a meeting in the Secretariat,
with the exception of two Kikuyus, all agreed that a site in the Race
Course Road area should be used for building an "African Mayfair",[28] or what the President of the African Civil Servants
Association called "a model village", which could later be opened to
"non-Government servants of about the same standard".[29] The
Africans agreed to this because it was a suggestion which would
solve their immediate difficulties, but the Christian Council, a few
other Europeans and a few educated Africans who lived near, but
outside, Nairobi, were appalled. Between Race Course Road and the
European and Asian residential areas was the business section of
Nairobi and if an 'African Mayfair' were built near Race Course
Road *apartheid* in housing in Nairobi would be firmly entrenched.
Two years later a senior European Administrative Officer asked
whether even senior Africans were "to be condemned indefinitely
to live in the worst part of Nairobi—in Nairobi's 'East End' ".
And he went on to say that "virtually the whole of Nairobi's African
population is segregated in the hot, flat, dusty, treeless, feature-
less plains in the eastern part of the city". So far so good, but he
continued, "would it not be a bold and sensible policy to allocate
land for better quality African housing in one of the better and more
agreeable areas of Nairobi?".[30] Such a scheme would have provided
good houses, but it would have still classed educated Africans racially
and would have still further established *apartheid*. The small group
of Europeans and Africans, who met each other in the Christian
Council and the United Kenya Club and who, because they were
not personally living in the "locations", were free from the
immediate personal problem, felt that better housing must wait
if its provision meant the still further strengthening of *apartheid*.

Some European areas were reserved entirely for Europeans
because they had been developed from European-owned land under
restrictive covenants, but other areas were closed to Africans for
economic reasons and municipal practice. All Africans were confined
to "locations" like Pumwani and Shauri Moyo, separated from the
rest of the town by what the sceptical might have called a 'cordon
sanitaire'. To walk at night across the waste space between Pumwani
and what was the edge of the business area of Nairobi in the late
nineteen forties was as dangerous as to walk across Blackheath in

eighteenth century England. The unemployed thug was the African counterpart of the highwayman and footpad. Public transport was meagre and the African members of the United Kenya Club therefore could not attend evening meetings unless they were fetched by Europeans or Asians in private cars, and on the whole their natural dread of being patronised ruled this solution out. "I hate being offered a lift in a car from the Club by a European or Asian", said an African member, "I can never pay it back".[31] This problem would remain until European thinking was willing to accept the idea of working class and higher income areas instead of African, Asian and European areas, because it was Europeans who controlled the Municipal Councils throughout Kenya and so could dictate the planning of residential areas.

The danger that urban *apartheid* would be permanently entrenched was defeated in an unexpected way when the difficulties which could arise from the restrictions on housing were shown by the case of Mashek Ndisi in 1955. This case resulted in drastic action which set a precedent for the future. Ndisi was a Senior Labour Officer, a Luo with a beautiful, sophisticated Kikuyu wife. They lived in Kaloleni, where his possession of a motor car made him an object of envy to his manual working class neighbours and to the wage earning population in general. During the Emergency there was considerable corruption in the Police Force and it was an intrusion by the Police into his house one night in 1954 that showed him and the Labour Department that it was unsafe for him to stay any longer in the "locations". But there were no other parts of Nairobi in which an African, however senior, could rent a house. The Commissioner for the Government of India came to the rescue at once and gave the Ndisi accommodation in his house, but Ndisi felt that he was being bought by Indian help and was anxious not to be under a debt to the Indian Commissioner. He admitted that he would not have felt the same if the offer of accommodation had come from a European. European friends then made enquiries and Ndisi was allowed to move to a temporarily unused European staff house at the Jeanes School at Kabete. For some months all went well, but then Ndisi was told that he must leave the house, although as a matter of fact it remained empty for some months before the next European occupant arrived. Mrs. Ndisi and their children went to stay with her parents, who were living at Eldoret, and Ndisi, unable to return to the "locations" and unable to stay any longer at the

Jeanes School, slept a night in his car. The following day the British Council Representative, who had been a friend of Ndisi's since 1947, heard what had happened and invited him to stay with him and then wrote to report the matter to C. H. Hartwell, the Acting Chief Secretary.

Hartwell knew about Ndisi's difficulty and had already told the European Housing Committee that "a senior African civil servant" would soon be needing a European-type house in a hitherto non-African area. The Committee's reply and Hartwell's marginal notes show how imaginative understanding had to contend with regulations and practices which could not meet the needs of the rapidity of African development. By that time the three fifths rule had been discarded and the Committee asked whether it was "really the Government's intention" that the allocation of European type housing "should no longer be made on a points basis according to salary, length of service, and the size of an officer's family". Here Hartwell wrote in the margin, "There will have to be exceptions". The Committee's reply continued, "it is obvious that an African or Asian Officer who could be described as a 'Senior Officer' in the old racial Service may not necessarily rank as such in the new non-racial Service where, presumably seniority will depend on status, salary and length of service, irrespective of race. If it is the Government's intention that certain African Officers who were previously the most senior in the purely African Civil Service should now be granted European *type* accommodation over the heads of European and Asian Officers (marginal comment, 'It is') who are far more senior in the non-racial Service, the Committee asks me respectfully to point out that this will inevitably cause serious repercussions in the European and Asian Staff Associations (marginal comment, 'Quite') particularly in view of the present length of the waiting list and very serious shortage of housing of all racial types". Another marginal comment showed that Hartwell did 'NOT' agree that allocation of houses should be made strictly on a basis of salary and length of service, which would put a senior African low down on the waiting list, and a comment at the end of the letter says, "The Committee can go on allocating European houses to European Officers, unless I ask them to do something different in particular cases".

The letter from the British Council enabled Hartwell to call a meeting immediately with the Nairobi European Housing Committee, "to discuss the general question of the allocation of suitable houses to senior African Officers" and to write to the appropriate authority that a house in Parklands which was "available for allocation" must be given to Ndisi. The Ndisi family went to live in Parklands and the danger of *apartheid* in housing was averted, because a precedent had thus been made for an African to live in an area where hitherto no African had lived except as a domestic servant.[32] Soon afterwards Mashek's father, the Rev. Isaac Ndisi, went to Nairobi to stay with his son and daughter-in-law and found them living in the house where he himself had been employed in former years as cook by a certain Captain Brook. Captain Brook had seen his potentialities and had set him on the road of education which led to his ordination as a minister in the Church. This earlier employer had acted as a good trustee for the progress of his African employee and later an enlightened Acting Chief Secretary swept aside regulations which, if strictly adhered to without imagination and liberal application, would have impeded the Government's fulfilment of its Trust for African advancement and equality. The allocation of a house in Parklands to an African was a small matter in itself, but it was important as a precedent in the campaign to eliminate racial discrimination.

Schools

Almost completely unanimously the Europeans were strongly opposed to the idea that any Asians or Africans might be admitted to schools attended by European children. Even the very few Europeans who believed that some lessening of educational segregation would help the cause of inter-racial understanding thought that change would have to come slowly and that the wisest course would be to admit pupils at sixth form level, unless it were possible to find a few African children who could enter a primary school on something like terms of equality with the European children. Disregard of practical considerations could only do harm. In the nineteen forties economic disparity was so great, differences in diet were so pronounced, home backgrounds so diverse, ability to learn in English so unequal that entrance at primary level could only have been very small. Even at sixth form level there would have been great difficulties. European children had opportunities which would have enabled them to reach sixth form standards at an earlier age than would have been possible for Asians and, even more, for

Africans and physical and emotional problems would accordingly have arisen.

It was said by some people in Britain that Government grants should be withheld from any schools which insisted on having only European pupils. Five thousand miles away from Kenya that seemed in theory to be a logical claim, but it ignored practical considerations and the aim of developing democratic parliamentary government. European opinion in Kenya was almost unanimously opposed to any infiltration of non-Europeans into European schools and the Government could only have insisted on their admission if it had overridden the European Elected Members in Legislative Council and disregarded European opinion in general. The course of parliamentary advance would have been interrupted by official disregard of the unofficial vote. Many leading members of the official side in Legislative Council would have resigned and European racism would have been increased. The European community was certainly numerically very small, but politically and economically it was very powerful and the value of European leadership was recognised by the majority of Africans. As with admittance to hotels and other vexed racial problems, many sincere inter-racialists felt that admittance of non-Europeans to European schools could best be achieved by changing European opinion.

Men like Raymond Barton, the Headmaster of the European Primary School in Nairobi, and Philip Fletcher, the Headmaster of the Prince of Wales School, were outspoken critics of European pride and prejudice, and Miss Janette Stott, the Headmistress of the Kenya High School, was no less liberal in her views and no less forceful in expressing them. Many teachers who went to Kenya from Britain were appalled by the attitude and behaviour of many European children who, as one Headmaster said, "do not think it is possible to be rude to a Native".[33]

Many Europeans were afraid that association at school would bring young people of different races together out of school and increase what they felt was the danger of inter-marriage, but "We do not consider", wrote an inter-racial group convened by the Provost of Nairobi, "that the fear of inter-marriage should in any way hinder closer friendship between all races".[34] Most Africans were like the Mbukusu who "would never wish to see his tribe full of half castes"[35] and were no more anxious than were Europeans to see inter-marriage. There were a few mixed marriages and they caused a serious educational problem. Even if the father was a European and so the child had a European family name, the European school committees were adamant in their refusal to grant admittance to a European school. The new Governor was deeply worried and in 1945 he called all the European Elected Members of Legislative Council together to discuss the matter. He told them that if the children "were 'near White' and came from good homes, it seemed wrong to exclude them from European schools"; but the problem facing him was that, if he over-ruled the school committees, such unpleasantness would result that the children themselves would suffer. The European Elected Members were adamant that children of mixed race should be excluded from European schools, but they admitted the need for education for them and suggested the building of another primary school near the Railway part of the town to which they could go.[36]

Four years later the problem of the education of their own children led John Karmali, a Moslem of the Ismaili community, and his English wife to take the bold step of founding a non-racial infant school. In February 1950 the Karmalis had an interview with the Governor about the project for which they had already made a start with ten children, six Asians and four Europeans. They first met in the house of a European family but, as these left Kenya a few weeks later, the class moved to the house of the Commissioner for the Government of India for a few months and then to the Karmalis' house, where it remained until it was installed in a wooden building on Hospital Hill in the grounds of Government House in September 1953. Mitchell, in accordance with his policy of trying to improve race relations, supported the project and told the Karmalis that he thought the United Kingdom Treasury might help.[37] The Kenya Government provided the land and buildings on Hospital Hill and the cost of structural alteration, and the provision of equipment was met from Colonial Development and Welfare Funds. For the next two years after the move to Hospital Hill there were no European children at the school, but eight were enrolled in 1955. The school received "a Government grant-in-aid in accordance with the rules applicable to all non-African aided schools", which meant four fifths of salaries, and a Board of Governors was appointed by the Director of Education. It was the only inter-racial school in Kenya. The Colonial Development and Welfare Fund gave £4,228 in capital grants in the first four years of its existence in its own premises. It had the following numbers of pupils:[38]

	Africans	Asians	Europeans	Total
1953	1	11	—	12
1954	7	18	—	25
1955	9	18	8	35
1956	12	20	9	39

In the early nineteen fifties the growth of African primary education resulted in a great increase in intermediate schools, and from this came an increase in the number of schools working for the School Certificate. This development affected Nyanza as well as the Central Province, but the Coast lagged behind and the secondary school at Shimo la Tewa continued to meet the needs of that area.

The allocation of funds for education was an issue which showed how communal rather than national was the thought of many Europeans. They forgot that in Great Britain and other democracies it was accepted that all should pay taxes according to their ability to pay and that the money thus provided should be used according to the needs of the whole community. In Britain the costs of state education were met from the general taxes, but in Kenya the poor were of a different race from the politically powerful Europeans, whose racial outlook blinded some of them to the normal principles of democracy, and who from time to time advocated that each community should pay for the education of its own children. At the Electors' Union Conference in 1948, for instance, a resolution was debated that "This Conference considers that each race should assume financial responsibility for the education of its children".[39] The small amount of money voted by Legislative Council for African education was a perpetual source of African complaint, but the most racially minded Europeans wanted to abolish it altogether. In 1946 the Director of Education had attacked this attitude in Legislative Council. The idea was not new, he said, because Indian and European education had once been financed "on a basis of communal taxation", but "the attempt failed".[40] Many Europeans condemned this racial outlook, but its existence was a fact which the progressives could never ignore.

The few educationalists and others who were working for the breaking down of racial barriers in education and social relations were all people with sincere religious convictions. They were practical people who saw that persistent effort was necessary and that they would have to advance patiently, step by step. Miss Janette Stott, who became Headmistress of the Kenya High School in 1942, believed that integration would be easier among girls than among boys, because boys always tended to discuss politics, whereas girls of all races were primarily interested in domestic concerns and found points of common interest along non-controversial lines. As early as 1944 girls from the African Girls School, Pumwani, and the Indian Girls High School ran in a relay race at the annual Sports Day at the Kenya High School and did the same each year afterwards, and there were no reactions from the European parents. Two years later African boys from the Alliance High School competed in a full sports meeting at the Prince of Wales School in Nairobi. This became an annual event and the Asian Duke of Gloucester School joined in three years later.

The Kenya High School

In 1947 Miss Stott wrote in a school publication that the parents of the girls "believe as I do that no scheme of development will succeed if the education of women, whether African or European, is neglected".[41] From the beginning she had hoped to be able to bring some Asian and African girls into the school and she started her campaign by announcing that the parents of her European girls, with whom she discussed educational matters, thought that the future of Kenya required the education not only of *their* daughters but of African girls also. She wisely tried first to get a few Asian girls into the school and in 1951 she suggested to the Department of Education that some Indian girls should be taken into the Sixth Form for science at the Kenya High School. Miss Stott circularised all the parents of her Sixth Form girls and all of them agreed that this experiment should be made. Bernard Astly, in the Department of Education, asked the Indian community for their views. The Asians were so pleased with the suggestion that they talked about it too publicly and the idea was reported in the newspapers. A great outcry was raised by the European public and pressure was brought to bear on the Department. A delegation from the East African Women's League went to the European Elected Members Organisation and said that "from correspondence which the E.A.W.L. had received it was obvious that there would be a storm of protest if the Government started "mixed racial schools",[42] and, although the parents of the Sixth Form girls themselves had raised no objections, the idea had to be dropped. The pattern was the same as had been experienced in the recent Finger-Print controversy.

Miss Stott suggested the same experiment in 1959, but again without success, and then in 1960 she discussed the question of integration with the Secretary of State's Adviser in the Colonial Office in London. They decided that the only hope of success lay in having a Board of Governors representing the public, although it would contain Government representatives also, and in getting such a Board to approve a policy of integration. The Minister for Education then formed a Board of Governors with representatives of the East African Women's League, the Parents' Association, the Treasury and the Ministry of Education, with Sir Philip Mitchell, the former Governor, in the Chair. The Parents' Association strongly opposed the idea of having Asian and African girls in the School and a rowdy meeting was held. The Chairman almost had to close it without a decision, but he managed to get the resolution passed by one vote, and in January, 1961, an Asian girl, Razir Ismail, the daughter of Dr. Ismail, a member of Legislative Council, became a pupil at the school. Four African girls followed in May. All of them started at the bottom of the school, the idea of Sixth Form entry having been abandoned. Their arrival was preceded by a circular to all parents from the Board of Governors, whose views, because they contained representatives of public organisations as well as of the Government, were accepted in a way which would have been impossible if the Ministry had still been in control with only an advisory School committee. After a year with good teaching and good food the African girls reached high places in their respective forms. They got on well with the European girls and there were no repercussions from European parents. Five more Asian girls were admitted and the School magazine reported without comment the "admission of our first ten African and Asian girls".[43] Miss Stott's persistence was then rewarded. Few people knew that in the early fifties she had held an unofficial discussion group in her own house, composed of some of her Sixth Form girls and some senior Asian girls, on Sunday evenings. European parents were bound to hear about this and to see that no harm resulted. Gradually in this matter, as in so much else, personal experience broke down racial prejudice.

In 1942 the Kenya High School had only 150 pupils. None of

them came from the richer settler families. They came from Tanganyika, Uganda and the Rhodesias as well as from Kenya. Their parents were Afrikaner farmers, missionaries, employees of the railway, such as engine drivers and engineers, and other junior Government servants. The daughters of leading settlers and other well-to-do Europeans went to schools in Great Britain or South Africa, or, if they stayed in Kenya, to the Limuru Girls School, a private school founded under the auspices of the Church Missionary Society by Mr. A. B. Macdonnell, who had his own daughters' education in mind. In 1943 the Limuru Girls School encountered financial difficulties and girls who would have gone there went to the High School instead; but many of the settlers who sent their daughters to the High School were apologetic about sending them to a Government school, but by 1951 the number of pupils had increased to 400.

In 1952 a modern side was started for girls who were still in primary schools at the age of fifteen and were taken into the High School without examination. They were given employment as clerical workers in banks and European businesses. Soon afterwards, however, Asian girls from the Duchess of Gloucester School began to be absorbed into commerce and banks and they were found to be better educated than the girls from the modern side of the High School, but because of racial salary scales they were paid less than the European girls, whom they began to overtake in competition for employment. Their infiltration into commercial employment proved to be so satisfactory to their employers that the subsequent equalisation of salaries did not affect their lead over those European girls who failed to pass the School Certificate examination. They won their leading position by their educational superiority over the less able of the European girls; their success tended to increase the general European dislike of Asians.[44]

The Prince of Wales School

The Prince of Wales School, like the Kenya High School, had not attracted the sons of the richer farmers before the War. They had gone to Public Schools in Britain or South Africa, or, if they were Afrikaners, to Afrikaans-medium schools in South Africa. Employees of the Railway, Post Office technicians and others, who could not afford to send their sons to Britain, sent them to the Prince of Wales, which between June 1940 and January 1942 had to move its day

boys to the upper floor of the Nairobi Primary School and its
boarders to Naivasha, while its own buildings were taken over by
the Army for use as a hospital. During the War it was impossible
to go to Europe and so, just as girls from richer families went
to the High School, so their brothers went to the Prince of Wales and
numbers rose from 150 to 450. They found that the School provided
a good education and after the War many, who would otherwise
have gone to Britain, stayed in Kenya and went to the Prince of
Wales or the Duke of York, which was founded in 1949 to meet the
need of providing places for greatly increased numbers. The ground
nuts scheme in Tanganyika took many men with high salaries to
East Africa. The two Nairobi schools had gained a sufficiently
good reputation for some of them to take their sons with them.
Some even took boys away from English Public Schools and sent
them to the Prince of Wales or the Duke of York. This was an
excellent development because they had no preconceived ideas,
whereas the normal Kenya European boy, who had no experience
of educated Africans, looked on all Africans as being like the farm
workers whom he knew in the holidays.

The European boys of low ability looked with growing fear at the
high standard being reached at the African Alliance High School
where a failure to obtain good results in the School Certificate
examination was unknown. They were afraid of becoming poor
whites and began to fear Africans as competitors; and the same
sort of tensions as were growing between European girls of low
ability and Asian girls began to be seen between these European
boys and the newly educated Africans. The poorer the home the
more racially rabid were the European boys. In the mid-nineteen
fifties Philip Fletcher, the Headmaster of the Prince of Wales
School, stressed the need for them to compete with boys of other
races on grounds of character and reliability: they could no longer
look for any monopoly of employment on academic grounds.[45]

Inter-Racial Meeting among the Young

The Boy Scout and Girl Guide movements were inter-racial and
throughout their history in Kenya inter-racial Scout camps and
Guide camps were held, and leaders were trained together. Ability
to overcome local prejudices has always been an achievement of
Scouting and Guiding all over the world. The Executive Committee
of the Scout Movement in Kenya was inter-racial; it was possible

there to have African interests represented by Africans many years before African women sat on the Executive Committee of the Guide Movement, but when in 1952 education made this possible, Miss Emma Njonjo became a member of the Guide Executive. The contribution to inter-racial co-operation and harmony made by Brigadier General Sir Godfrey Rhodes, the Chief Scout Commissioner, was great and was shown by him also through the St. John's Ambulance Brigade. This organisation and the Red Cross Society were outstanding examples of the possibility of inter-racial work. The creation of inter-racial understanding was carried on also by the Outward Bound Movement with its inter-racial courses at Loitokitok. It was established in Kenya in 1956 after an exploratory visit by Major Spencer Chapman, who held a meeting under the auspices of the British Council in the National Theatre in 1954.

During the nineteen fifties boys and girls in the schools in and around Nairobi were continuously finding themselves sitting next to boys and girls of other races at functions of various kinds. The annual Kenya Music Festival was an entirely inter-racial affair. There was an annual tea party and musical recital at the house of the British Council Representative, where care had to be unobtrusively taken to see that seating space on the chairs and on the floor respectively was equally distributed among the races. In 1954 the Mayor of Nairobi, R. S. Alexander, himself educated at the Prince of Wales School, gave a tea party at the Town Hall to senior pupils of all races.[46] In 1953 Professor Vincent Harlow, at that time Beit Professor of the History of the British Commonwealth at Oxford, gave a lecture on behalf of the British Council in the National Theatre and chose as his subject Britain's part in the abolition of slavery, when the questions asked came with equal intelligence from boys and girls of all races. Other similar meetings were held and in 1959 an annual Schools Drama competition was inaugurated. Competitors and the public of all races thronged the theatre and colour was a factor of no account.

These developments were not the result of chance. Creech Jones and Mitchell were proved right in their demand for a National Theatre in 1947. The Theatre was in fact a gift from Britain to the cause of inter-racial co-operation in Kenya. It provided a place in the centre of Nairobi, opposite the Norfolk Hotel, which had always been the meeting place of Europeans from all over Kenya, where racial considerations did not apply and where intellectual and cultural functions could be held on a basis of quality alone. After the Emergency, when it was possible to raise money for additional building, the Cultural Centre was built and the Conservatoire of Music, the Orient Art Circle, a school of ballet and other organisations acquired offices and practice rooms there.

The Kenya Drama Festival

The Kenya Drama Festival, which had an offshoot in the Schools Drama Festival, was the result of a plan put into operation in 1951. The British Council had to win the goodwill of Europeans and do what it could to help them to keep at a high standard the cultural heritage of Britain. Drama was a cultural activity enjoyed by both actors and audiences and it was also an activity in which Africans and Asians engaged. It was hoped that through the theatre the goodwill of the European community could be gained, European cultural standards could be helped, and, later on, members of the different races could be brought together by participation in a common pursuit which they all enjoyed. In 1951 at the request of its Nairobi office the British Council sent to East Africa Mr. Charles Thomas, an expert on the theatre, to lecture on drama and to advise European dramatic societies on the building or adaptation of little theatres and on dramatic production. As a result of this tour the Mombasa Amateur Dramatic Society adapted a building to form a theatre and theatre club and similar work was carried out at Moshi, Kitale and elsewhere. Four European dramatic societies said they would like to hold a competition in the following year. This was organised by the British Council in 1952. In 1953 the African Dramatic Society of the Jeanes School and an Asian Society decided to compete also and the British Council realised that it would have to form a society to run what was clearly going to be an annual Drama Festival. So the East African Theatre Guild was formed with separate Kenya and Uganda branches. The Schools Drama Festival was started in 1959.[47]

The Kenya Arts and Crafts Society

The East Africa Conservatoire of Music was founded on an interracial basis in 1944 and the annual Music Festival was open to all races. In the Drama Festival also all races came together, but the annual Art Exhibition was confined to Europeans, with the exception of a guest section for other races. The Kenya Arts and Crafts Society, whose exhibition it was, refused to become inter-racial right up to the last years of the colonial era, even though some of its members made great efforts to persuade the majority to be progressive and accept the necessity of change.

The Society's name, the Kenya Arts and Crafts Society, and its constitution which stated that the object of the Society was "to encourage Arts and Crafts in all their branches", when looked at in conjunction with the clause which stated that the membership should consist of "an unlimited number of Europeans", elected in accordance with the rules, showed the old attitude of mind that in such matters the Europeans were the only people of Kenya to be considered. The Society was in fact a European Arts and Crafts Society, existing to encourage art among Europeans. When Asians and Africans produced artists and craftsmen of a quality entirely suitable for membership, the constitution prevented them from joining the Society, because it confined the membership to Europeans, although the name of the Society was not the European Arts and Crafts Society, but the Kenya Arts and Crafts Society. Great ill will began to be felt when the best sculptor in East Africa was an African and John Karmali, an Ismaili Moslem, proved that he was the equal of the best European photographers in Nairobi but was not able to join the Kenya Arts and Crafts Society, which existed "to encourage Arts and Crafts in all their branches".

By the mid-fifties opinion in the Society was sharply divided. The question of opening membership to other races was debated in 1956, and in 1958 a postal ballot produced a majority of 151 to 120 "for the inclusion of artists of all races", but the opponents then raised legal objections on the plea that the constitution required a unanimous decision of all the members of the Society for a fundamental change like the admission of members who were not Europeans.[48] The real objection of many members, which was never admitted in public, was that Asians and Africans would have to be allowed to attend the life class, where they would sometimes have Europeans as models. Those who objected to this possibility, however, saw no objection to Africans being used as models for a European life class.

The issue in the Arts and Crafts Society was subsequently allowed to drift. There is no minute recording the change of the Society to inter-racial membership, but in 1961 "ways and means of attracting

Asian and African membership were discussed",[49] and non-Europeans did become members in the early sixties. When Asians and Africans became members it was the former opponents of inter-racial membership, such as Mrs. Lulu Dyer, one of the best artists in Kenya who, more than any others, tried to make them feel at home in the Society.[50] On a national scale the same thing happened when some Europeans, who had most strongly opposed the entry of Africans into the White Highlands, accepted the inevitable and became particularly good neighbours of the new farmers.

The East African Women's League

The East African Women's League, like the Arts and Crafts Society, had a misleading name. It was not an East African organisation, but was a League of European Women in Kenya. It did much useful work for the European community, but the educated women of the other races sometimes wondered how an organisation whose constitution confined its membership to "any women of white races" could be called the East African Women's League, unless its members thought that no non-European women were worthy of consideration. It was certainly not till well on in the nineteen fifties that there were African women with an education which could reasonably enable them to be members of a society of that character, but there were Asian women who would have profited greatly from being included as members. They were for the most part shy and often not at ease in the English language, but, if Kenya was to develop as a multi-racial nation, European leadership could have helped the leading Asian ladies to become acquainted with the life of the western world, towards which Kenya was moving, and then could have welcomed the African women elite as they began to appear on the stage of national life.

In 1959 Elizabeth Erskine, the wife of Derek Erskine, resigned from the E.A.W.L. and decided to direct her "energies to the organisations which are genuinely made up of members of all three races in the Colony", as she said in her letter of resignation. An Inter-racial Liaison Committee had been formed some years earlier, but it was "pushed into the background". She believed that that Committee might "have gone a long way to breaking down the appalling prejudicies and misunderstanding held by so many of the white people of Kenya", but in fact she felt that it had merely been "a make-belief idea which has done little else than save the face of the League from heavy outside criticism".[51] It was not till September, 1962 that a postal referendum was held. Then 756 members voted for the inclusion of women of any race, 238 voted against and 5 abstained. At the Annual General Meeting on the 19th March, 1963, the amended constitution, omitting the words, "any women of white races", was passed and membership of the League was open to women of all races.[52]

Problem and Cure

When Sir Philip Mitchell said that "the overwhelmingly great" problem was the human problem he put his finger on not only the basic cause of many of Kenya's troubles but also on the means of curing them. The economic and political problems could not be solved unless people got together as fellow human beings respecting each other's human personality and trying to understand the cultural background which conditioned each other's approach to the economic and political problems of the day. Fear was an ever-present factor: the fear felt by the Africans that the scales of progress would always be weighted against them by European power, the fear of the Europeans that they would lose, not just their privileged position, but everything they had, if African numerical superiority was reflected in political influence, the fear felt by the Asians that they would always suffer discrimination from the Europeans and fail to win the friendship of the Africans. Fear and arrogance, racial discrimination, a sense of grievance and frustration, stood in the way of inter-racial co-operation. The goodwill and harmony which were so greatly needed to ensure a peaceful passage to Independence could not be evoked by legislation. The work of the legislators had to be based on a solution of "the overwhelmingly great" problem of human relations.

1. Sir Andrew Cohen: *British Policy in Changing Africa*, p. 8.
2. Letter from Rev. Canon Donald Howes, 19th July 1970.
3. Interview with Dr. Beecher (formerly Archbishop) 15 Mar. 1971.
4. Western Aberdare Chaplaincy News Letter, September, 1955 (Copy in possession of the Rev. Canon Donald Howes).
5. Interview with Dr. Beecher, 15 Mar. 1971.
6. ibid.
7. Note in Frost papers, corroborated by Rev. W. Owen in an interview on 18th February, 1970.
8. Interview with the Rev. W. Owen, 18 Feb. 1970.
9. Interview with Archbishop Beecher, 20 Mar. 1970.
10. Mr. C. N. Millington of Molo to R. A. Frost, 1954.

11. Roland Oliver: *The Missionary Factor in East Africa*, pp. 291–2.
12. Miss Clarke's Diary, 18 May 1957.
13. Interview with Dr. Beecher, 15 Mar. 1971.
14. Interview with the Rev. John Gatu, General Secretary of the General Assembly of the Presbyterian Church of East Africa, 20 Mar. 1970.
15. Paul Foster: *White to Move*, p. 116.
16. Interview with Archbishop Otunga, 18 Feb. 1972.
17. From a sermon printed in full in K.W.N., 3 Feb. 1956, pp. 40–41.
18. E.A.S., 11 Mar. 1955.
19. E.A. & R., 5 July 1945, p. 1055.
20. L.C.D. 20 Jan. 1949, col. 1166.
21. E.A.S. 15 Jan. 1954.
22. Sir Philip Mitchell's Diary, 2 Oct. 1945.
23. Minutes of the Working Party on African Housing in Nairobi held at the C.M.S. Guest House on 25th November, 1954. Church Missionary Society deposit No. 1/229 in the Kenya National Archives.
24. *Report of the Committee on African Wages* (*F. W. Carpenter, Chairman*) Parts 1–3. Nairobi Government Printer 1954, p. 71. Cf. Dr. Trowell in 1947, Chapter 2.
25. Alderman G. A. Tyson, *A Talk on African Affairs given to the Members of Young Kenya Association*, Nairobi, May 1961. A copy is among Mr. Tyson's papers.
26. Richard Frost, "Nairobi", *The Geographical Magazine*, November 1950, p. 287.
27. R. A. Frost to Deputy Governor.
28. P. P. Narracourt for Member for Development to Deputy Chief Secretary. Office of Chief Secretary, Deposit No. 8/1736 in Kenya National Archives.
29. John Muchura to Chief Secretary: 1 Oct. 1953, file ibid.
30. Acting Officer-in-Charge Nairobi Extra Provincial District to Acting Administrative Secretary, 13, Aug. 1955, file ibid.
31. Richard Frost: 'Nairobi', *The Geographical Magazine*, November 1950, p. 287.
32. This correspondence is in Office of Chief Secretary Deposit No. 8/1738 in the Kenya National Archives.
33. E.A. & R. 1 Apr. 1948, p. 821.
34. E.A. & R. 7 Jan. 1954, p. 574.
35. E.A.S. 15 Jan. 1954.
36. Sir Philip Mitchell's Diary, 1 May 1945.
37. ibid, 22 Feb. 1950.
38. Details taken from a Note sent to the Chairman of the European Elected Members Association by the Minister for Education. A copy is in Blundell 15/3.
39. Havelock file: *The Electors' Union* (*1948 Conference and After*), in the Kenya National Archives.
40. L.C.D. 10 Jan. 1946, col. 724.
41. *The Kenya High School 1942–1960*, p. 1.
42. European Elected Members Organisation: Minutes of Meeting on 27 Nov. 1952, Blundell, 14/3.
43. *The Kenya High School Magazine*, 1961, p. 5.
44. These paragraphs are based on interviews with Miss Stott on 19 and 20 Aug. 1969.
45. Interview with Philip Fletcher, 28 Aug. 1969.
46. E.A.S. 17 Sept. 1954.
47. British Council Nairobi Office file 341/7, folio 49.
48. Information contained in the minute and record books of the Society.
49. Minutes of Meeting on 25 Sept. 1961.
50. Information supplied by the former Secretary, Mrs. Gwen Streets.
51. Elizabeth Erskine to the President of the E.A.W.L., 17 Apr. 1959: copy of letter in file in possession of Lady Erskine.
52. Information supplied in April, 1970 from the E.A.W.L. Minute Book.

9

THE NINETEEN-FIFTIES: A DECADE OF PROGRESS

European Disagreements not recognised outside Kenya

The work done by organisations and individuals to enlighten opinion and bring about co-operation between the races would have been of only academic interest if it had not achieved a fair measure of success. During the nineteen fifties there was a great increase of liberalism and progressive thought within the European community and the moderate, co-operative centre between the extremes of African nationalism and European die-hard immobility increased. In the second half of the decade the results of liberal progress in thought were seen in many ways and in Legislative Council the European Elected Members voted for measures, such for instance as the ending of racial discrimination in hotels, which might have cost them their seats ten years earlier.

The increase of liberal thought was not fully recognised outside Kenya. Writing in 1958, Carl J. Rosberg in America said that what he believed to be attempts by all the Europeans to hold on to past privileges and power would drive "the African elite . . . to exploit the possibilities of African nationalism".[1] The Europeans, however, were far from united in their views and aims and only a section of them were trying to hold on to the power of earlier years. Developments within Kenya and the implementation of the Lyttelton Constitution, which for the first time gave ministerial responsibility to an African, showed the nationalists that the erosion of European privilege and monopoly of power had begun. It is true that the first reaction of Tom Mboya, who was soon to become the leader of nationalist militancy, was anger that the Lyttelton Constitution gave two Ministries to the Asians but only one to the Africans,[2] but he and his colleagues soon saw that the break-through had been made and that the number of educated Africans would grow and the balance would gradually swing over to an African majority in the Government. The nationalists' determination to gain the predominance of political power was due not so much to fear of

European reactionary policies as to the realisation that the prize was in sight and to the consequent desire to get it quickly.

During the nineteen-fifties European willingness to accept inter-racial co-operation steadily increased at the expense of die-hardism. This was plain to African politicians like Mboya and Ngala but was less apparent overseas. "It is significant", wrote Rosberg in the same essay, "that though European leadership has become politically divided in the last five years, this division has not been centered around basic goals and objectives, but has related to tactics, procedures and means for maintaining and entrenching European formal influence in Kenya. Clearly the European settler is disposed to resist any constitutional reform that recognises a decline in his formal influence in the parliamentary system".[3] In fact, however, what was really significant was that the divisions in "European leadership" *were* based on basic goals—on inter-racial co-operation on one side or on attempts to maintain "European formal influence in Kenya" on the other, but the speeches of the European reactionaries and the silence of the large number of moderate Europeans, who seldom attended political meetings, obscured the change which was taking place.

The main constitutional history of the nineteen fifties can be quickly outlined. African representation in Legislative Council was increased from two to six nominated members; the Lyttelton Constitution brought an African and two Asians into the ranks of Ministers; the Lennox-Boyd Constitution followed; Specially Elected Members were introduced; European parties, multi-racial parties, African parties were formed and dissolved and replaced by others; inter-racial co-operation and non-co-operation were violently opposed to each other; after the publication of the Coutts Report on African franchise[4] African Representatives in Legislative Council were elected in 1957 instead of being nominated; they numbered eight. Led by Tom Mboya, they soon demanded fifteen more seats. Then, unexpectedly quickly, in 1960 the First Lancaster House Conference produced the blueprint for Independence.

The Vincent Committee

At the beginning of the nineteen-fifties most European politicians still hoped that the authority of the Colonial Office could be lessened and power be transferred to them, although even then there were differences of opinion about the future. In 1952 the Elected Members appointed a committee under the chairmanship of Sir Alfred Vincent to consider plans for constitutional advance. In its Draft Interim Report[5] the Committee stated, "The gradual assumption of more responsibility by the European community is, we believe, sufficiently provided for in our proposals, whilst allowing due opportunity for other races and affording special safeguards for the protection of "African interests", and they felt that "any constitutional change must be gradual rather than a leap in the dark". As so often, European politicans seemed to think that *they* could decide how Kenya should develop. They forgot the trusteeship of the Imperial Parliament and sometimes seemed to believe that the Devonshire Declaration was merely "a scrap of paper". K. E. Robinson, Reader in Colonial Government at Oxford, who was their adviser, pointed out the psychological mistake of a provision which implied "the suggestion that the Government is likely to seek to injure African interests", and he foresaw "a time when European rights will need protection". And so he recommended that safeguards "for universal rights or interests" were "preferable to specific safeguards".[6]

With one exception the European Elected Members thought differently and "recognised that delegation of further responsibility to the Kenya Government from the Secretary of State would entail special safeguards for other races".[7] Mervyn Cowie, who was at that time a Member of Legislative Council, wrote a reservation to his acceptance of the Interim Report. He suggested that in future it was likely to be the Europeans rather than the Africans who would need protection, because they were "not on the privileged side of the colour bar".[8] He alone among the members of the Committee seems to have accepted the fact, which was clear to the consitutional adviser from Oxford, who advocated a Bill of Rights, that power would pass into African hands and that the once powerful minority might need protection. Eight years later the African Elected Members declared that a Bill of Rights would be necessary in the independent Kenya which was soon to be created. In preparation for the first Lancaster House Conference in 1960 they wrote that "the concept of minority safeguards is self-contradictory and self-defeating. On the one hand it seeks guarantees from the majority government that special rights or privileges will be observed and on the other it states that the majority government cannot be trusted to look after the welfare of all its citizens".[9]

Although on the Vincent Committee Mervyn Cowie's was the
only voice in disagreement with the views of the other members,
even before then there were signs of policies which would split the
European community before long. In 1951 Havelock wrote to the
Chairmen of all European District Associations to say that, if the
Europeans wanted to press for the appointment of more Members
from the unofficial community, that is Members in charge of
Departments or Ministries, they must not forget that the other
races would advance in ability and would be eligible for appointment to responsible posts.

"It seems to me," he wrote, "that the ultimate choice lies between
the majority influence in the legislature being awarded to those
with the merit and ability and the system of partition or apartheid.
It must be understood that if we are to accept the former principle,
should members of other races show the ability and merit, that
the door must not be closed in their faces and we may have to
accept the inclusion in the Executive and Higher Administrative
positions of Asians and Africans in the future."[10]

Blundell and New Policies

Already the European politicians were becoming divided.

In February 1952 the Governor noted that relations between
Keyser and Blundell, the old fashioned and the progressive elements
among the Elected Members, had become very strained.[11]
In December of that year Keyser had to give up the position of
Leader because of illness. It is significant that it was not one of the
conservative Members who was elected in his place. Blundell was
chosen to succeed him. There were graduations of liberalism and of
reactionary ideas among the Elected Members. Humphrey Slade,
who was to become one of the Europeans most respected and liked
by Africans, was not one of Blundell's admirers, but as early as
March 1952 it was noted that he had "come out openly and strongly
for the Common Roll".[12]

One of the first things which Blundell did as European Leader was
to get Members of all races to agree on a statement of policy aimed
at "strong suppression of M.M. but attention to housing, wages,
etc., no more Colour Bar in hotels, civil service salaries", as Mitchell
wrote in his Diary.[13] Such a policy was bound to be unpopular
with the European die-hards, but inter-racial agreement seemed to
Blundell to be of greater value than a facade of European unity.

He felt sure that "his dissident group", who were uncompromisingly opposed to what they called "appeasement" of African aspirations, would break away from the other European Elected Members,[14] and three months later, in March 1953, a split was accepted as inevitable. "I think we are likely to get an extremist European party forming as a result of our troubles", wrote Blundell, "but it will free more moderate opinion".[15] The subsequent formation of the extremist White Highlands Party was to be welcomed, because it freed Blundell and the European Elected Members who followed him from the need to try to carry with them the die-hard fringe of the European community and so made it easier for him to express his beliefs in his speeches, which became noticeably more liberal. The more die-hard the fringe became the more obvious it was that European unity was impossible to achieve and that all attempts to bring the extremists along the road of moderate opinion were useless. A complete split in the European ranks was preferable to attempts to produce an impossible compromise, which could only result in lukewarm and ineffective policies. At the beginning of the year Mitchell had come to the conclusion that "the Europeans must split or be for ever sacrificed to the die-hards".[16]

The split in the European ranks, which arose from fundamental differences of view on future policy, was not due to the announcement of the Lyttelton Constitution in 1954. That made it all the more definite, but there had been a split on basic principles at least a year earlier. The Lyttelton Plan was not an innovation suddenly imposed on the Europeans of Kenya by a hostile Secretary of State. The fundamental innovation, the inclusion in the Government of an African Minister—a step which could lead only to ultimate African supremacy—was the result of suggestions already discussed in Kenya. After the introduction of the Lyttelton Constitution some people thought that Blundell had worked on the proposals with Lyttelton during his periodic visits to London in 1953. Lyttelton subsequently denied this,[17] but correspondence passed between them and Blundell had "protracted discussions" with the Governor at the end of 1953 and could "give a rough outline of the picture which Oliver Lyttelton would be willing to accept".[18] Blundell told the Secretary of State that he thought that an African ought to be included as a Minister in the Government and Lyttelton replied in November, "I am glad to hear you were thinking of including an African Minister in the proposed Government. It would win a great deal more support to your scheme over here".[19] The scheme, which later became public as the Lyttelton Plan, was conceived in Kenya. The proposals were not sprung on the Elected Members as a *fait accompli*. Blundell discussed with them at every step what he had discussed with the Secretary of State and the Governor. He stressed the point that, if the unofficial side of the Government was to acquire more power, Asians and Africans would have to be brought into ministerial ranks: there could be no increase of European power by itself. Although this fact of trustee-ship was made clear for all the European Elected Members to see, there was opposition from the more reactionary Europeans to the suggestion that Africans and Asians should be given full responsi-bility. In January 1954 George Usher, European Elected Member for Mombasa, said that he would agree to the appointment of African Under Secretaries, "but no executive authority for Asian or African",[20] but Havelock, who was Blundell's close follower, told the European Elected Members on 2nd February, 1954, that "Associating members of other races in the capacity suggested by the European Elected Members Organisation, i.e. without portfolio and advisory, will not produce that community of interest which shared responsibilities develop", and he maintained that only by having African and Asian Ministers would they get "the beginning of the nation".[21]

During the later years of his Governorship Mitchell had seen the futility of the European attempts to hold on to power instead of sharing it with the emerging elite among the other races. He was an inter-racialist and deplored the discriminatory attitude of Executive Council and "urged on them the importance of promoting some Asians and Africans to better posts. We cannot just go on saying we are going to", he wrote, "and never doing it".[22] After his retire-ment he lived, like Blundell, at Subukia. Both men were progressively and inter-racially minded and Mitchell's long experience was always at Blundell's service. In December 1952 he advised Blundell to form a party of all races,[23] and a month later Blundell accepted the idea and was ready to form an inter-racial party,[24] but he decided that the majority of the European electorate was not yet ready to accept such an innovation. Disagreement between the reactionaries and the progressives was growing into bitter hostility and after Blundell's acceptance of the Lyttelton Constitution some of the European Elected Members went so far as to announce publicly that he was no longer their leader.[25] Throughout 1953 his opponents kept up a campaign against him on political platforms and in the Press. "I have never for a moment dreamed", wrote J. A. Couldrey to Blundell in May 1953, "that the Press in Kenya could sink so low, not even Vigar's mouthpiece, *Comment*."[26] Blundell wrote to Hugh Fraser, the Parliamentary Secretary to the Secretary of State in the House of Commons, that "an attack of mounting proportions has been launched on me by a small group of extremists in Nairobi" and he went on to say that they had "bought a paper".[27] *Comment* became a mouthpiece of views most sharply opposed to Blundell's policies of moderation and liberal progress towards the elimination of racial prejudice.

But liberal efforts to educate European opinion had not been without effect and the Rev. David Steel assured Blundell in January, 1953, that he had "a very large measure of support for moderate policies . . . among the majority of the settlers who would never dream of attending political meetings. The fact that the majority don't attend political meetings may be deplored, but it would be a mistake to ignore them".[28] And Rawson Macharia praised his "wise leadership" later in the same year. But Blundell was well aware that there was "a great move in Nairobi" to get rid of him and put Grogan in his place.[29] In the Trans-Nzoia Gerald Smallwood, a farmer of liberal views was defeated in a by-election by Ray Letcher, "a South African with almost Malanite views".[30] The Royal Commission was in Kenya and people were wondering what its recommendation would be. Mau Mau was active and at the beginning of the year the march to Government House after the murder of the Ruck family showed the uncertainty of tempers among some members of the European community. The Federal Independence Party were determined "to oppose multi-racialism at all costs".[31] Liberalism had to pay attention to political possibilities, and the United Country Party, composed of Europeans who asked for co-operation with Asian and African political parties, seemed to Blundell to be all that was possible at that time, although he would have liked to form an inter-racial party.

The Editor of *East Africa and Rhodesia* and Colonel David Stirling, founder of the *Capricorn Africa Society*, attacked him strongly for not including all races in the United Country Party.[32] David Stirling became more realistic during the next few years and, when speaking in London to the Royal African and Empire Societies

even as late as in 1957, said, "The point I especially want to empha-
sise is that any measure of constitutional reform proposed by
European settler politicians calculated to get African support
would quite certainly lose these politicians the basis of their political
authority which is the European voter. Equally, if Africans put up
any proposition which they reckon had a ghost of a chance of
achieving European support for the sake of creating common ground,
then they would as surely lose their African support".[33]

In this address Colonel Stirling showed that he had tempered the
impractical idealism which had activated his attack on Blundell
for not making the United Country Party an inter-racial political
party in 1954. But the negative tone of his remarks suggested a
failure to appreciate the change in thought which had been taking
place among many Europeans. In 1955 a European Member of
Legislative Council said that the concept of multi-racialism had
"destroyed everything for which he had worked throughout his
life". His aim had been the creation of "a White Dominion of East
Africa".[34] In January 1955 Cavendish-Bentinck, wrote Mitchell,
"faced the fact that dreams of a settler independent Kenya have
come to nought and are now seen to be vapour, unsubstantial things
of little account". Mitchell's comment on that was "Of course;
but there are great things to look for in the future, once the mind is
adjusted to realities".[35] At the end of the decade Leo Vigar, in his
capacity of Chairman of the Federal Independence Party, wrote to
Blundell. "In our opinion your political record over the last ten
years fixes firmly and squarely upon your shoulders the responsibility
for the mess in which this country now finds itself". Blundell, he
wrote, was "the Kenya Architect of the Blue Print on which the
present ruinous state of the country has been built up".[36] Blundell
"fought so hard" for the Lyttelton Constitution because he "believed
that the only solution to the problem of Kenya was eventually to
create a non-racial society".[37] Multi-racialism would merge into
non-racialism as the Africans reached what were regarded as
European standards, and so Blundell felt that what was needed
was "the concept of a Kenya Citizen, whether black, white or
brown".[38]

The violence of the opposition to progressive policies and to
Blundell's acceptance of the Lyttelton Constitution gave the
impression outside Kenya that most Europeans were still intent on
entrenching European power in the constitution, but a keen observer

in Kenya formed a different judgement. George Tyson, a leading member of the business community, wrote to Blundell, "I believe you have 80 per cent of the European community behind you in your determination to make the plan work and work smoothly".[39]

Mau Mau did not impede progress
Serious disagreements within the European community were seen before the outbreak of the Mau Mau revolt. After the effects of the initial shock had worn off, the Emergency, instead of bringing communal unity in European opinion, tended to increase the differences, and efforts to promote understanding and co-operation between the races continued. The cultural campaign reinforced the claim for recognition made by education. The Royal Commission of 1953 had an African member, part of whose education had been at Oxford;[40] in law and in medicine Africans and Asians had proved their ability to meet British requirements; Africans were reaching high standards in the arts; and nothing but prejudice could maintain that Europeans were intrinsically a superior race. To deny that they *were* ahead was folly, but that did not prove that they always would be ahead, and efforts were made throughout the late forties and fifties through cultural and functional activities to bring the Europeans to a better understanding. Some remained arrogant and aloof, but others began to appreciate the advance of the African elite and to see the wisdom of keeping them in contact with the culture into which they had been educated. An African Member of Legislative Council said that "Kenya became an African state at the time of the Lancaster House Conference".[41] It was an African state which had learned much of the culture and ideals of the Trustee.

Official lack of feeling
The work of creating understanding between the races was not always helped by officialdom. Even before the Declaration of a State of Emergency officialdom seemed to lack a sense of feeling for African reactions. Co-operation cannot be achieved by force. Unwilling acquiescence is something different. An instance of such lack of feeling occurred in August 1952. David McDowell Wilson, the Editor of *Baraza*, was in touch with African thought and saw the folly of sending the Kenya Regiment through the African "locations" in Nairobi in August 1952, two months before the declaration of the Emergency, because the Kenya Regiment was

composed of young Kenya Europeans and contained no African soldiers.

"I think", he wrote, "that the recent decision to send the Kenya Regiment through the African locations in Nairobi was a psychological blunder of the first magnitude. To have sent a column of African troops or a mixed column of African and European troops would have been a sound move, but the sending of European troops only will certainly be interpreted as a threat on the part of the Europeans to maintain political supremacy by force and I think that the repercussions of this are certain to be felt in any further deliberations regarding the constitutional future of Kenya, appearing as a more intransigeant attitude on the part of the African spokesmen".[42]

The Emergency was declared in October 1952. The conflict was between the forces of order and modern civilisation and a movement with many atavistic features in the Central Province, but it was increasingly made to appear a struggle of White against Black with Brown being allowed to be second class helpers for White.

Isolation of African Leaders

In April 1953 the British Council Representative invited Michael Blundell, who was leader of the European Elected Members, Wycliffe W. W. Awori, who was Acting President of the Kenya African Union, and Wilfred Havelock and James Gichuru to lunch. In the middle of lunch Blundell said, "You know, Awori, we ought to do this again. We have never talked together like this before. We've only met each other in debate in Leg. Co.[43] But if my constituents knew that I was having lunch with the President of K.A.U., I'd be thrown out at the next election". "I quite agree", said Awori. "It's very valuable for us to meet in a friendly way like this, but if my Africans knew that I was lunching with Mr. Blundell, I'd have a knife in my back". All four agreed that they should meet again in similar circumstances but, they asked, "where except in Dick Frost's house could we do it"? It was possible for Blundell and Awori, the leader of the European Elected Members and the Acting President of the Kenya African Union, to meet for lunch and to discuss affairs in a completely open and friendly way, even though in so doing they were ahead of the majority of the population, but at that time Awori was given no official encouragement to support the Government.

After Kenyatta was arrested, Walter Odede, a Luo, was made Acting President of the Kenya African Union and, when he was sent to detention at the Coast in March, 1953, he was succeeded by W. W. W. Awori, Member of Legislative Council, who was a Luyia from the extreme west of Kenya. The membership of K.A.U. was mainly Kikuyu and it was thought by many to be to a great extent a reincarnation of the Kikuyu Central Association which had been banned in 1940,[44] but its *leadership* was more widespread. On the Committee, in addition to the Kikuyu members, there were such men as J. D. Otiende, a Maragoli, J. Z. Murumbi, half Masai and half Goan, and Richard Achieng Oneko, a Luo. The country-wide nature of its leadership was highlighted by the fact that its Heads were in succession a Kikuyu, a Luo and a Luyia, although, to keep the image of Kenyatta as Leader, Odede and Awori had the title of Acting President.[45] Instead of bringing Awori into any sort of co-operative contact the Governor, who saw him from time to time during November and December, 1952, ceased to see him in January, 1953.[46] In May 1953 the British Council Representative wrote to the Governor at Awori's request to ask the Governor to see him "and discuss his various difficulties and possible solutions".[47] This request did lead to an interview, but it is noteworthy that the President of the Kenya African Union did not meet the Governor for four months and, even then, was only accorded an interview at the request of a European friend. A similar sense of being excluded was felt by Clement Argwings-Kodhek, a Luo who returned to Kenya in 1951 as the first African from Kenya to be called to the English Bar. He said that leading Africans found it was no longer possible to have any contact with members of the Government. In particular the Member for African Affairs had repeatedly refused to see him.[48] Of course the Government was suspicious of the Kenya African Union because so many of the leading people in Mau Mau were members of it, but within the limits allowed by security it would surely have been possible for the authorities to make it clear that the revolt was a war between the forces of order and an atavistic movement in the Central Province. The refusal to meet the President and leading officers of the Union, however, added to the feeling that the struggle was regarded by the Government as a war between Black and White.

A year later official unwillingness to consult the Africans or listen to Europeans who understood the African point of view was

found still to be equally strong. When Oliver Lyttelton was Secretary
of State and went to Kenya on the visit which preceded the
introduction of the Lyttleton Constitution, Bishop Beecher wanted to
see him. Beecher had been Member Representing African Interests
in Legislative Council at an earlier date, his knowledge of African
thought and custom was immense, and his personal contacts with
leading Africans were numerous. The previous Governor, Sir
Philip Mitchell, had regarded him as "the man whose views I really
trust and value."[49] To a Secretary of State who wanted to learn as
much as he could about Kenya before issuing a new Constitution
no one could have been of greater interest. The Christian Council of
Kenya asked that Bishop Beecher should meet the Secretary of
State, but after several telephone calls to Government House the
Council was told that the Secretary of State could not see its spokesman. No reason was given.[50] Lyttelton was thus deprived of advice
which would have been based on almost unique knowledge.

African Grievance

It is little wonder that during these years the leading Africans
should feel, as Awori said in Legislative Council, that all that was
possible for them was to express their views in Council but that they
could *do* nothing. "Is Government asking for co-operation?"
he asked. "No! Government is not asking for their co-operation
at all."[51] A year later in Legislative Council Mathu expressed the
feeling of frustration and exclusion which continued to affect the
leading Africans. "Our plea", he said, "is that we want closer
association with the Government as a public service from the bottom
level to the top level and that the contribution we can make is
greater than some people believe. All we want is greater opportunity
to help to run this country for all communities together."[52]

In the early nineteen fifties the leading members of the Kenya
African Union became increasingly imbued with a feeling of
frustration and were despondent at their inability to get any active
response from the Government when they expressed their hopes
and their grievances. Section 4 of the 17 Points drawn up by the
Executive Committee in May, 1952, and expanded to 24 Points in
October, 1952, shows clearly that they were not asking for control
of the Government but were only asking to be heard. Almost
immediately afterwards the Emergency was declared. Moderation
had failed to make any impression on the Government; Mau Mau

had resorted to violence; and a very different note was sounded in the Memorandum submitted to Oliver Lyttelton, the Secretary of State, on 4th November 1952.

"We are of the opinion", this Memorandum began, "that much of the present trouble is due to the fact that Africans are not adequately associated with the machinery of Government to make them feel that they are a real part or partners in the Government of the country. This has the twofold effect of denying to the Government the benefit of considered African opinion in the making of Government policy; and on the other hand of creating an impression in the minds of the people that the Government, because of its composition, does not work in the interests of Africans. During the last thirty years, while the requests of the European community have been readily conceded, the requests of the African community have been consistently ignored. This has led the ordinary African to believe that only if he has a government of his own can he benefit and not otherwise. He refuses to believe that his interests can be safeguarded by the European Community."

The County Council Ordinance was cited among grievances because, as the Memorandum said, it enabled Europeans to dominate local government and the settlers, it was claimed, had opposed training in improved agricultural techniques "on the grounds that a policy aimed at making the Reserves remunerative and self-sufficient would deprive them of cheap labour". That had certainly been the opinion of Lord Delamere and leading settlers of the early days. This contention that the European settlers were opposed to agricultural training for Africans showed how the sins of the past caused suspicion and bitterness in the present. The Memorandum complained that the banning of 52 African newspapers, of public meetings and political parties prevented the Africans from expressing their opinions and their grievances. It ended by asking why Kenyatta and other leaders had been removed "during the critical hour when their calming influence would have had a most salutary effect." The Memorandum was submitted on behalf of the Provisional Executive Committee of the Kenya African Union, and it was significant that the Acting National President and the Acting General Secretary, who signed it, were neither of them Kikuyus.[53]

Confusion in Race Relations

After the declaration of a State of Emergency the behaviour of certain sections of the Security Forces caused great concern to those people who prized justice and civilized standards. The Emergency was, as Blundell said in a letter to the Secretary of State for Commonwealth Relations, a struggle of "the supporters of Government of all Races against people who for one reason or another have become temporarily completely barbaric,"[54] but the fact that the Governor ignored the President of the Kenya African Union and the lack of any signs that African co-operation was desired in high places caused many to feel that the struggle was purely racial. Carey Francis, the Headmaster of the Alliance High School, had so many African contacts and so much information coming from the boys in the school that his opinions were always very near the truth. "A tragedy of the present situation", he wrote in December 1953, "is that the Police are shunned and hated by even the best loyal Africans, and that more and more the fight is being made to seem what Mau Mau wants it to seem, a fight of Black v. White".[55]

Brutality committed by some members of the Security Forces could only do great harm to relations between Africans in general and Europeans, and in the same letter Carey Francis wrote about "irresponsible Kenya settlers, especially—but not only—young fellows in the Police, whose wild and unjust statements and actions, and contemptible contempt for Africans, inflame the many wounds."[56] There were also, however, British officers in the Police and the Army whose behaviour was of the highest standard, and there were Kenya Europeans in the Police and the Kenya Regiment who showed not only great courage but true comradeship with their African colleagues. As a District Commissioner wrote in his Annual Report for 1956, "Many were the bonds of friendship between people of various races which had been strengthened in the sharing of hardship and adversity in the forests and on the farms."[57]

There were also Europeans who were not in the armed forces who were fighting a moral battle for justice and true humanity. "Fighting a difficult battle on the side of right are not only the Christian Church and the administration but many responsible settlers," wrote Carey Francis.[58] Unfortunately inadequate public relations failed to show the spirit of harmony which existed among people of all races who were actively concerned with the maintenance of high principles. One of the difficulties facing them was what the

Governor, Sir Evelyn Baring, called "arrogance on the part of Europeans and suspicion on the part of Africans."[59]

The Emergency shattered complacency and made many people think seriously about matters to which they had previously given little serious attention, and moderate members of all races reacted to the racialism of Mau Mau by showing a willingness to think together about the causes of African unrest. In February 1953 it was possible to bring together in a conference on Rural Development convened by the British Council such men as the Professor of Agriculture at Makerere, the Director of Agriculture in Kenya, Eliud Mathu, Harry Thuku, the leader of an African nationalist movement in 1921 and subsequently a successful, large-scale farmer at Kiambu, Major F. H. Sprott, a farmer at Karen and Chairman of the African Affairs Committee of the Electors' Union, and other Africans and Europeans and two Asians in an attempt to reach constructive conclusions to be included in a report and sent for information to the Government.[60] Whether or not the Government paid any attention to the suggestions made in the Report, the fact that it was possible to hold a conference, attended by leading people of all races, during the Emergency was an indication of the existence of the goodwill which continued to grow throughout the decade.

Indian Support for Africans

The social isolation of so many of the "emerging" educated Africans and the Government's failure to make the African leaders feel that they were needed in the Government of a multi-racial country led to their turning for help to Indians who were themselves embittered by European exclusiveness. New regulations and legislation were often complicated and most of the African politicians were inexperienced. "As regularly as clockwork the Indians turned out for them long duplicated memoranda, going through the Bills clause by clause and putting the worst construction on everything."[61] The political liaison, or at any rate the willingness of the African politicians to use Asian expertise and experience when they needed them, was shown particularly clearly when a new Draft Constitution for the Kenya African Union was drafted by Indians.[62] But at the same time the African politicians were anxious not to seem to be dependent on the other races for the details of political planning. In June 1952 the first Inter-territorial East African Political Conference was held in Nairobi. Among the items on the Agenda was the creation of a society or category called "Servants of Africa" which was to have a special membership in each territory. It was to be confined to Africans and was intended to dispel any idea that any but Africans were the architects of federation.[63]

Growth of European Liberalism

In spite, however, of the official failure to encourage those Africans who were opposed to violence, a failure which caused a sense of frustration and helped the Indian campaign of co-operation with Africans against the Europeans, goodwill between Africans and British residents continued to grow. A greater number of Europeans outside the official ranks came to understand and accept the fact that the progress of Africans meant that the European monopoly of power was gone for ever, and a spirit of liberal co-operation joined forces with this realistic acceptance of the inevitable. European opinions and politics became more and more divided. Discerning Africans saw that a steadily increasing number of Europeans were showing a more liberal outlook than had existed in the past. As early as March 1953, Awori, then Acting President of the Kenya African Union, told a reporter from the *East African Standard* that Africans knew that there were "thousands among the European community" who subscribed to the Africans' "policy of democratic government", but that what was needed was action by that liberal element,[64] and a European observer wrote in November of that year that at a meeting called by Blundell "one couldn't help being impressed by the liberal atmosphere of the meeting" where leading members of the White Highlands Party "and one or two even beyond that pale got a very hot reception and were decidedly unpopular."[65] Blundell found support among many of the younger Europeans. "You must educate your young men in this Colony", wrote an African, "that they must carry Africans with them".[66] The change in attitude among the younger Europeans was noted by Sir Philip Mitchell, who discussed it in October, 1954 with Mervyn Hill, the Editor of the *Kenya Weekly News* who, he wrote, "agrees that Michael's stock is high with the young Europeans who are sick and tired of the pesky old White Highlanders and their perpetual nagging at Indians and Africans".[67] Bishop Beecher told a group of journalists in London in August, 1954, that "the large majority of European farmers and business men in Kenya were well disposed towards African advancement and the achievement of a plural society". "Liberalism", he said, "has advanced markedly in recent years" and it would be wrong to judge the Europeans by "the extravagant utterances of vocal minorities".[68] It was frustrating to those Africans who saw and were heartened by this change in European attitudes to find so little official encouragement after the retirement of Sir Philip Mitchell.

European arrogance and rudeness had often been noticed by the Governor and visitors from abroad and by liberal Europeans in Kenya itself. "A comparative new-comer" wrote about "the rude and aggressive attitude of my fellow Europeans towards Asians and Africans".[69] They caused great harm but were not characteristic of all Europeans and steadily decreased during the fifties. Even the organisers of Mau Mau admitted that there were "good" Europeans, but for the purposes of their campaign they had to declare that all Europeans were the enemies of African progress. In actual fact in the farming areas especially many Europeans won the respect, and some the affection, of their African neighbours. The settlers who were magistrates in the White Highlands were the counterparts in Kenya of the Justices of the Peace in Britain, and the members of the local committees were doing in Kenya what they would have done in the United Kingdom. Fair and impartial dealing characterised their work as it characterised the work of an English Bench. The Africans appreciated this quality and contrasted it with what they feared they would experience if Asian magistrates were appointed. In Kenya, with the great differences in economic standards which seemed to be synonymous with race, the influence of the individual was particularly far reaching. ". . . the crux of the matter", wrote Dr. Clive Irvine, a famous missionary of the Church of Scotland at Chogoria on the eastern slopes of Mount Kenya, "is the attitudes of the individual European towards the individual African. It is far more a European problem than an African problem."[70] Impartial decisions by magistrates and the maintenance of high standards played an invaluable part in the establishment of friendly relations between the races, a part which can be regarded as a manifestation of an *unofficial* co-Trusteeship with Britain on the part of *some* Europeans for the development of the Africans in Kenya.

It was because of many years of devoted work that, when Mr. E. N. Millington handed over the management of his farm to his son-in-law in March 1955, the Kikuyus of Molo gave a tea party to

express their admiration of him and his wife and presented them with
an Address saying that their lives were "a testimony to the truth
of the saying, 'Never become tired of doing good'".[71] In the same
year of the Emergency a farmer named Harold Hill died at Hoey's
Bridge. He was one of those who, as an African had written,
encouraged Africans "to believe that colour discrimination among
Europeans and Africans is beginning to be removed."[72] It would
be naive to suggest that such happy relations existed everywhere.
They did not, but there were many others who were appreciated
for their benevolent interest in the welfare of their employees and
their families, such as Frank Joyce of Ulu, of whom Lord Portsmouth
has written that "he devoted much of his land and his life to helping
his squatter workers and . . . his public services were devoted almost
entirely to helping African land development", and that "all this
was done with loving sympathy".[73]

Problems facing co-operation

In 1936 Lord Moyne in his Report on the financial situation in
Kenya had written that he had been "much impressed by the amount
of good feeling evident between natives and settlers".[74] The good
relations were between Europeans and "the working classes", as
they would have been called at that time in Britain, because the
number of educated Africans was very small. After Hitler's War
there was a continuous increase in the number of Africans with
secondary or higher education. Social mixing was made all the more
difficult because these "new" Africans were mainly young men and
because economically they had to live so far below European
standards. There were therefore barriers of age and material
conditions as well as race to be overcome. In Kenya the factor of
race aggravated the results of history. The Europeans were employers
and the Africans with whom they mainly came into contact were
the employed, while the Asians were at all economic levels. A
table in the Development Plan 1964-1970, giving the Income Groups
in 1962, shows the immense differences in income between the races.

Percentage of Taxpayers

Income Groups	Africans	Arabs & Somalis	Asians	Europeans
Under £120	91.4	86.0	11.0	1.5
£120–£159	4.7	7.2	4.3	3.2
£160–£199	1.7	1.9	3.3	0.6
£200–£399	1.7	2.0	13.0	2.5
£400 and over	0.5	2.9	68.4	92.2
Total	100	100	100	100[75]

As late as 1962 almost all Europeans were at an economic level which put them on a totally different social plane from almost all Africans. In 1958 11,600 Europeans, 24,800 Asians and 149,600 Africans were reported as employed. The following table shows the financial make-up of the European population.

£ per annum	Private Industry and Commerce	Public Service
up to £599	3.6 per cent	1.3 per cent
£600–£1,199	33.3 ,, ,,	32.6 ,, ,,
£1,200–£1,799	38.1 ,, ,,	47.7 ,, ,,
£1,800–£2,399	14.6 ,, ,,	12.6 ,, ,,
£2,400 and over	10.4 ,, ,,	5.8 ,, ,,
	100.0 ,, ,,	100.0 ,, ,,[76]

The rate of progress along the path of inter-racial co-operation was affected by two political brakes. On the one side were those Europeans who wanted to retain their traditional position of privilege and power and on the other side was the new force of African nationalism, which aimed, not at inter-racial co-operation, but at complete African supremacy. The right wing Europeans could not believe that a European could be what they called pro-African without being anti-European and so opposed the liberals in their own community. At the same time African nationalism attacked as "black Europeans" those Africans who believed that all who were sincerely loyal to Kenya and wished to improve conditions for all Kenyans irrespective of race could work together for the common good.

Economically and culturally some Asians and Africans had come closer to Europeans and some small social contact had been established. In Nairobi by the mid-fifties Africans and Asians were no longer excluded from the best hotels. The Music and Drama Festivals were completely non-racial affairs and the Europeans who were invited to Government House and receptions at other official places found many fellow guests of other races. At Kitale young Europeans who attended a political meeting in 1955 spoke against Keyser and many assured Blundell after the meeting that they supported him and his ideas "and were not at all interested about what the old buffers were thinking about the past."[77] The Royal Commission issued its Report in 1955 and advocated the removal of all land barriers: the White Highlands and the African Reserves alike ought, it said, to be open to the best farmers of any race. This attack on "the sanctity of the White Highlands" increased the fears of some Europeans that European settlement was doomed unless by some means or other the whiteness of the Highlands could be guaranteed for ever. A few, a very few, Europeans had said even in the late nineteen-forties that a European farmer in the White Highlands, who wanted to sell his farm, should be allowed to sell it to anyone, irrespective of race, who had the necessary capital and agricultural knowledge to enable him to farm it well, the Highlands Board being the arbiter of quality; and during the nineteen-fifties their number gradually increased. It was among the younger Europeans especially that agricultural ability slowly began to be seen as what really mattered and as early as 1953 Graham Greene found that "younger men agree that unused land in the Highlands will one day have to be sequestered".[78]

In 1954 the Editor of the *Kenya Weekly News* admitted that he thought it would be desirable to allow competent farmers of non-European race to farm in the White Highlands,[79] but open advocacy of this by Blundell, especially when his support of the Lyttelton Constitution antagonised many Europeans, would have been political suicide. The fact that some Europeans no longer felt that the "whiteness" of the White Highlands was "a sacred trust" made others all the more passionate. The Editor of the *Kenya Weekly News*, wrote that Group Captain Briggs feared that, "if the present checks and controls were removed, some settlers might be tempted to accept a favourable offer for their farms from an Asian buyer. After the meeting", continued the Editor, "I was surprised to hear a group of settlers agree that a percentage of their fellows cared so little about the principle of the White Highlands that they might well do so".[80] This fear of possible "treachery" within their midst would have made the majority all the more antagonistic to Blundell if he had advocated a change of policy at that time. What was most needed was the extension of inter-racial participation in common projects and of the introduction of Asians and Africans into hitherto European preserves. Little by little die-hard European antagonism would be worn down and progressive Europeans would be strengthened in their efforts to effect inter-racial co-operation. But there was a sad irony in the situation. As European willingness to co-operate grew greater, so too did African nationalist refusal to share power and to co-operate with the other races. In 1957 the *Kenya Weekly News* pointed out that "A peculiar feature of the political scene in Kenya is the common ground between a section of European opinion and the African nationalists. Neither has any use for the Lyttelton Constitution nor for any form of multiracial government".[81]

1956—A Year of Innovation

In 1956 the seeds sown in the past began to produce their fruit. In January the Government announced measures to enable Africans to become Army Officers and to commission men of all races into the East African Land Forces instead of into British regiments. This was an East African scheme under which the East African Territories would supply many of the officers needed for their military forces and would send them to Sandhurst for training.[82]

In the same month R. P. Maini was appointed a resident magistrate in Nairobi. He was the first Asian to sit as a resident magistrate in Kenya.[83] In January also the *East African Standard* printed a photograph of an Asian wedding in its social columns.[84] European social events were no longer to have a monopoly of attention. A fortnight later a Goan wedding was reported with a photograph and after that the reporting of the weddings of leading Asians became normal practice. Even more revolutionary was the inclusion of a picture of an African wedding in Uganda in February. Blundell had been to see the Editor of the *East African Standard* and had asked him to report Asian and African social events.

He had also asked him to leave out any mention of race when crimes were reported in the paper. Instead of reporting that "an Asian, Mr. A. E. Patel", or "a European, Mr. B. C. Smith", had been robbed, mention of the race of criminals or the victims of crimes, Blundell asked, should be omitted. If any readers were interested in the race, the name itself would supply the answer, but he was anxious that people should be treated as Kenyans and not as members of particular races.[85] He had also written to the Chief Secretary on 6th January 1956 suggesting that newspapers should print "Shopkeeper in Dock and indicate afterwards that the shopkeeper was an Asian by giving his name and background".[86]

In April C. M. G. Argwings-Kodhek, the President of the Nairobi African Congress, spoke at the weekly snack-bar luncheon at the New Stanley Hotel, where he was introduced by Colonel E. S. Grogan. Argwings-Kodhek told his audience that Africans had been "Faithfully and well served by Britain" and Colonel Grogan, commenting on the frustration suffered by "up-and-coming Africans" who had learned to live according to western standards but were not accepted socially by Europeans, urged Europeans to entertain "these symbols of the new Africa" in their homes.[87]

In August the President of the Kenya Indian Congress urged the Indian community "to take stock of its short comings and set about overcoming them". The time had arrived, he said, when Indians should "declare an end to (their) 50-year-old feud with the European community and bury the hatchet" and he went on to say, "We have often flattered ourselves by claiming that we have supported African aspirations", but, he continued, "it would be a tragedy, for us of all people, if the British lion in Kenya dies of an ass's kick."[88]

In October Duncan Nderitu Ndegwa, who was about to return from the University of St. Andrew's, was appointed a statistician in the East African Statistical Department. He was the first African recruited by the Colonial Office for service with the East African High Commission.[89] In the previous year Charles Njonjo on his return from England, where he had been called to the Bar, had been appointed to a job suitable for a newly called barrister and carrying a salary proper to its responsibilities. He subsequently became Attorney General. The days were gone when an African could return from an overseas university or professional training and be offered a salary geared to a two-thirds standard of living.

A Kenya Citizenship

At the end of 1956 Blundell advocated the creation of a Kenya citizenship, within which all could work together. He believed that the success of attempts to create such a citizenship would depend on sufficient time being available and on "the acceptance of the idea that standards and culture can run across the barriers of race".[90] Fear and ambition, one on one side and one on the other, stood in the way. "The truth is", he wrote, "we have two tasks—one to hurry up European thinking and the other to slow down the Africans. It is immensely difficult, and so dimly perceived by most people who really seem to have no imagination whatever in regard to these racial problems".[91]

The idea of a common citizenship without regard to race was not new. In 1952, a few months before the declaration of a State of Emergency, a group of people of all races had tried to overcome the racialism of politics by founding the Kenya Citizens' Association. The initiative came from the African side. Mbiyu Koinange met Sir Charles Mortimer one day in Nairobi and told him that he and Kenyatta wanted him to be Chairman of a Conference to found an organization to tackle the problems of tensions between the races. Koinange suggested that the Conference should be composed of ten members from each of the three main races, but Mortimer preferred a larger number, and it was agreed that twenty representatives of each race should be invited. The Conference met in the Desai Memorial Hall. Speeches were made by leading politicians, including Kenyatta, who said that the chief trouble arose from fear. The Europeans were afraid of the Africans and the Asians were afraid of both the Africans and the Europeans. He declared that they must get to know each other better and get rid of fear. An executive Committee composed of five people from each race was formed. Kenyatta was a member. Derek Erskine was elected President of the Association and the Editor of the *East African Standard* agreed to invite all the vernacular journalists, who issued mimeographed news-sheets, to form an educational club for members of the Press.[92]

The Kenya Citizens' Association policy was founded on the belief that "in National Unity lies the only key to progress". "In Kenya today", wrote the President, "'party' politics are 'racial' politics", but, whereas in the western democracies a man can change his party allegiance if he alters his political beliefs, "the Racial Politician cannot change his race, so he will not change his prejudices". It seemed clear to the members of the Association that "the system of communally elected representatives tends always to widen the rift between the races, since each community sends its champions to the central legislature, for the principal purpose of fighting for its own racial aims, as opposed to the good of the country as a whole." They approved of the innovation in the interim constitution of June, 1951, whereby the Governor added to the Government Benches ten members, selected regardless of race, with "especial regard to their qualifications as potential legislators". And they aimed at providing a meeting ground "for liberal minded persons of all races" where politics, economics and "new trends of thought" could be discussed.[93] Hopes of success were high, but Mau Mau activities soon cast doubts about the sincerity and basic assumptions of the association.

The Mau Mau insurrection put an end to the Kenya Citizens' Association, but the idea of Kenya citizenship was kept alive and at the end of 1953 a study group was formed by the Electors' Union in conjunction with the European Elected Members, under the Chairmanship of Humphrey Slade, to discuss the question of Kenya Citizenship.[94] Nothing concrete came out of the discussions, but they added to the growing fund of co-operative ideas.

Blundell revived the idea of a Kenya citizenship. He wanted to create a society in which any one with the necessary qualifications could say, "I am a Kenya citizen", just as St. Paul had claimed, "Civis Romanus sum". Any one having Kenya citizenship would be able to own land in the White Highlands. Africans and Asians would be able to acquire this citizenship by fulfilling certain requirements, such as reaching certain educational standards, owning a requisite amount of property, displaying a record of public service and having a character of accepted merit. But who, it might be asked, was to be the judge? The judges would be drawn from all races. Some Asians and Africans would clearly satisfy the requirements from the start and so right from the beginning they would sit on the panel with Europeans. It was hoped that such a Kenya citizenship would be free from the suspicion, which some people felt, that the "merit and ability" stipulation advanced by the European non-racial group was a blocking device intended to keep matters in their own hands.[95]

It was a period when in Legislative Council and at many political meetings inter-racial co-operation seemed to be far away but when individuals, both politicians and others, were more and more overcoming racial antagonism on a personal level. In September 1957 Humphrey Slade stayed with Oginga Odinga in Central Nyanza.[96] Two years earlier Odinga had aimed at "eliminating the immigrants in the shortest possible time". Was there now a change of heart or a change of tactics? Slade and arap Moi shared a political platform at Thomson's Falls where arap Moi paid tribute to the European contribution to progress in Kenya.[97] African nationalism swept on quickly to power and it is surprising that in the highest Government quarters, although not among prominent unofficial Europeans, few efforts seem to have been made to effect co-operation with it. In 1953 the President of the Kenya African Union had been cold shouldered and as late as 1959 Mboya was able to write with reference to the controversy arising from the Lennox-Boyd Constitution of 1957 that "on every occasion on which they (the African Elected Members) met the Governor it was at their own request".[98]

Although for tactical political purposes Mboya, who became the leading African politician, took every opportunity of attacking Blundell and although racial discrimination, which still existed to some extent, and the arrogance of the hard core of out-dated Europeans were naturally the target of African criticism, there was in general little animosity among Africans against Europeans personally. Mboya's position was difficult and was similar to Blundell's. Both had extremists around them, whom they could not safely ignore, but whose aims were a hindrance to their own more co-operative policies. Both sets of extremists vehemently opposed the Lyttelton and Lennox-Boyd constitutions and any suggestions of multi-racialism, but Blundell himself only supported multi-racialism as a step towards the ultimate elimination of racial considerations in politics, and Mboya saw that universal suffrage was certain to come in the end. In the meantime Mboya attacked multi-racialism "on the grounds that its existence is dependent on the maintenance of racial groups and as such is an impediment to the establishment of democratic rights" and also because he thought that "the present multi-racial form of government is forcing a conflict of policies based on self-preservation".[99] In December 1957 Mboya wrote to Sir Alfred Vincent asking that he and other African Members of Legislative Council might address European electors.

"I feel that a meeting of this sort", he wrote ". . . may go a long way in helping the Europeans to understand and appreciate the African view point",[100] but this approach seems to have had a poor response. "The small group amongst the Elected Members who seem to believe that racial and intransigent opposition is a method of achieving their wishes"[101] were active throughout the nineteen fifties and, the more extreme African speeches became, the more difficult became the task of the moderate European politicians to arrange any form of inter-racial co-operation.

A few years later Blundell came to appreciate Mboya's difficulties. "Although Mboya makes truculent, aggressive and negative speeches", he wrote in 1960, "I am increasingly coming to the conclusion that he is a moderate and is fighting a desperate battle with the atavistic 'back to the golden days' boys who maintain everything was wonderful before the Europeans came here".[102]

Unpopularity of Indians

When arap Moi spoke at Thomson's Falls with Humphrey Slade and said that Europeans "had not come to Kenya to exploit the Africans and had imparted knowledge to the African community", he went on to say that "the same could not be said of the Asian community", who "had brought to the country a knowledge of trade and commerce but had done very little to put back the money they had made in the Colony'.[103] Accusations of the Asians' exploitation of Africans and of their failure to commit themselves wholeheartedly to Kenya and demands for their exclusion from the African Reserves and for their confinement to the towns were made regularly at all levels of African society and, although politicians might accept Asian help when it was convenient, there was little general good-will towards Asians.

The Indian politicians tried to overcome this dislike by vieing with African extremists in launching verbal attacks against Europeans and the Government. The Muslims seldom joined them in this and the Ismailis allied themselves with the Government. It was the Hindu politicians who encouraged African nationalism and uttered anti-European outbursts during the Emergency, apparently in the belief that they would thereby win future favours. *The Times* referred in retrospect to "the difficult position" in which the Commissioner of the Government of India to East Africa found himself in being accredited to a colonial territory while the newly independent

Government of India was offering "all possible assistance to African nationalism" and wrote of "his methods in sponsoring extreme nationalist leaders when the Mau Mau revolt was at hand".[104] But the most astonishingly mistaken outburst was provided by the Kenya Indian National Congress in August 1954, when it passed a resolution by the huge majority of forty-two votes to five in favour of "soliciting the aid of the Indian Government in ending the Mau Mau Emergency'. The motion was proposed by the retiring President, D. D. Puri, who thought that the Government of India ought to "interfere" in Kenya to end the Emergency and went on to say, "We in India have obtained our independence. Why cannot Africans do the same?" He claimed that 150 million Africans had great faith in Mr. Nehru and in India and looked to that country for guidance. A. B. Patel, who was praised by *East Africa and Rhodesia* for leading "the moderate Hindu section so sensibly and courageously"[105], was one of the five members of the meeting who opposed the forty-two. "What", he asked "would Mr. Nehru say if it were suggested that Britain or the United States should interfere in the dispute between India and Pakistan?"[106]

At the same meeting of the Congress N. S. Mangat, Q.C., the new President, delivered a violent attack on the European community and followed this by asserting that Indians in Kenya owed a loyalty to India transcending any loyalty they owed to the Colony. This caused considerable consternation in Asian circles, and the Sikhs, followed by the Indian Christians, demanded that Mangat should withdraw part of his anti-European speech; but the memory of it could not be erased. This meeting was held a month after the formation of the United Country Party. It must have strengthened the view that the formation of an inter-racial party was not yet possible. What *was* possible was to form a party which expressed willingness to work with Africans and Asians. This had two effects. It forced European politicians to think more carefully about inter-racial co-operation and to distinguish between the die-hards and the progressives, and it invited the other races to join with Europeans in an inter-racial approach to the development of Kenya. The party was short-lived. In 1957 the European politicians disbanded their political parties, but they could not dispel the differences in their racial attitudes. In 1958 the Specially Elected Members' Association was formed and the New Kenya Group and the New Kenya Party carried the aims of the United Country Party to the further stage of inter-racial politics, which would not have been possible in 1953. Throughout this period outside the field of politics members of the various races had been meeting each other, African cultural achievements had been brought to the notice of Europeans and African educational progress had shown to all who had open minds that the discriminations of the past had become unrealistic in the present. Largely unnoticed overseas and scarcely perceptible to the Europeans in Kenya themselves, liberalism and a co-operative outlook had increased among them. Such a change in the electorate was essential if the more liberal and progressive European politicians were to advocate co-operative measures, leading to a national rather than a racially divided policy. It was not academic theory but practical observation which led Sir Andrew Cohen to write, "However, important policy and policy-making may be, human relations are still more important in successful government and development."[107]

 1. Carl J. Rosberg: "Political Conflict and Change in Kenya" in *Transition in Africa: Studies in Political Adaptation*, ed. Gwendolen M. Carter and William O. Brown, p. 119.
 2. Tom Mboya to R. A. Frost, March 1954.
 3. Rosberg. op. cit. p. 119.
 4. *Report of the Commission appointed to Enquire into Methods for the Selection of African Representatives to the Legislative Council* (*W. F. Coutts Commissioner*), 1956.
 5. *The Constitutional Committee Interim Report*, Kenya National Archives.
 6. European Elected Members Organisation: Minutes of meeting on 14 Jan. 1953, Blundell 14/6.
 7. ibid.
 8. ibid.
 9. *The Stand of the African Elected Members of Legislative Council*. A copy is in Havelock file H3/6 in the Kenya National Archives.
10. Letter from Havelock to District Chairman, 28 May 1951, Havelock file 89/EM/51, in the Kenya National Archives.
11. Sir Philip Mitchell's Diary, 5 Feb. 1952.
12. Blundell to Joelson, 3 March, 1952, Blundell 24/2.
13. Sir Philip Mitchell's Diary, 18 Dec. 1952.
14. ibid. 18 Dec. 1952.
15. Blundell to Sir Richard Acland, Bt., M.P., 1 March 1953 Blundell 12/3.
16. Sir Philip Mitchell's Diary 12 Jan. 1953.
17. Lyttelton to Mervyn Hill, 24 March 1955. Blundell 3/2.
18. Blundell to Sir Godfrey Huggins, 19 Dec. 1953. Blundell 5/1.
19. Lyttelton to Blundell, 26 Nov. 1953. Blundell 17/3.
20. Note written on 8 Jan. 1954, Blundell 17/3.
21. Blundell 17/3.
22. Sir Philip Mitchell's Diary, 4 April 1952.
23. ibid, 14 Dec. 1952.
24. ibid, 12 and 18 Jan. 1953.
25. ibid, 25 Nov. 1954.
26. J. A. Couldrey to Blundell, 2 May 1953. Blundell 3/1.

27. Blundell to Hugh Fraser, M.P., 2 May 1953. Blundell 2/3.
28. Rev. David Steel to Blundell, 16 Jan. 1953, Blundell 3/1.
29. Blundell to Alan Clarke of the Daily Herald, 1 May 1953, Blundell 12/2.
30. Kendall Ward's Diary: Kenya National Archives.
31. Major B. P. Roberts at Limuru, E.A.S. 29 Sept. 1954.
32. E.A. and R. 22 July 1954, p. 1509.
33. Lecture to Royal African and Empire Societies in London, 7 March 1957. "The Capricorn Contract", *African Affairs*, Vol. 56, No. 224, July 1957, p. 192.
34. Michael Blundell: "Making a Nation in Kenya", *African Affairs*, Vol. 58, No. 232, July 1959, p. 221.
35. Sir Philip Mitchell's Diary, 13 Jan. 1955.
36. Vigar to Blundell, 4 April 1959. Blundell 20/7.
37. Blundell to Mrs. Eirene White, M.P., 22 June 1956, Blundell 4/3.
38. ibid 4 May 1956.
39. Tyson to Blundell, 14 March 1954, Blundell 17/3.
40. Chief Kidaha Makwaia of Tanganyika, who had spent a year at Lincoln College.
41. Minutes of Joint Committee of the Kadu and Kanu, 10 Aug. 1961, para. 22, Blundell 23/2.
42. D. McDowell Wilson to Blundell, 29 Aug. 1952, Blundell 17/2.
43. Legislative Council.
44. George Bennett: "The Development of Political Organizations in Kenya", *Political Studies*. Vol. 2, No. 2. Issue 1957, p. 128.
45. Carl J. Rosberg calls both Odede and Awori Luos and misses the point that K.A.U. had a Luyia President, following a Luo, who followed a Kikuyu. The same mistake was made by O. F. Engholm, Lecturer in Political Science in the University College of East Africa (now the University of Nairobi). Writing about the African elections of 1957, he said, "In *Nyanza North*, Mr. W. W. W. Awori, who is a Jaluo . . ." (*Five Elections in Africa*, ed. W. J. M. Mackenzie and Kenneth Robinson) p. 453.
46. Awori told Miller this: memorandum by Miller, 15 Jan. 1953: Miller papers. Lt. Commander J. P. B. Miller, GC of the Education Department was allowed by the Government in 1952 to be a member of the Study Group of the Kenya African Union. He acted as Secretary of the Group.
47. Frost to Governor, 8 May 1953: Frost papers.
48. Argwings-Kodhek to Miller, 2 Jan. 1953: Miller papers.
49. Sir Philp Mitchell's diary 25 Jan. 1952.
50. E.A. & R. 8 May 1954, p. 994.
51. L.C.D., 13 Oct. 1953, col. 230.
52. ibid. 15 Dec. 1954—col. 1152.
53. A mimeographed copy of the Memorandum is in Commander Miller's papers. The Acting National President was Walter Odede, a Luo, and the Acting General Secretary was J. Z. Murumbi, half Goan, half Masai.
54. Blundell to Patrick Gordon-Walker, 30 Jan. 1953, Blundell 12/3.
55. Letter from Carey Francis "to Friends", 20 Dec. 1953.
56. ibid.
57. Annual Report for 1956 by N. G. Hardy, District Commissioner, Naivasha, ADM/15/1 in the Kenya National Archives.
58. op. cit.
59. Address to African Civil Servants Association, *Times* 13 April 1953.
60. The Conference was held at the Jeams School at Kabete on February 7th and 8th, 1953 (Mimeographed Report).
61. Letter from Miller to Frost. 9 Nov. 1952: Frost papers: carbon copy in Miller papers.
62. ibid.
63. Miller papers.
64. E.A.S. 21 March 1953.
65. Vivian Giffard to Miller, 19 Nov. 1953: Miller papers.
66. 20 Dec. 1953, Blundell 3/1.

67. Sir Philip Mitchell's Diary, 13 Oct. 1954.
68. E.A. & R. 8 May 1954, p. 994.
69. E.A.S. 28 March 1952.
70. ibid, 1 June 1945.
71. The Address is in the possession of Mr. Millington.
72. E.A.S. 8 Dec. 1955.
73. The Earl of Portsmouth, *A Knot of Roots*, p. 280.
74. *Certain Questions in Kenya: Report by the Financial Commission (Lord Moyne)* Cmd. 4093, 1932, p. 4.
75. *Development Plan:* 1964–1970, p. 34.
76. *Report on Wages and Employment in Kenya 1958.* East African Statistical Department Kenya Unit, July 1959 (Mimeographed).
77. Blundell to Kendall Ward, 23 June 1955. Kendall Ward Deposit in Kenya National Archives.
78. *Sunday Times*, 27 Sept. 1953.
79. K.WN., 26 April 1954, p. 7.
80. ibid. 25 March 1955, p. 7.
81. ibid. 5 April 1957, p. 4.
82. E.A.S. 6 Jan. 1956.
83. ibid. 26 Jan. 1956.
84. ibid 27 April 1956.
85. Interview with Sir Michael Blundell, 14 April 1970.
86. Blundell 5/3.
87. E.A.S. 27 April 1956.
88. ibid. 27 April 1956.
89. ibid. 5 Oct. 1956. Ndegwa became Head of the Civil Service and later Governor of the Bank of Kenya.
90. Article by Blundell in K.W.N. 20 Dec. 1956.
91. Blundell to Mrs. Rebecca Fane, 15 April 1955. Blundell 3/2.
92. Interview with Sir Charles Mortimer, 12 Dec. 1969.
93. Derek Erskine: *The Kenya Citizens' Association: An Analysis of its Purpose* 23 July 1952 (Mimeographed): Frost papers.
94. Electors' Union Newsletter, January 1954.
95. Interview with Sir Michael Blundell, 14 April 1970.
96. E.A.S. 20 Sept. 1957.
97. E.A.S. 27 Sept. 1957.
98. Tom Mboya: *Kenya Faces the Future*, p. 19.
99. Tom Mboya: *The Kenya Question: An African Answer* (1956) p. 32.
100. Havelock file H 5/2. vol. II., Kenya National Archives.
101. Blundell to Joelson, 4 Nov. 1955, Blundell 4/3.
102. Blundell to Edward Thomson, Burton-on-Trent, 14 Dec. 1960. Blundell 5/5.
103. E.A.S. 27 Sept. 1957.
104. The Times, 2 June 1969.
105. E.A. & R. 2 Sept. 1954, p. 1705.
106. ibid. 5 Aug. 1954, p. 1576.
107. Sir Andrew Cohen: *British Policy in Changing Africa*, p. 64.

10

ST. JULIAN'S COMMUNITY

A Conflict of Views

At the end of 1956 a proposal to establish an inter-racial religious community at Limuru in the White Highlands produced a controversy which showed how divided European opinion had become. It showed the views of the reactionaries and the liberals concentrated on a single issue and demonstrated the ultimate responsibility of Britain as Trustee.

As early as 1953 Michael Blundell told his colleagues in Legislative Council that "the European's existence in Kenya depended entirely on his relationship with the African",[1] but the die-hards continued to believe that Europeans could live a satisfactory life only in a white island in a black sea and were unable to see that in willing co-operation and mingling with Africans at a time when the tide of African nationalism was running so strongly lay their only real chance of survival. Even the Capricorn Africa Society, which had a plan based on the maintenance of existing European areas in East Africa and Rhodesia, was regarded by such Europeans as highly dangerous and objectionable because it advocated multi-racial government based on a qualitative franchise. The President of this Society in Kenya was a leading surgeon, Michael Wood. In 1956 he offered his house at Limuru for sale to the St. Julian's Community. This proposed incursion into the White Highlands by a religious community which would admit people of all races was regarded by the die-hards as an utterly unacceptable invasion of their white reserve, made all the more suspect because of the Woods' support of the Capricorn Africa Society in which members of all races met as equals. But by that time the die-hards were outnumbered by the realists, many of whom accepted the progress of Africans and Asians in a spirit of friendly co-operation. The sale of the Woods' house to the St. Julian's Community produced a confrontation between the traditional demand for the retention of a position of privileged exclusiveness, which remained among some

Europeans, and an enlightened realism and adherence to moral principles, which had begun to outweigh the old European outlook of the past, the outlook of those who failed to see that in their refusal to accept the inevitability of change lay the certainty of their own destruction.

"A Venture in Kenya"

In 1941 Miss Florence Allshorn established a meeting place and rest centre under the auspices of the Church of England at Coolham in Sussex. It was given the name of St. Julian's and it soon became a centre for rest and rejuvenation and spiritual refreshment for men and women suffering from the strains and stresses of overwork. In 1956 Miss Dorothy Alton of St. Julian's, who had spent part of a legacy on instruction in flying, flew to Africa and felt that a St. Julian's would be useful in Kenya. She came in touch with Mr. Michael Wood and his wife, and decided that their house at Limuru, which they wanted to sell, would be an ideal place for a second St. Julian's, and returned to England to prepare for this new venture. On 9th October she and Miss Mary Phillipson left for Kenya.

On that very day a cloud, which might have seemed no bigger than a man's hand, appeared in the form of a paragraph in *The Times* under the heading, "A Venture in Kenya"—"Four women members of the St. Julian's Community, Coolham, Horsham, Sussex, are flying to Kenya to pioneer the establishment of a 'multi-racial meeting place' at Limuru, fifteen miles from Nairobi."[2] Someone in Nairobi read the paragraph and the storm burst. It was the word 'multi-racial', at that time anathema to a certain section of the white population in Kenya, that was at the bottom of the trouble. On the 12th October the *East African Standard* announced that a letter of protest had been sent to the Chief Secretary by the Limuru District Association.[3] The storm, which lasted for the next eight months, was of truly tropical intensity.

Miss Alton and Miss Phillipson were joined by Miss J. E. Clarke and Miss Dinah Hart. This story of four women and twenty acres at Limuru is like a microscope under which we can study the fears and emotions, the hopes and the prejudices which beset the progress of inter-racial harmony in Kenya. The word 'multi-racial' was certainly anathema to a certain section of the white population, but it was also anathema to many of the politically-minded Africans, to whom it implied the perpetual retention of European and Asian communal quotas and so stood in the way of African power. The proposal to establish the Centre at Limuru forced people to study the legal basis of the 'whiteness' of the 'White Highlands' and gave frenzied expression to the fears of those who wanted to keep the 'White Highlands' as a white island for ever. The argument showed the struggle which went on continuously between liberal aspirations and racial arrogance, between acceptance of the reality of change and blind hope that a privileged isolation could be maintained for ever.

When the four ladies arrived at Limuru the sale of the house had not been completed, but Mr. and Mrs. Wood agreed that they should start on the establishment of a St. Julian's centre while the legal negotiations were proceeding. The battle fought by the opponents of the scheme was to prevent the sale from being allowed on either legal or political grounds. Miss Potts quoted the opponents of the establishment of the Community at Limuru as saying that it would "prejudice future sales of land and result in the depreciation of land values. It might be an undesirable influence on African employees and would be the beginning of the end of the White Highlands".[4] A centre like St. Julian's would obviously be used only by educated people, whatever their race might be, and only a refusal to accept the realities of change could imagine that the 'White Highlands' could always be kept so white that they could not contain an inter-racial religious centre just inside their border. "If we give way on this issue" wrote the weekly paper *Comment*, "it will probably mean the end of British Settlement in Kenya".[5] There were certainly some who were scandalised by the thought of an African or Asian staying in a house in the White Highlands, but there were others who objected on other grounds. If Africans attended conferences as fellow members with Europeans, it was feared that they would become upstarts, regarding themselves as equal to Europeans, and, as they were seen walking around the neighbourhood, they would cause the farm labourers to become upstarts on a lower rung of the social and economic ladder.[6] That danger must be prevented. The opposition admitted that they were afraid. Looked at under the microscope provided by this controversy, this fear shows the true character of the European slogan that Kenya must advance under European leadership. There were some Europeans who sincerely wished to lead the Africans up the slopes of development, but there were others to whom the words "European leadership" meant

"domination by Europeans". The rivalry of these two sections of
the European population is at the heart of the history of the
nineteen fifties.

Die-hard European Opposition

At that time Mrs. Susan Wood, who had beautiful auburn hair,
was a candidate for a seat in Legislative Council and the Woods
were leading members of the Capricorn Africa Society, which,
because of its inter-racial aims, was bitterly opposed by the die-
hard Europeans. In the same number of *Comment* was a drawing of
an exaggeratedly fearsome Mau Mau fighter against a notice labelled
"White Highlands" which was plastered over by two smaller notices.
One read "Limuru Rest House" and the other, which was torn off
on one side, read "Vote for Ginger S" and "Good old Caprico".
Although the notice was torn, no one would be unable to guess
what the name was intended to be which started with an 'S' nor
how the word 'Caprico' should be finished. "The Community",
wrote Miss Potts, "was at best ridiculed as a group of naive do-
gooders—at worst its members were accused of being supporters
of 'Mau Mau' ".[7]

There is an area of Limuru called Tigoni. The extreme right wing
element in Limuru were known as the Tigoni Tigers. Many of them
were charming, courteous people, kind to their European friends
and neighbours and helpful in a feudal manner to the African
employees; but the sight of a black or brown face in the European
area, other than those of African employees or Asian tradesmen,
excited them to a fury scarcely equalled by the most vicious bull
at the sight of a red cloak in a Spanish bull ring. The battle was
fought in the Limuru Association, in the meetings of the European
Elected Members' Organisation, in the Press, in Government House,
in the House of Commons, and even in Lambeth Palace, where the
Archbishop of Canterbury had to write to the Community a letter
of encouragement with a plea for patience and co-operation over
terms of occupation.

Many years earlier, in 1930 St. Paul's Divinity School for the
training of African clergymen had been founded in the Limuru
area at Tigoni as a joint venture of the Anglican Church and the
Church of Scotland, which later became the Presbyterian Church
of East Africa. This had not been done without opposition and in
order to avoid allowing African residential training to take place

in the 'White Highlands' the compound had been legally excised from the Highlands, although geographically it was within the Highlands area, and the same expedient had been employed in the case of the Roman Catholic Loretto Girls School for Africans, which, like St. Paul's, was situated at Limuru. When the European Elected Members Organisation found that legally it seemed to be impossible for the Highlands Board and the Land Control Board to raise objections to the sale of the Woods' property to the St. Julian's Community, the view was expressed that "If the case went through, there must be an excision".[8] In the previous year the European Elected Members Association had been told that Lady Eleanor Cole wished to find funds "to establish a high-class boarding school for African boys near Gilgil township, that is in the High-lands", and they agreed that "the best procedure would be to have the land in question excised and added to Gilgil township".[9] The scheme, however, did not materialise. An excision of land near a township might have been geographically acceptable to the Europeans, but the Woods' house was not near a township and the bitterness of the opposition in Limuru was hardly likely to be appeased by that expedient. Whatever the legal or administrative arrangements might be, Africans and Asians would stay at St. Julian's and that was the fact against which opposition was raised. The opposition was so fierce that "sinister remarks" were made "about threatened road blocks",[10] and it was rumoured that Michael Wood's patients were "dropping off as part of the campaign against the sale".[11]

An Earlier Wrong

Tigoni had been the scene of an unhappy incident just before the War when Kikuyu peasants were removed from the area. Shirley Victor Cooke, who had recently been elected as Member for the Coast in Legislative Council, took up the cause of the Tigoni clans and wrote to Colonel La Fontaine, the Chief Native Commissioner, to protest about their removal. It was the Carter Commission of 1933 which had recommended their removal from Tigoni,[12] and, as Dr. Louis Leakey wrote to Cooke, this was "because settlers objected to having an island of Reserve among them".[13] As the Carter Commission's recommendation, wrote Dr. Leakey, "was a *recommendation* in favour of the Europeans and *against* the native it was fully implemented at once. On the other hand a clear *recommendation* (Para. 413 last half) in favour of Kikuyu is *NOT CARRIED* out and instead the people concerned are given a bit of comparatively useless land". The Lari massacre in 1958 was a terrible result of this evil transaction.[14]

The episode showed an unhappy bias on the part of the Administration in favour of the European settlers. "In the case of the right holders", wrote the Chief Native Commissioner to Cooke, ". . . the move was completely voluntary as they were aware that if they refused to move there would be no compulsion at any rate until the Native Lands Trust Ordinance was brought into force".[15] The last words made nonsense of the claim that the Kikuyus left voluntarily. "If you contend", wrote Cooke, "that the Tigoni clans left *without resistance*, then I agree with you, but to contend that they left voluntarily and of their own free volition would be simply outrageous. The plain truth is that they left because they knew that otherwise they would be turned out 'bag and baggage' and they were urged to this 'wise decision' by chiefs who knew that they would lose their jobs if they did not support Government".[16] "Incidentally", wrote Dr. Leakey, "natives have been out of Tigoni for over a year (I think it is that anyway or very nearly a year) and no attempt has been made to use the Tigoni land for any other purposes, so that natives say it was just dog in the manger attitude and because it was good land. They thought when they were forcibly and hurriedly ousted from Tigoni a year or so ago that it was because it was to be used, not just that it should lie idle when they need it so much".[17] By 1956 many Europeans in Limuru had become more progressive in their views, but the Tigoni Tigers and other reactionaries in the Limuru Association even then objected to any educated African or Asian staying in the District, although they were happy for the farm labourers and domestic servants, whose existence was essential for the maintenance of their economy and social life, to live and bring up families among them.

The Racism of Some Europeans

Before the Community left England the Anglican chaplain at Makerere, the University College of East Africa in Uganda, had suggested that a group of students should help the Community by erecting a prefabricated chapel. They arrived two days after Christmas. Instead of being respected as a group of young men who were giving some of their vacation as a voluntary contribution to a religious project, they were regarded as the first wave of an African invasion of the White Highlands. One European neighbour so far forgot the normal code of decency as to listen in to a telephone conversation on a party line concerning arrangements for this group and called at St. Julian's to protest at this breach of the sanctity of the White Highlands.[18] In 1948 J. K. arap Chemallan, an African Member of Legislative Council, had stayed at Limuru with the British Council Representative and his family. Soon afterwards their European nurse gave notice and left and a leading member of the East African Women's league said, "I hear you had an African to stay with you in your house. You couldn't expect her to stay with you after that, could you?" At that time the majority of residents would have agreed with her, but by 1956 a large number were in sympathy with the aims of St. Julian's and those who "tiraded against St. Julian's" and who "when they heard that Makerere students had been here were enraged afresh",[19] were probably in the minority; but the Member for Kiambu, the Constituency which contained Limuru, said a few weeks later that the visit of the Makerere students showed people that the Community was "going to be dangerous", because Makerere students and some of the Makerere staff were suspect.[20] In the opinion of the most extreme members of the reactionary Europeans any educated Africans ought to be kept away from the White Highlands. The Committee of the Limuru Association asked two members of the Community to meet them. "They were quite frank", reported Miss Clarke, "and said they were afraid. They were prepared to meet educated Africans in Nairobi but not in the White Highlands".[21] It is interesting to compare this die-hard element in 1957 with the liberal settlers at Njoro who were anxious to meet educated Africans eight years earlier.[22] In fact, however, liberalism had increased during the nineteen fifties and the snarls of the Tigoni Tigers did not express a majority attitude in the Highlands as a whole.

A non-racial attitude depended to a considerable extent on the absence of fear, and the reactionary members of the Limuru District Association were not alone in being afraid. An anonymous memorandum written for the New Kenya Party early in 1959 ably described the situation. "Fear", it said, "is really the dominant note, a conscious fear of the Africans' prodigious majority and an unconscious or more correctly, subconscious fear of his behaviour. This fear colours European politics, thought and expression".[23]

Division of Opinion

The Royal Commission on Land and Population had issued its Report in 1955. It recommended that land barriers should be removed throughout Kenya, but by 1957 nothing had been done to accept and implement its recommendations. The publication of the Commission's Report added to the fears of those who were determined to preserve what they called "the sanctity of the White Highlands". The Commission was a Royal Commission appointed by the United Kingdom. By 1955 it was clear to all except the blindest that any hope that self-government would be granted to a European-dominated Kenya could no longer be entertained. The Mau Mau Emergency had shown that the local Europeans could not rule Kenya and that Britain would not spend money and effort to keep them in perpetual power. In the long course of history the sixty years of the White Highlands will seem to be like

". . . the snow-fall in the river,

"A moment white—then melts for ever"[24]

but during the nineteen fifties, while an increasing number of Europeans saw in partnership or inter-racial co-operation their only hope of survival, others still clung to the hope of white domination for "an unforeseeable future". It was against this unrealistic hope that liberal Europeans inside Legislative Council and in the country at large, struggled to create a fund of co-operation with the other races. The Mau Mau Emergency showed how right S. V. Cooke had been when, as he recalled, "Time after time I quoted to the European Elected Members Edmund Burke's dictum, that 'You will later have to yield to force what you now refuse to concede to reason' ".[25] The story of St. Julian's showed that by the middle of the fifties the fund of goodwill was large enough to prevail against the die-hards, as exemplified by the Tigoni Tigers; and the general events of the period were evidence that an enlightened realism was spreading throughout the European community, although some Europeans remained as isolationist as ever and fought to the last against the incoming tide.

In 1953 Lawrence Machonochie-Welwood, European Elected Member for Uasin Gishu, had said that he thought that "people in Kenya were not interested in principles but only in policy".[26] Loyalty to principles entered fully into the story of St. Julian's three years later. On the one side were the "Pesky old White Highlanders", as Sir Philip Mitchell called them, represented by the

Tigoni Tigers and others in the Limuru District Association, and on the other side were those who would not betray their religious principles.

"St. Julian's", wrote the Chairman of the St. Julian's Board to the Chief Secretary, "is a Religious Foundation and as such cannot by its very nature accept discrimination on purely racial grounds".[27] The Chairman of the Limuru District Association also claimed that the opposition was based on "matters of principle" and not on any antagonism to "the motives of the Community". "Our opposition", he said at the annual meeting of the Association, "has been based entirely on the ground that the St. Julian activities do envisage people of other races *living* in the building which they are taking over in the White Highlands. The Association feels that this is the first step towards the abrogation of the spirit and intent of the Highlands Ordinance. That is the only reason why the Community proposal has been opposed".[28]

But the opposition was not universal, although the 9.00 p.m. wireless news on the 24th January announced that seventeen other District Associations had sent in protests against the St. Julian's Community.[29] Only the most politically conscious were regular attenders of District Association meetings and the seventeen Associations which sent in protests were probably no more representative of their Districts as a whole than was the Limuru District Association of all the Europeans of Limuru, where in March two leading residents wrote to the Chief Secretary to say that "influential public opinion was not with the Tigers",[30] and another farmer told the ladies of the Community that "the feeling at Limuru about [their] staying had changed a lot".[31] In the opinion of Roy Howard, Church Warden at Limuru for over twenty years and at one time Chairman of the District Association, true opponents of the scheme were only a minority, though a vociferous minority of the European residents of Limuru. Other Europeans with many years residence at Limuru, like Mr. and Mrs. Arnold Curtis, were in agreement with this view.[32]

Among the European Elected Members of Legislative Council opinion was divided. Politicians have to think of the next election and the situation was certainly awkward; but Sir Alfred Vincent, the Chairman of the European Elected Members Organisation, was "very sympathetic".[33] Clive Salter, who had been a leading protagonist in the fight against national registration by finger-printing for all in 1949 was, wrote Miss Clarke, "100% with us and anxious we should rally supporters" and "should say in our statement to the H.B.[34] that we have many supporters whose names we are willing to divulge if required",[35] and Michael Blundell told the Archbishop of Canterbury that refusal to allow the St. Julian's Community to buy the property "would offend all his Christian principles".[36]

There was also the existence of common sense. At the very beginning of the controversy at a meeting in the Vicarage on the 30th November "everyone said that no harm had come" from having St. Paul's Divinity School at Limuru.[37] The Woods' house was near the edge of the settled area, but St. Paul's was much further in and yet its existence had not shattered the foundations of European Society. Opinion had changed since 1948 and African clergy in training could attend services in the church at Limuru without causing offence;[38] and at the same meeting the ladies of the community were assured that "the Tigoni Tigers and Committee of the Limuru Association were politically active and vocal but did not speak for all".[39]

Political Implications

But the matter had important political implications and not only the European Elected Members who opposed it but also the St. Julian's Trustees and other advocates of the establishment of the Community at Limuru saw the fundamental political importance of the decision. Group Captain Briggs said at a meeting of the European Elected Members Organisation that "the St. Julian's Trustees wished to treat this matter as a test case and were not interested in land excised from the Highlands".[40] It seemed that there was bound to be an uproar whichever way the final decision went. As Archdeacon Bostock said, if the sale of the property were not allowed to go through because the Community was not allowed to open a Centre in the White Highlands, there would be an uproar "from the Church and people of other races, who are all watching the issue".[41] It had been proved that legally there was nothing to stop the sale. The Attorney General had said that "the Governor was required by law to *consult* the Highlands Board concerning dispositions of land in the Highlands (as to which he has powers of veto under Crown Lands Ordinance Section 88) but is not legally bound to accept the advice of the Board in such matters".[42] If then,

although there was no legal reason against the establishment of the
Community at Limuru, the Trustees agreed to give up the struggle
and abandon the project, they would "be failing the Africans" and
they agreed that it would be entirely wrong to give in to "the settlers
because they made such a fuss about the matter".[43]

The European Elected Members appreciated the dilemma which
faced them. Those who supported the sale and those who opposed it
all realised that, if the sale were allowed, a section of the Europeans
of the Colony would create such an uproar that race relations would
be greatly embittered, while if it were refused, not only would even
more harm be done to race relations in Kenya but a "very dangerous
situation" might be brought about "because of public opinion in
Britain" and it "might cause the whole Highlands issue to be
opened".[44]

The European Elected Members decided that attempts should be
made to persuade the St. Julian's Trustees to withdraw their
application for the purchase of the house and a deputation was sent
to talk to the Bishop. At the same time it was suggested that, if the
Trustees refused to withdraw their application, the European
Elected Members Organisation should "see the representatives of
the Limuru Association and point out to them the dangers of the
case".[45] Michael Blundell thought that withdrawal would be the
worst solution because it "would cause a major crisis with Indians
and Africans". He told Miss Alton that the European Elected
Members were not unanimous in asking the Community to leave
Limuru and that "it would be against Christian principles for
[them] not to be allowed to stay".[46] Another site had in fact been
suggested in the Karura Forest nearer Nairobi but the St. Julian's
Trustees had turned it down on principle.[47] Then a majority of the
Elected Members decided to advise the Highlands Board to "advise
H.E. the Governor to withhold his consent to this transaction".[48]
The Governor, who had supported the scheme in principle at the
beginning, subsequently told the Bishop that the Community
would have to accept conditions which the Bishop told him were
against all Christian principles. At that the Governor got so angry
that he hit the table so hard that papers bounced off it on to the
floor.[49] But the logic of religious principles prevailed. The Bishop
refused to agree to the terms, and when the Highlands Board
"recommended to the Governor that the scheme should be turned
down" he sent the matter back for recommendation and it was

"agreed with certain safeguards".[50]

The violent opposition of the Tigoni Tigers was based on the die-hards' determination to keep the White Highlands white for ever, but others like the Governor and some of the European Elected Members were afraid also from quite a different point of view. Many years before, Archdeacon Owen in Nyanza and the Reverend Handly Hooper in the Central Province had openly allied themselves with the African cause. They refused to accept the current situation in which, as Francis Thompson once wrote, God had become "a constitutional Deity with certain state rights of worship but no influence over political affairs".[51] Archdeacon Owen was instrumental in founding the Kavirondo Taxpayers Association and was the champion of the Luo people of Nyanza, while Hooper agreed to help the Kikuyu Central Association if it were conducted on lines of reason. In these two men the state authorities saw the Church allying itself with an oppressed people against the Administration. It was feared that St. Julian's might become the focal point of a new tension between Church and State. The Governor wanted to impose a condition to the effect that no discussions might ever be held in the Centre on political matters and that somehow or other the Government should prevent what they might regard as the wrong type of people from going to St. Julian's. Obviously these restrictions could not be accepted by the Bishop. Refusal to allow the sale of the house to St. Julian's would have had serious repercussions in Britain as well as in Church circles in Kenya and so agreement was the only possible course, but it was reached only with serious fears about a revival of tensions between Church and State, to which the sermons of the Provost of the Anglican Cathedral and the Minister of St. Andrew's Church in Nairobi gave touches of reality.[52]

The Imperial Parliament Intervenes

In fact, however, the ultimate decision had passed out of the hands of anyone in Kenya. The matter had been brought to the notice of the Trustee, the British House of Commons. During Question Time on 13th March a Labour Member, Kenneth Robinson, "asked what decision had been reached by the Highlands Board and the Land Control Board of Kenya regarding the proposal of the St. Julian's (Church of England) Community to establish a multi-racial rest centre at Limuru". The Secretary of State for the

Colonies, Alan Lennox-Boyd, replied that "Neither the Highlands Board nor the Land Control Board has yet tendered advice on the proposal to the Governor". Kenneth Robinson then asked, "Would not the Minister agree that the noisy opposition coming from the reactionary minority to this very modest project is really making things very difficult for the more moderate elements who genuinely want to see a multi-racial society in Kenya, and would he use his influence on the side of moderation?". "I made it perfectly clear", replied the Minister, "that I gave my support to a branch of the St. Julian's Community in Kenya".[53]

Even the Tigoni Tigers thought the Community's "motives truly laudable",[54] and Lennox-Boyd's answer avoided the point at issue, which was not concerned with the establishment of a St. Julian's centre in Kenya, but with its establishment at Limuru in the White Highlands. However, as the matter had been raised in the British House of Commons, the fears of some of the European Elected Members that "public opinion in Britain" might be raised and refusal to allow St. Julian's to buy the house "might cause the whole Highlands issue to be opened"[55] had been realised and public opinion in Britain could be enlisted to support the project if it were turned down in Kenya. Permission for the purchase of the property by the Community was given in June 1957. The proposal to establish a St. Julian's Community house at Limuru was made just half way in time between the publication of the Report of the Royal Commission and the opening of the White Highlands to other races in 1959.

Changes of Opinion

Opinion was changing so widely that, even during the turmoil over St. Julian's, Blundell, the Leader of the European Elected Members, was able to write a memorandum for his colleagues, in which he said, "if we think rationally instead of tribally or racially we cannot afford to have the potential output of the land sterilised by old-fashioned barriers"; and he went on to say, "in other words, I should like to educate our community on the lines of the Royal Commission Report".[56] In scope the St. Julian's proposal was half way between European exclusiveness in the White Highlands and their opening to farmers and other residents of all races. It was, as Kenneth Robinson said, "a very modest project", a proposal to establish, not a farm, but a residential centre in which Africans and

Asians as well as Europeans could stay. The violent opposition with
its talk of road blocks showed that die-hard opinions were still
strong, but the support which the proposal evoked in Limuru and
elsewhere was evidence of a great change of outlook among the
Europeans during the previous ten years.

During the next two years opinion moved further and the New
Kenya Group demonstrated that non-racialism had become a
political possibility. "The retention of land by any tribe or race",
wrote Blundell, "for its own exclusive use which is not fully utilised
for economic production is, therefore, indefensible on moral,
economic, and agricultural grounds, if elsewhere there is excessive
population pressure and inadequate land for cultivation".

"When the Royal Commission on Land made a report to this
effect in 1954, it was clear that they had reached this view after
consideration of economic factors alone. There are others, however,
equally important. There are deep tribal and racial feelings about
land similar to those which existed in Europe some centuries ago,
which will only become subordinate to pure economics in the course
of time and experiment".[57]

At that time, in April, 1959, Blundell and Group Captain Briggs,
who, as *The Times* said, was "the leading critic of Mr. Blundell's
policy"[58] held meetings in their constituencies. At Nyeri Briggs
"won an overwhelming vote of approval on a show of hands"[59]
while at Nakuru three major meetings approved Blundell. At one
of them, an African, Musa Amalemba, the Minister of Housing,
shared the platform with Blundell and *The Times* reported that his
"witty and urbane speech was well received except by a small
vocal minority".[60] The education of their constituents was an
important task facing Kenya's politicians. European politics were
very personal and were greatly influenced by the personality of the
Member. Many constituents were apt to support their Member and
accept his policies because it was he who advocated them, but in-
directly this cult of personality could not help influencing
fundamental outlooks. These meetings were perhaps a measure of
the success achieved respectively by Briggs and Blundell.

Fundamental Issues seen in the Controversy
The battle over St. Julian's was fought in a period when outlooks
were swiftly changing. Some Europeans clung to the hope that
their only security lay in keeping the White Highlands exclusively

White, but others had come to believe that their future in Kenya
could be secured only by inter-racial goodwill and were beginning to
understand that inter-racial goodwill and the White Highlands
policy were incompatible. Some agreed with the resolution proposed
by the Trans Nzoia delegation at the Electors' Union Conference in
February 1955, "That this Conference deplores the recent speech
made by Mr. C. J. M. Alport, M.P., in which he refers to the Kenya
Highlands as 'a political and economic anachronism'."[60]; but
there were others who saw that an exclusiveness, however tenable
when higher education among Africans was non-existent, had
become arbitrary *apartheid* by 1955, and who were beginning to
accept the fact that European farming could continue only if
European settlers were members of a farming community in which
African farmers could be their neighbours.

Fear and uncertainty, understanding of the truth but refusal to
admit it, were evident in much European thinking in the middle and
later nineteen fifties. The story of the establishment of St. Julian's
at Limuru shows them focused on one small issue. Quite early in the
controversy a lady resident of Limuru, wrote Miss Clarke, "put the
point of view of the settlers who were fearing that the land they had
worked on for years would be taken away from them and given to
Africans". They opposed the establishment of a multi-racial centre
in the White Highlands "because they saw it as a first step to the
realisation of their fears. But she also said that everyone realised
that the Africans must come into their own eventually, and she
admitted that it was better to face this now and start working
towards a solution of friendly co-operation, rather than fight a
desperate and losing battle to keep the status quo".[61] This view was
midway between the opinion of the most liberal Europeans and the
blind policy of the die-hards. Ten years earlier Mrs. Grant of
Njoro had publicly declared that African supremacy would come
in the future.[62] The liberal realists, who accepted the fact that British
democratic principles would lead to rule by the majority believed that
friendship was the only security for those Europeans who wanted to
make Kenya their permanent home and that the removal of racial
barriers was the best insurance against confiscation of land. Even
after Mau Mau had shown that European power was insufficient
for the maintenance of perpetual domination, the die-hards believed
that they could live apart in a Kenya in which every year saw the
emergence of more and more Africans with education and

qualifications of many kinds. They admitted that educated Africans
existed. They even said that they were agreeable to meeting them
in Nairobi, but they refused to meet them in the ivory tower which
they sought to build for themselves in the Highlands. They were
afraid of the future and thought that they could find security in
isolation.

In July 1957 *New Comment* had a cartoon of Blundell pushing a
wooden horse, called "African Tenant Farmer Scheme", into the
White Highlands, while another wooden horse, labelled "St. Julian's
Centre", is standing on that holy soil. Blundell's bag, labelled "To
London", is on the ground where lie sheets of paper marked
"Appeasement". In the distance is a scene meant to represent
Tom Mboya speaking to an African audience in the Desai Hall in
Nairobi, where he had addressed an enthusiastic election meeting
two months earlier.[63] In a previous number of *New Comment* Mboya
had written, "Africans read papers, listen to overseas and local
radio broadcasts; some travel; others come back here after several
years at University. And of course locally, Makerere, the Secondary
Schools, and more recently the Royal Technical College, are playing
their part in the process of building an enlightened and knowl-
edgeable African public opinion".[64] The question which had to be
decided in a future, which was coming nearer with increasing speed,
was whether African political power would sweep everything out
of its way or whether there was by now an element of enlightened
realism among the Europeans large enough to influence African
public opinion and enable inter-racial co-operation to temper the
exuberance of African political success.

1. European Elected Members Organisation: Minutes of Meeting 29 Oct.
   1953, Blundell 14/3.
2. *The Times*, 9 Oct. 1956.
3. E.A.S., 12 Oct. 1956.
4. Margaret I. Potts: *St. Julian's Community: An Experiment in Two Continents*,
   London. S.C.M. Press Ltd., 1968, p. 27.
5. *Comment*, No. 31, 2 Nov. 1956, p. 6.
6. Interview with Archbishop Beecher, 20 Mar. 1970.
7. Margaret I. Potts, op. cit. p. 27.
8. Minutes of Meeting of European Elected Members Organisation, 12 Dec.
   1956.
9. European Elected Members Association: Minutes of Meeting, 31 Aug. 1955
   Blundell 15/1.
10. Miss Clarke's Diary, 16 Nov. 1956.
11. ibid, 19 Nov. 1956.
12. Cmd. 4556 (1934) paras. 408 and 413.

13. L. S. B. Leakey to S. V. Cooke, 16 Mar. 1939, in file belonging to S. V. Cooke.
14. cf. chapter 6.
15. C.N.C. to Cooke, 24 Mar. 1939, file cit.
16. Cooke to C.N.C. 11 Mar. 1939, file cit.
17. L. S. B. Leakey, file cit.
18. Miss J. E. Clarke's Diary, 29 Dec. 1956.
19. Miss J. E. Clarke's Diary, 2 Jan. 1957.
20. ibid, 1 Feb. 1957.
21. ibid, 2 Jan. 1957.
22. p. 79.
23. *Towards a Future For Kenya* (6 pages mimeographed). There is a copy among Mrs. J. Raw's papers.
24. Robert Burns: *Tam O'Shanter.*
25. Note on cover of confidential file in the possession of S. V. Cooke.
26. European Elected Members Organisation: Minutes of meeting on 29 Oct. 1953 in Havelock File E.E.M.O. in Kenya National Archives.
27. Ven. Archdeacon Peter Bostock to Chief Secretary. 14 Mar. 1957. File at St. Julian's.
28. E.A.S. 2 Feb. 1957.
29. Miss Clarke's Diary, 24 Jan. 1957.
30. ibid, 19 Mar. 1957.
31. ibid, 22 Mar. 1957.
32. Interview with Mr. Howard, 30 Mar. 1970.
33. Miss Clarke's Diary, 8 Feb. 1957.
34. Highlands Board.
35. Miss Clarke's Diary, 23 Jan. 1956.
36. Archbishop of Canterbury to Miss Potts, 8 Mar. 1957, in file at St. Julian's.
37. Miss Clarke's Diary, 30 Nov. 1956.
38. cf. pp. 175–6.
39. Miss Clarke's Diary, 30 Nov. 1957.
40. European Elected Members Organisation: Minutes of Meeting on 13 Feb. 1957. Havelock File H.5/2 Vol. II in Kenya National Archives.
41. Miss Clarke's Diary, 1 Feb. 1957.
42. European Elected Members Organisation: Minutes of meeting on 30 Jan. 1957, Havelock file H 5/2 vol. II in Kenya National Archives.
43. Miss Clarke's Diary, 1 Feb. 1957.
44. European Elected Members Organisation: Minutes of meeting on 12 Dec. 1956, Havelock file H 14/1 in Kenya National Archives.
45. European Elected Members Organisation: Minutes of meeting on 12 Jan. 1956, Havelock file H 14/1 in Kenya National Archives.
46. Miss Clarke's Diary 14 Mar. 1957.
47. European Elected Members Organisation: Minutes of Meeting, 13 Feb. 1957, Havelock file H 5/2 vol. II in Kenya National Archives.
48. European Elected Members Organisation: Minutes of Meeting, 14 Feb. 1957 Blundell 15.
49. Interview with Archbishop Beecher 20 Mar. 1970.
50. European Elected Members Organisation: Minutes of Meeting, 13 May, 1957, Havelock file H 5/2 vol. II.
51. Francis Thompson: *Essay on Shelley.*
52. Interview with Archbishop Beecher, 20 Mar. 1970.
53. H.C.D., Vol. 566, col. 1121, 13 March 1957.
54. Miss Clarke's Diary, 2 Jan. 1957.
55. European Elected Members Organisation: Minutes of meeting, 12 Dec. 1956, Havelock file, H 14/1 in Kenya National Archives.
56. Blundell to European Elected Members, 2 Jan. 1957 in Havelock File H 5/2 vol. II in Kenya National Archives.
57. Note, April, 1959 in Havelock File, 'The New Kenya Group' vol. I in Kenya National Archives.
58. *The Times,* 16 Apr. 1959.

59. The Times, 16 Apr. 1959.
60. Havelock file, "Electors' Union", in Kenya National Archives.
61. Miss Clarke's Diary, 24 Nov. 1956.
62. p. 64.
63. *New Comment*, No. 67, 12 July 1957.
64. *New Comment*, No. 59, 17 May 1957.

11

THE FINAL YEARS

The Capricorn Africa Society

Opposition to the sale of a property within the White Highlands to a non-racial community was an out-moded minority attitude in 1957. The die-hards regarded the transfer with particular suspicion because Mr. and Mrs. Wood were leading members of the Capricorn African Society, an organisation which throughout the fifties had played an important part in bringing people of different races together on equal terms. This personal human aspect of the Society was its greatest contribution and was strong enough to enable Asians and Africans to forget that its original document, the Salisbury Declaration, was based on the maintenance of the European areas in Kenya and Southern Rhodesia and could be described as "*Apartheid in sugar icing*, but not the less *Apartheid* for that."[1]

The creation of goodwill between the races depended so largely on a change in European thought, which itself depended so much on experience of the educational advance of Africans and Asians, that a society which included on equal terms people of every race was bound to have much influence in the quest for inter-racial harmony. As one African member said "The organisation sprang up from the ranks of Europeans after our founder had worked ceaselessly to start an organisation that would fight for equality of opportunity for all irrespective of colour, creed or race".[2] Tom Mboya admired the inter-racial attitude of the Society[3] and was the first President of the Kenya Branch. Clement Argwings-Kodhek went to the Capricorn Conference at Salima, but the African political campaign of non-co-operation forced them both to resign. Although the political extremes grew further apart and increasingly bitter as the nineteen fifties wore on, social barriers between the races became less and less rigid and contact between Europeans and Africans increased. After the first Lancaster House Conference in 1960 the African Affairs Officer of the Nairobi City Council believed that in spite of the violence of political speeches and in spite of the gap between the financial status of most Africans and of most Europeans there was "a fund of goodwill to be tapped."[4] The Capricorn Africa Society had great influence in fostering this goodwill and in promoting the idea of common citizenship. Its membership was considerable and its work was carried on in London as well as in Kenya. In this way it helped to make people in Britain more aware of Africa and African problems and its non-racial basis undoubtedly strengthened the co-operative elements in the different races.

African political nationalism

A few years earlier inter-racial co-operation had met strong opposition from African political nationalism. The European Elected Members Organisation made several attempts to arrange talks with the African Elected Members, but, they wrote to the Secretary of State, "Unfortunately, except for one preliminary meeting, our endeavours have been unsuccessful."[5] In May 1957 the Chairman of the European Elected Members Organisation had approached Ohanga and Mboya "both of whom were willing to meet E.E.M.O. for constitutional discussions",[6] but African non-co-operation subsequently hardened. An important bar to political co-operation was misunderstanding of the possibilities presented by the Lyttelton Constitution. It was a multi-racial constitution, because its creators believed that the introduction of a common roll was a political impossibility in 1954 but that African educational advance would lead to an increasing number of African seats and ministries and that a non-racial society with a common Kenya citizenship would later take the place of multi-racialism. The African nationalist politicians, however, saw the Lyttelton Constitution as a multi-racial plan to prevent them from attaining power. The declarations of Humphrey Slade and others that the introduction of a common roll should be the aim of political policy, the suggestion of a common Kenya citizenship, the thought of a steady increase of African ministries after the first Minister had shown that Africans were capable of filling such posts—such moves towards the introduction of non-racialism were disregarded in the face of the fact that the first step, the Lyttelton Constitution, was multi-racial; and the African Elected Members wrote to the Governor, "We have as our ultimate objective the development in this country of society and Government where all regardless of race or colour have equal rights and opportunities. Thus we want to assure you and all other racial groups that our move is not motivated by any desire towards black domination;" but, because the Lyttelton Constitution was based on multi-racialism, they added, "Our decision regarding non-participation in the Lyttelton plan remains unchanged."[7]

Later that year Alan Lennox-Boyd, who was then Secretary of State, visited Kenya. One of the results of his discussions was the introduction of Specially Elected Members, four Africans, four Asians, and four Europeans, elected by the Legislative Council sitting as an Electoral College. In this way each of the twelve Members, whatever his race, was elected by a body composed of all races. The scheme originated in Kenya and was an attempt to produce Members who owed allegiance, not to a racial electorate, but to all races equally.

When the African nationalists saw that power was passing from European to African hands, they became as racially minded as the Europeans of former years and the die-hards who still remained unchanged. Other Africans, no less patriotic, were willing to accept all true Kenyans, whatever their colour. Professor Plamenatz has succinctly expressed the difference between the two outlooks. Patriotism, he says, is "a love of one's own people which does not carry with it hostility to strangers, whereas nationalism is emotionally in arms against the foreigner, the intruder, the outsider."[8] Few Europeans shared the attitude of the settler who wrote that Blundell recommended "Appeasement by way of Cannibals for the Cabinet,"[9] but there was a European element which to the last resisted any suggestion of inter-racialism. In general, however, as the nineteen fifties wore on, a spirit of goodwill between Africans and Europeans grew stronger and, if the African nationalists were to acquire complete power, it was necessary for them to attack any African who believed that co-operation with other races and the creation of a common citizenship would bring the greatest benefit to Kenya. They denounced any African who might be willing to stand as a candidate for a Special seat, but yet, as Lennox-Boyd told the House of Commons, "More Africans put themselves forward for the specially-elected seats than did members of any other race."[10] Political co-operation was achieved among a multi-racial group within Legislative Council, but African nationalism made it

impossible to bring about co-operation in the Council as a whole.
The Specially Elected Members, especially Musa Amalemba who
accepted office as Minister of Housing, had to be discredited as
"Black Europeans".[11] Indeed not only were the Specially Elected
Members "Black Europeans" and "betrayers", but any Africans who
associated with them would be "betrayers" themselves and ought to
be boycotted.[12] In 1961 Amalemba stood successfully for an open
seat. His Luyia constituents did not regard him as a "betrayer" and
he rightly claimed that he was then a Member freely elected by
Africans and could not be called a European stooge. The later
nineteen fifties were years during which the idea that real democracy
should be established in Kenya had been accepted, but when the
means of achieving it were a matter for heated debate. In 1956 a
Labour Party pamphlet in Britain said, "The peculiar problem of the
plural society is not whether, but how it should become fully
democratic".[13]

African Political Intemperance and American Animosity

African politicians who wanted to acquire absolute power saw
that they had to persuade the electors that there was no further
need for Europeans and Asians in Kenya. As the prospect of
African political supremacy was seen to be coming quickly nearer
realisation, they began to throw truth to the winds in some of their
speeches. If Africans were to demand Independence with an African
Government, it was necessary to show that they were capable of
filling all the high offices in the Government and the Civil Service.
For that an adequate supply of well educated Africans was essential.
In 1955–56 seventy-six Africans from Kenya were studying in
Britain, but in 1957 Argwings-Kodhek told an African audience
that there were "10,000 Kenya students studying in the United
Kingdom,"[14] and he also declared that "Africans must be prepared
to spill blood, which is necessary liquid for mixing the concrete of
freedom."[15]

By 1959 American antagonism to British colonialism was
increasing. "I ought to warn you," wrote Granville Roberts, the
Kenya Information Officer in London, to Havelock, who was at
that time Chairman of the inter-racial New Kenya Group, "that in
America there is a rising crescendo of public opinion, which, to say
the least of it, is not favourable to even moderate multi-racialism
in Kenya,"[16] Americans had no responsibility for Kenya, but, as

Sir Andrew Cohen told an American audience in 1959, there were "still quite a number of people . . . who in this cold world find anticolonialism a comfortable blanket to wrap themselves up in."[17]

Two years after Argwings-Kodhek announced that 10,000 Kenya students were studying in Britain, Tom Mboya departed equally far from the truth when addressing an American audience in New York. As Chairman of the All Peoples Conference he gave an address on African Freedom Day, 15th April 1959, in which he said, "the Government has reserved the entire cool, fertile highlands for white settlers only—refusing to allow Africans to farm even unoccupied sections—while as many as 700-900 are crowded per square mile into the poor semi-desert areas not wanted by the whites".[18] The most remarkable thing about this statement is not its lack of truth but the fact that his American audience could have believed that 700-900 people per square mile could live in semi-desert places.

American animosity and lack of understanding and anti-European bias continued even after the Lancaster House Conference had given an assurance of African supremacy in the near future. The maintenance of inter-racial goodwill was important for the peaceful and efficient administration of Kenya, which was so soon to be independent. A sad example of lack of understanding and appreciation of the reality of the situation was shown in 1961 by Mennon Williams, the American Assistant Secretary of State for African Affairs, when he visited Kenya. At a party given by the American Consul General in Nairobi, to which Ministers of all races had been invited to meet him, Mennon Williams snubbed the European guests, whom he pointedly avoided, but posed for American television cameras with his arms round the shoulders of African Ministers.[19] The need for European advice and expertise in the early stages of Independence was clear to people of all races in Kenya itself, all the more so in view of the speed with which the British Government was determined to hand over power to an African Government. What was required after the first Lancaster House Conference was the stimulation of European confidence as well as the most intensive training of Africans for positions of responsibility. Fortunately the goodwill which had grown between Africans and Britain and the progressive Europeans in Kenya itself was not injured by American animosity.

Difficulties of Political Leaders

The African nationalist attack on the Lyttelton and Lennox-Boyd constitutions was, like the European opposition to the constitutional proposals in Paper 191 in 1946, activated by a refusal to share power with people of other races. Mboya wrote that "Britain holds ultimate responsibility for Kenya and must account for itself to every racial group".[20] The British Government believed that through a multi-racial constitution, becoming continuously more African, Britain could best fulfil that responsibility, but Mboya, while maintaining that the responsibility was hers, vehemently opposed her plans for carrying it out. But, as Blundell realised, Mboya was more moderate than some of his speeches made him seem to be. Leaders of racial parties could not ignore their extremists. Blundell had for many years had the difficult task of leading as many Europeans as possible along lines more liberal than some of them agreed with, and Mboya could only restrain his most violent supporters if they accepted him as a true nationalist without any taint of appeasement.

Both Africans and Europeans were divided. In the late nineteen-fifties the Federal Independence Party among the Europeans and the African nationalists among the Africans were equally opposed to any real inter-racial co-operation and the Indian National Congress was sometimes the scene of bitter anti-European speeches; but outside politics and in parts of the political field also a great deal of co-operation existed. In April 1958 the Specially Elected Members Association was formed "with the primary object of promoting policies for the benefit of Kenya as a whole without any racial or sectional bias".[21] Havelock was elected Chairman of the Association. Eighteen months later he told the Association that the New Kenya Group had stemmed from the Specially Elected Members Association.[22] Humphrey Slade, who had opposed Blundell in the past, joined forces with him and Havelock. Musa Amalemba and Wanyutu Waweru, Chunilal Madan (later Hon. Mr. Justice Madan) and Ibrahim Nathoo were among the Africans and Asians who became members of the inter-racial group, which had "a political policy which set out to create a nation of all races in which Africans played the major part".[23]

The beginning of training of Africans for responsibility

The Politics of Inequality, the title chosen by Professor Gwendolen

Carter for a book on South Africa, would not be inappropriate for
a book about Kenya in the earlier days, but it would be misleading
if applied to the period between the Second World War and the
attainment of Independence. During that period a belief was
growing among Europeans that inequality should give way to a
non-racial system based on merit and a qualitative franchise for
Africans should lead in time to a common roll. Such a change
in European thought—a change which split the European community
in the fifties—would hardly have come about unless an increasing
number of Europeans had appreciated the rapid development of
the African elite. Much was done during the period to bring that
development to the notice of Europeans, but already at the end of
the War the inevitability of African progress was being accepted
here and there and the need to train Africans for positions of
responsibility was beginning to be recognised, although in a small
way, in official and private quarters.

The Government saw the need to train Africans for executive
positions in the Administration and started to implement this idea
by appointing Africans as Administrative Assistants in the
Administration. At the same time the "new" Africans, the products
of secondary education and Makerere, injected a new factor into
the labour market and a few employers in the private sector led
the way in the employment of Africans with a view to their becoming
executives and colleagues of Europeans. The first company to enter
this field was Bovill Matheson and Co. Ltd., who paid for the
education of two Africans at Makerere in 1944 and 1945, "our idea
being", said Mr. E. W. Bovill in a lecture to the Royal African
Society in London in 1951, "that they should take the place of
junior Europeans". The partners, he said, "took great precautions
to protect them against racial prejudice". But, he continued, after
a good start, they began to ask for increased salaries and then
declared that they would not stay unless they were made branch
managers. Both left the firm under a cloud of disappointment and
ill will.[24] The two Africans were B. M. Gecaga, who was subsequently
helped by a European friend to read for the Bar in London, became a
barrister, director of companies and Chairman of the Council of the
University of Nairobi, and John Mwangi who was given a scholarship by the Kenya Government and qualified as a chartered
accountant in Scotland and later became a partner in a previously
purely European firm in Kenya and Chairman of the Kenya Road

Authority. His view did not tally with Mr. Bovill's. After being paid 120/- a month for two years he was offered 170/- a month. He and Gecaga saw young Europeans with no better qualifications promoted above them and when Mwangi asked for an advance of 30/- to pay the fee for a course in book-keeping at the Nairobi Continuation Classes, the European accountant at Bovill Mathesons said to him, "Don't waste your money. You have got enough education for any job you are likely to get in this organisation and in any case I can't see you sitting over a European for a long time". That seemed to be the signal for resigning from the firm. As was found elsewhere, in the police force, for instance, the intentions and behaviour of the most senior members were not always copied by those lower down. The two young Africans were not so foolish as to demand to be branch managers, but they wanted to know whether such promotion would be open to them later on or whether, as the accountant said, such hope was unreal. It was not difficult for the partners to be given a prejudiced account, and disappointment and bitter recrimination were the sad result of a liberal and progressive experiment.[25]

In 1947 a young African from Meru, George Muketha, was taken on for executive training by the Calico Printers of Manchester. The possibilities ahead were made clear to him, training and promotion were co-ordinated, and he subsequently became Sales Manager for East Africa of Nytil Ltd., the organisation formed by the Calico Printers of Manchester to carry on their enterprise in modern East Africa. In the late nineteen forties a few other firms began to train Africans for executive positions. Gilbert J. Macaul Ltd. appointed Luke Obok with this end in view and, after working for the City Council, Tom Mboya was employed by Overseas Motor Transport Ltd. . The East African Standard employed Africans as journalists and under the supervision of David McDowell Wilson, the liberal-minded Editor of *Baraza*, Musa Amalemba, Joseph Thuo and Laurence Kibui, received efficient training and were treated as colleagues.

In the fifties other commercial companies also saw that it was necessary to train Africans for executive positions. David Kamau, who became Commercial Manager and a Director of Gaily and Roberts, started as an accounts clerk in 1953, and the British American Tobacco Company appointed Ambrose Lukhalo to an executive post on his return from the University of St. Andrews in

1955. Throughout the fifties the practice of appointing Africans
to posts which would enable them to reach the highest positions
was followed by other commercial firms and increased after the
first Lancaster House Conference showed what the political future
would be like.

The early nineteen fifties were a period when the number of
Africans who went to universities was small and therefore firms
which wanted to train Africans for executive positions could not
always demand a university degree as a necessary qualification.
In the late forties and early fifties the Shell oil company appointed
African sales representatives who had not had university training,
but this led to resentment in university circles. In 1953 Shell made
no such appointments, but in 1954 three men who had just taken
their London External B.A. degrees at Makerere were appointed.
As all were Kikuyus and the Emergency was at its height their
appointment was a bold move and was due to the determination of
E. T. Jones, who was then General Manager of the Shell Company
of East Africa. Of these three Mwai Kibaki subsequently left Shell,
went to the London School of Economics, entered politics and
became Minister of Finance and Economic Planning, Joseph Kariuki
went to King's College, Cambridge, and reached high status in the
Kenya Civil Service, and Nicholas Muriuki stayed with the Company
and is now the General Manager of the Company in Kenya. The
idea that Africans could and would occupy high places in commercial
enterprises had been firmly accepted by 1960.[26]

Although in the late nineteen forties a small beginning was made
of bringing Africans into the Administration as officers, "the
leisurely time-tables for political advance"[27] in the colonies had not
caused the Colonial Office or the Kenya Government to institute
schemes for the quick and large-scale training of Africans in Government service. The imminent advent of Independence after the first
Lancaster House Conference caused a sudden acceleration and in
the final years a number of African officers were sent to Oxford and
Cambridge or London for training and returned to take up senior
posts. Jeremieh Kiereini, for instance, was already District Commissioner at Embu when the National Assembly met in June 1963;
S. O. Josiah was Assistant Provincial Commissioner in the Rift
Valley; and Paul arap Boit was District Commissioner at Kakamega.
Geoffrey Kariithi, Sila arap Boit, John Michuki, and others were
in the Districts or in senior posts in Ministries, of which they were

soon to be the Permanent Secretaries. They were very successful and showed to people of all races that educated Africans were capable, with training, of holding the highest posts. Unfortunately in the Civil Service as a whole, as Commander Miller was told, official policy had been against training young Asians and African graduates on the job in the manner of the British Civil Service and so enabling them to become qualified to fill the higher posts. Only a year before the Conference met at Lancaster House, as Blundell pointed out, "in January, 1959, the official policy was a slow and unspectacular constitutional advance for these [East African] territories with Kenya comfortably last."[28] The policy propounded at Lancaster House by Iain Macleod, the Secretary of State, of "full speed ahead for quick independence" caused great shock, because people in Kenya did not realise how strongly in the previous few months "the wind of change" had blown through the windows of Whitehall and Downing Street. Failure in Kenya to appreciate the changed mood of Whitehall was matched by failure in Britain to appreciate the extent to which inter-racial goodwill had increased in Kenya during the fifties. As late as May 1959 Harold Macmillan, the Prime Minister, told Blundell that the situation was not understood outside Kenya. "He told me," wrote Blundell, "that to the outside world I appeared very much on my own".[29] There was nothing new in that. The gradual growth in inter-racial harmony since the War had not been noted while the bitterness of the European die-hards and the violent speeches of the African nationalists and the Mau Mau Emergency held the front of the stage.

Inadequate Meeting between Politicians

Although in many fields people of different races were meeting each other in the fifties, there was one area in which unfortunately little contact had been made. The grant of a franchise to Africans in 1956, which was followed by the first African elections in 1957, brought to the fore many African political leaders, who previously had not been prominent on the national stage. It is true that some of the European Elected Members knew the leading African politicians, but they were in the minority.

Oginga Odinga and Arap Moi were among the Africans elected to Legislative Council in 1957. Towards the end of that year Humphrey Slade stayed with the former and shared a political platform with the latter. Blundell knew Mboya, Ngala and the rest, but most European Members saw them only in the debating chamber of Legislative Council. When at a meeting of the European Elected Members Organization in May 1957 it was proposed that "a meeting should be held with Members of all races" to discuss "a re-starting" of the United Members Organization, Norman Harris, Elected Member for Nairobi South, said that "it was difficult to go into important negotiations with people one did not know."[30] If the European politicians did not know the Africans who had recently become their fellow Members of Legislative Council, still less did they know the African politicians who, although not elected to the Council, were influential people in the towns and reserves. This lack of contact deprived most European politicians of any deep knowledge of African nationalist thought and desires and of the extent of inter-racial co-operation in politics which might have been possible in the months before the Lancaster House Conference. If there had been more contact between the European political leaders and the African nationalist politicians in the late nineteen fifties, some measure of agreement on policies might have been achieved in Kenya before the delegations went to London. A definite attempt was in fact made in 1959, but it was unsuccessful.

The Kenya Party was formed in 1956 to provide a political voice for the ideas of the Capricorn Africa Society, which itself was forbidden by its constitution to indulge in politics. The Executive Committees of the Kenya Party and of the Capricorn Africa Society were composed largely of the same people. Susan Wood stood as the Party's candidate for a Nairobi seat and the connection between the Party and the Society was the cause of *Comment's* scurrilous cartoon referred to in the last chapter. The Kenya Party, of which Ernest Vasey was a member, did not aim at achieving political power but rather at influencing other parties and people. They were trying to achieve inter-racial co-operation in political policies. In the homes of members of the Party many meetings were held with African Members of Legislative Council, who in 1957 were elected by African voters, and in December 1959, when Iain Macleod was in Kenya, the Committee of the Party were able to send him a draft constitution with electoral proposals which would have produced a Legislative Council composed of 24 Africans, half of them from reserved constituencies, in which Asians and Europeans would have been prominent among the voters, and 12 from open constituencies with a basically African electorate; 12 Asians from reserved constituencies, voted on by Europeans, Asians and Africans; and 12 Europeans elected in the same way. This document recommended Independence in 1966. With the exception of the date it was not very different from the proposals imposed by Macleod. Among the signatories were Ernest Vasey, John Karmali, the Ismaili founder of the first inter-racial school, Wycliffe Awori's brother, A. M. Awori, Boaz Omori, subsequently Editor-in-Chief of *The Nation* newspaper group, and S. T. Thakore, a prominent Asian business man.

This document was discussed with Dr. Kiano, Tom Mboya, Ronald Ngala and other African Elected Members, who said that, if it was accepted by The New Kenya Party, they too would accept it in good faith. The two groups were meeting at opposite ends of the same corridor in the Legislative Council building and Mrs. Raw, the Hon. Secretary of the Kenya Party, carried messages from one room to the other, but the Committee of the New Kenya Party rejected it, saying that they had no intention of going so far so fast. European Members refused to "take the thumb from the dam", as they expressed it. Tom Mboya then said, "Very well, we will now ask for the whole cake and with luck we'll get three-quarters of it." In fact the Africans were given more than the cake they were asking for. Mboya, who was very much of a realist, was embarrassed by the speed of Macleod's plans for Independence and tried to get a slower time-table with an intensive programme of training for Africans. He said that he would have liked a period of five to ten years leading to Independence. The Imperial power, however, had grown tired of colonial responsibilities and hustled Kenya into Independence with a speed which Mboya and others thought to be unwise. The trustee at the last relinquished the trusteeship before the ward felt quite ready to be independent.[31]

Reactions to the Lancaster House Conference

If there had been more friendly contact between African and European politicians, the two groups meeting on the same corridor might have discussed the proposals together instead of communicating only through Mrs. Raw. A month later, five thousand miles away from home, when the very fact that they were away from Kenya evoked a common feeling among them, the progressive Europeans and the Africans did have discussions with each other at Lancaster House outside the Conference room. These informal meetings in London enabled the groups to discuss political proposals and plans among themselves, but their most important result, wrote Blundell, was that the politicians "came alive to each other as individuals, with ideas, hopes, and fears, and, above all, a love of Kenya common to them all."[32] It had not been possible to create such inter-racial appreciation before Macleod's drastic plans showed the delegates that the ship was so soon to be pushed out of the Imperial harbour into the rough seas of Independence.

Tom Mboya was not alone in thinking that the time-table was too fast. Africans studying at universities in the United States were alarmed by American ignorance of the situation and the resulting pressure on Britain to grant Independence quickly. They felt that the United States Government believed that there were far more Africans in Kenya already qualified for high office than was actually the case.[33] In other fields also African capacity was still limited. Doctors, lawyers, teachers, engineers were gaining qualifications overseas, but their numbers were not sufficient for the needs of an independent country.

When they first heard the news from Lancaster House, many Europeans besides the die-hards were aghast. Some settlers thought that an African Government created in such haste would confiscate European farms; some felt that lack of training and experience would cause an African Government and Administration to show such inefficiency that life would become economically impossible. Most of the Afrikaners and others, who could not accept the thought of living under African authority, prepared to sell up and leave Kenya.[34] The thirty pieces of silver flung at Blundell's feet at the airport on his return to Nairobi, the eggs and tomatoes thrown at him during an election meeting at Londiani in the following year, the backs turned on him and his supporters at social gatherings showed the strength of feeling against the European liberals held by the die-hard element; but, as had been the case during the last decade, the violence of the reactionaries obscured the moderation of the more co-operative section of the European community. After the first shock was over, the majority of Europeans decided to stay in Kenya, to live and work there under an African Government. Indeed by the end of 1961 Blundell felt that "80 per cent of the European community would like to stay" and he thought that probably half of that 80 per cent were behind him and his political colleagues and that the other half would feel the same "if the African political front could settle down". And he wrote, "My impression is that a great many Europeans are tuning in to the thought of living in Kenya under an African government. With one or two wise statements from the Africans the whole of the 80 per cent would be behind the new pattern".[35] A few months later the District Officer in the Molo Division of the Nakuru District reported, "I find about 98 per cent of the European Community are fully co-operative. . . . We have, unfortunately, a 2 per cent extremist element amongst the Europeans who are in my opinion a source of danger to both security and confidence".[36] The release of Kenyatta in August 1961 removed a principal cause of inter-racial tension. Rivalry between the African political parties, Kanu and Kadu, became the major political issue and, when independence with an African government became an early certainty, inter-racial antagonism largely faded away. The great majority of European civil servants, lawyers, doctors, businessmen, and farmers accepted the new situation with good grace, and Kenyatta and other African leaders assured them that an independent Kenya under an African government would be glad to see them stay. It would probably not have been so if members of the different races had not been brought into friendly contact with each other outside the political arena during the preceding ten years.

Independence

The late nineteen fifties saw the beginning of a congested period of decolonisation throughout the colonial world, in the French and Belgian and Dutch Empires as well as the British. For the most part the colonies were countries administered by metropolitan powers in tropical areas which Europeans did not regard as "White Man's Countries." Inter-racial difficulties arose in colonies with large Indian communities. Mauritius and Fiji, for instance, faced the certainty of Indian majorities, which would cause conflict between the indigenous inhabitants, who owned the land, and the Asian political majorities who preponderated in politics. It is, however, the Colonies of European settlement, the Colonies where the "dominion" and "trusteeship" concepts existed in the same territory, which have particular relevance to the subject of this book.

The decolonisation of such territories is in the main a story of violence and ill will. In Indonesia the Dutch resident community had not been able to win the friendship of the Indonesians. It is recognised that the Japanese conquest terminated Dutch endeavours to solve "the human problem", along lines of co-operation and harmony, and so, when independence came, the Dutch community had to leave amid Indonesian rejoicing and the Dutch language was abandoned until the first violence of the storm had passed. Indo-China won independence from France through a most bloody war and the Belgian withdrawal from the Congo led to chaos and bloodshed. The French colonies in West Africa were tropical countries which did not lure Europeans to settle in them, but, in North Africa, Algeria, a colony of large scale settlement, where certain admirable efforts to promote inter-racial co-operation had not been sufficiently successful, was subjected to a merciless civil war which soon had manifestations in metropolitan France itself and which ended only when De Gaulle abandoned the French settlers. The proximity of Algeria to France itself gave it a special position which was not seen elsewhere. In the British Empire in Africa the countries which were for a time brought together in the Central African Federation faced the problems of a plural society with a settler population, but the virtually independent status of Southern Rhodesia was not paralleled in other parts. Uganda had almost no agricultural settlers and Tanganyika had no central settled area analagous to the White Highlands of Kenya, where from the early years the settlers had used their social contacts at Westminster and their persistence in Kenya to win for themselves a position of great political power.

Even after the Second World War the majority of politically-minded Europeans still hoped that they might be able to "be entrenched in power by the terms of the constitution", and the Electors' Union declared that "our undeviating purpose is the control of our own affairs." At the same time, however, Africans were beginning to maintain that Kenya was "a black man's country" and the Africans "must see that it remains so for ever".[37] Would the river of conflict sweep two races away or would it be turned into a stream on which all races could sail together to independence?

Sir Philip Mitchell saw at the very beginning of his Governorship that the danger would not be averted unless conscious efforts were made to bring the leading members of the various races together and to create opportunities for them to meet as fellow human beings, interested in common subjects and engaged in common enterprises.

A few Europeans in Kenya shared his views. Creech Jones, the Secretary of State, and the Colonial Office, whose African Department was led by Andrew Cohen, appreciated the need for improving human relations. The approach had to be along functional lines. Opportunities had to be created for educated people of different races to do things together. Purely social meeting would follow when economic disparity was lessened. It was hoped that inter-racial co-operation would nourish a liberalism in the European community which would agree to the abandonment of discriminations which stood in the way of inter-racial harmony. Then the central body of inter-racial co-operation, which was so grievously small in 1945, would grow at the expense of European diehardism on the one side and African racial nationalism on the other.

The key to inter-racial co-operation lay with the Europeans. They had power and privilege, self-sufficiency and, too often, racial arrogance. They had to be willing to share with the other races many of the monopolies which they enjoyed. Conscious efforts were required to influence their minds and so to alter the thinking of a sufficient proportion of the European electorate that their members in Legislative Council could vote for the co-operative and liberal measures which were increasingly required as the colony moved towards independence. The work of the Churches, of the British Council, of cultural societies and above all of individuals all tended to bring people together and so to enable them to understand each other. Through such an understanding and contact, through perticipation in cultural pursuits and the gradual growth of a sense of community a remarkable measure of harmony was reached and independence came with a spirit of goodwill which it seemed scarcely realistic to hope for in 1945. In the earlier years of the period under review this process, this growth of liberalism and co-operation, was scarcely visible. The work done during these years began to have its effect in the nineteen fifties, when the more liberal European politicians were able to suggest to their electorates that power would one day have to be shared. The consequent split in the European political ranks was to be desired because it enabled liberalism to advance without having to continue to take with it the reactionary element of the electorate.

In this book the gradual growth of a spirit of co-operation has been traced. It was impeded many times by elements of fear and selfishness, of a thirst for power and greed for privilege, of lack of understanding and sympathetic consideration of the problems of other races. The failure of trusteeship which led to the Mau Mau civil war and the outstanding service loyalty in the Civil Service in the early fifties have both been noted. The work of individuals and groups and its impact on community thought has been used as evidence to support the claim that the promotion of closer intercourse between, above all, Africans and Europeans during the years between the end of the Second World War and the granting of independence played an indispensable part in making possible the eventual peaceful transfer of power in Kenya.

When Kenyatta became Prime Minister of the self-governing Kenya, he told Malcolm MacDonald, the Governor-General, that he wanted bitterness to be forgotten. This was a principle which he stressed to his African colleagues also. The friendship and trust which had grown up between Kenyatta and MacDonald and the spirit of co-operation which had been created between all but the extremists of the African and European races blessed the beginning of the era of Independence. Sadly the Asians were not similarly regarded by the Africans. Great as had been their contribution to the economic development of Kenya, there had been a failure in human relations and they were not included in the goodwill which existed between Africans and Europeans. As had been the case throughout the nineteen fifties, the growth of friendship between the Africans and the British was not realised overseas. The speeches of the extremists on both sides were what caught the attention of journalists and the steady and patient increase of goodwill received scant recognition, and the tactic of accepting multi-racialism as a first step towards the elimination of communal politics was not understood. It was fortunate that long association had formed a bond between Africans and the British residents and the officers of the Administration which was not harmed by lack of understanding overseas.

A month or two before Independence the members of an African boys' club in one of the poorest districts of Nairobi wrote a play which they wanted to act in the Uhuru Stadium during the Independence celebrations or, if that were not possible, on successive evenings in the social halls in the various parts of the City. The play was an ignorant travesty of history and was intended to create hatred of Britain and the Colonial Administration. The matter was brought to the attention of Tom Mboya, the Minister responsible for the Independence celebrations. He asked to see the script and immediately banned its performance anywhere. "That", he said, "is not the spirit in which we want to enter Independence."

Writing to the Secretary of State in 1947, Sir Philip Mitchell had expressed his view of the responsibility of Britain as a Colonial power. "Colonial responsibilities," he wrote, "which had been consciously pursued since the end of the Second World War, are a task requiring all our fortitude and tenacity of purpose, all our humanity and long experience; a task which will expose us to much criticism and obloquy, but which is tremendously worth while."[38] The efforts to create inter-racial co-operation in Kenya, had achieved a considerable measure of success when Britain relinquished the responsibility of trusteeship on the 12th December, 1963. Whether discrimination had died or whether, like the chamelon, it only changed its colour will be for future historians to decide. The story of Kenya since Independence is not the subject of this book which has been concerned with some of the human problems and relationships within the multi-racial Colony and the attempt to create a society in which loyalty to the nation would be stronger than considerations of race. When the flag of the new Kenya flew in the Uhuru Stadium on that December day, the new nation was acclaimed with general goodwill. Not only did the majority of private Europeans choose to stay and work in Kenya under an African government, but in the Administration and specialist departments, such as Agriculture and Education, British civil servants were willing to step down and remain to help with their experience and expertise the Africans whom they had trained to replace them. Many causes had hastened the advent of Independence, but it is reasonable to claim that the peaceful transfer of power owed much to the successful efforts to promote inter-racial goodwill and co-operation which were pursued since the end of the Second World War by both organisations and individual people.

1. Sir Philip Mitchell's Diary, 10 April 1952.
2. A Verbatim Report of Capricorn Africa Society General Council Meeting held at St. Julian's, Limuru, on 21/22 January, 1961, p. 17. The founder was Colonel David Stirling.
3. Mboya said this to Mrs. Joyce Raw. Interview with Mrs. Raw, 17 February, 1970.
4. Eric Wilkinson to Jonathan Lewis, 27 September 1960, Hughes Papers.

5. European Elected Members Organisation, Minutes of Meeting on 15th October 1957, Havelock, H. 3/4 11.
6. Minutes of Meeting on 29 May 1957.
7. Letter to Governor, 28 March, 1957, Havelock file H 3/411.
8. John Plamenatz: *On Alien Rule and Self Government*, p. 13.
9. Major J. O. K. Delap: *Kenya as I see it*, a pamphlet circulated to members of Parliament in London, K. W. N., 14 October 1955, p. 5.
10. H.D.C., Vol. 587, col. 1398, 8 May 1958.
11. e.g. Mboya at a meeting on 26 August 1958, Blundell 8/1.
12. Oginga Odinga at a meeting on 18 April 1958, Blundell 8/1.
13. *Labour's Colonial policy: One: The Plural Society*, July 1956, p. 30.
14. K.W.N., 24 May 1957.
15. E.A.S., 24 May 1957.
16. Granville Roberts to Havelock, 3 April 1959, Havelock file, "The New Kenya Group", vol. I, in Kenya National Archives.
17. Sir Andrew Cohen: *British Policy in Changing Africa*, p. 116.
18. A photostat copy of this speech is in Havelock file, "The New Kenya Group", Vol. I, in Kenya National Archives. Mboya's visit to America was made "in order to launch in company with Mrs. Eleanor Roosevelt, the African Freedom Fund." (*Economist*, 11 April 1959).
19. *Daily Telegraph*, 23 February, 1961.
20. Tom Mboya: *Kenya Faces the Future*, p. 26.
21. Specially Elected Members Association, Minutes of Meeting on 23 April 1958. Kenya National Archives.
22. ibid., Minutes of Meeting on 12 November 1959.
23. Sir Michael Blundell: *So Rough a Wind*, p. 251.
24. E. M. Bovill: "East Africa Today": *African Affairs*, Vol. 50, 1951, pp. 225–226.
25. Information collected in 1948 and confirmed by John Mwangi on 11 April, 1970.
26. Interview with A. Weaver and George Muketha of Nytil Ltd., K. L. Mackenzie, Sales Manager of Machinery Services (Gaily and Roberts), David McDowell Wilson, formerly Editor of *Baraza*, J. H. Oyugi, Director of Personnel and Public Relations, Shell Company of East Africa.
27. Margery Perham: *Colonial Sequence 1949–1969*, p. xviii.
28. Sir Michael Blundell: *So Rough a Wind*, p. 262.
29. ibid., p. 264.
30. Minutes of Meeting of European Elected Members Organization, 29 May 1957, in the Kenya National Archives.
31. Mboya said this both to Mrs. Raw, Chief Editor of Hansard and S. V. Cooke. (Interview on 27 Oct. 1971 and 2 Jun. 1970).
32. Sir Michael Blundell: *So Rough a Wind*, p. 273.
33. Interviews with Nathan Fedha, Chief Archivist, March 1970. He was at Wisconsin University at the time of the Lancaster House Conference.
34. In 1961, 6,052 Europeans left Kenya. (E.A.S. 27 July 1962).
35. Blundell to Miss Joan Vickers, M.P., 8 November 1961. Blundell 19/5.
36. Handing over Report: Molo Division, Major W. K. Barrow to Mr. G. M. Crabbe, 26 August 1962.
37. cf. Chapter 1.
38. *Confidential No. 16:* Sir Philip Mitchell to Secretary of State, 30th May, 1947.

SELECT BIBLIOGRAPHY: Great Britain

Cmd. 3562, H.M.S.O. 1907 — *Correspondence relating to the Flogging of Natives by Certain Europeans at Nairobi.*

Cmd. 1922, H.M.S.O. 1923 — *Indians in Kenya:* A Memorandum

Cmd. 2387, H.M.S.O. 1925 — *Report of the East Africa Commission* (Hon. W. Ormsby-Gore, M.P. Chairman)

Cmd. 2904, H.M.S.O. 1927 — *Future Policy in Regard to Eastern Africa.*

Cmd. 3378, H.M.S.O. 1929 — *Report of Sir Samuel Wilson, G.C.M.G., K.C.B., K.B.E. on his Visit to East Africa, 1929* (to see how closer union 'would be administratively workable')

Cmd. 3234, H.M.S.O. 1929 — *Report on the Commission for Closer Union for the Dependencies in East and Central Africa* (Sir E. Hilton Young, Chairman)

Cmd. 3573, H.M.S.O. 1930 — *Memorandum on Native Policy in East Africa.*

H.C. Paper No. 156 H.M.S.O. 1931 — *Report of the Joint Select Committee on Closer Union in East Africa*, 3 vols.

Cmd. 4093, H.M.S.O. 1932 — *Report by the Financial Commission (Lord Moyne) on Certain Questions in Kenya*

Col. 91, H.M.S.O. 1934 — *Kenya Land Commission. Evidence and Memoranda*, 3 vols.

Cmd. 4556, H.M.S.O. 1934 — *Kenya Land Commission Report, 1933* (Sir Morris Carter, C.B.E., Chairman)

Col. 116, H.M.S.O. 1936 — *Report on the Commission appointed to Enquire into and Report on the Financial Position and System of Taxation in Kenya* (Sir Alan Pim, Commissioner)

Col. 191, H.M.S.O. 1945 — *Inter-Territorial Organisation in East Africa.*

Col. Off. H.M.S.O. 1946 — *Labour Conditions in East Africa.* Report by Major G.St.J. Orde Browne, C.M.G., O.B.E.

Col. 210, H.M.S.O. 1947 — *Inter-Territorial Organisation in East Africa —Revised Proposals*

Cmd. 9081, H.M.S.O. 1954 — *Report to the Secretary of State for the Colonies by the Parliamentary Delegation to Kenya, January 1954* (Rt. Hon. Walter

	Elliot, Chairman)
London,	*Report of the Commission on the Civil*
1954	*Service of the East African Territories and*
	the East African High Commission 1953-54.
	Under the Chairmanship of Sir David
	Lidbury, K.C.M.G., D.S.O.
Cmd. 9103, H.M.S.O.	*Kenya Proposals for a reconstruction of the*
1954	*Government* (*Lyttelton Plan*)
Cmd. 9475, H.M.S.O.	*East Africa Royal Commission 1953-1955*
1955	*Report* (Sir Hugh Dow, Chairman)
Cmd. 309, H.M.S.O.	*Kenya Proposals for New Constitutional*
1957	*Arrangements* (Lennox-Boyd proposals)
C.O. Inf. Dept.	*Kenya: Statement by Secretary of State for*
1953	*the Colonies,* 8.11.53, No. 13.
Cmd. 369, H.M.S.O.	*Kenya Despatch on New Constitutional*
1958	*Arrangements* (to Acting Governor from
	Secretary of State)
Cmd. 1030, H.M.S.O.	*Historical Survey of the Origins and Growth*
1960	*of Mau Mau* (F. D. Corfield)

Colonial Reports, Kenya—annually
House of Commons Debates

OFFICIAL PUBLICATIONS: Kenya

Govt. Printer,
Nairobi

1936	*Report on Native Taxation* (G. Walsh, C.B.E., Treasurer and H. R. Montgomery, C.M.G., Chief Native Commissioner.)
1945	*Arthur Phillips: Report on Native Tribunals*
1945	*Report of the Civil Service Commission* (L. C. Hill, C.B.E.)
1945	*Proposals for the Reorganization of the Administration of Kenya*, Sessional Paper No. 3.
1945	*Land Utilization and Settlement. A Statement of Government Policy.* Sessional Paper No. 8.
1946	*Man Power, Demobilization and Reabsorption Report 1945*
1946	*General Aspects of the Agrarian Situation in Kenya.* Despatch No. 44 of 1946 from the Governor to the Secretary of State for the Colonies.
1946	*African Social Welfare in Kenya*
1946	*Report of the Development Committee* 2 vols.
Conference of East African Governors 1946	*A Report on a Fiscal Survey of Kenya, Uganda and Tanganyika*, 1946 (Sir Wilfred Woods, K.C.M.G., K.B.E.)

Govt. Printer
Nairobi

1947	*The Agrarian Problem in Kenya.* Note by Sir Philip Mitchell, G.C.M.G., M.C., Governor of Kenya.
1947	*Sir Philip Mitchell to Secretary of State, 30th May 1947*, Conf. No. 16.
1948	*Report of the Committee on Educational Expenditure* (*European and Asian*) (Sir Bertrand Glancy, Chairman)
Cent. Regis. Office, 1948	*Registration of Persons: National Registration: What do They Mean?*

Govt. Printer
Nairobi
1949   *African Education in Kenya. Report of a Committee Appointed to Enquire into the Scope, Content and Methods of African Education, its Administration and Finance, and to Make Recommendations* (Ven. Archdeacon J. Beecher, Chairman)

1949   *Report of the Select Committee on Indian Education*

1950   *Report of Committee on Agricultural Credit for Africans*

1950   *Report on Whitley Councils* (W. J. Haimes)

1950   *Report of a Commission of Inquiry Appointed to Review the Registration of Persons Ordinance, 1947, and to Make Recommendations for any Amendments to the Ordinance that he may consider Necessary or Desirable.* (Sir B. J. Glancy, Commissioner)

Mimeo
1950   *Report on African Housing in Townships and Trading Centres* (E. A. Vasey, C.M.G.)

Govt. Printer
Nairobi
1951   *Report of the Planning Committee*

1953   *Report of Inquiry into the General Economy of Farming in the Highlands* (L. G. Troup, O.B.E., Commissioner)

1953   *Some Aspects of the Development of Kenya Government Services for the Benefit of Africans from 1946 onwards*

1954   *Report of the Kenya Police Commission 1953*

1954   *The Implementation of the Recommendations of the Kenya Police Commission 1953,* Sessional Paper No. 24

1954   *Report of the Committee on African Wages* (F. W. Carpenter, Chairman)

1954   *A Plan to Intensify the Development of*

African Agriculture in Kenya (R. J. Swynnerton, O.B.E., M.C., Assistant Director of Agriculture.)

1954   The Psychology of Mau Mau (Carothers, Dr. J. C.)

1955   Report of the Commissioner appointed to Enquire into Methods for the Selection of African Representatives to the Legislative Council (W. F. Coutts, Commissioner)

1958   Report on Asian and European Education in Kenya 1958

1958   Report of a Working Party on African Land Tenure 1957–58

1959   Land Tenure and Control Outside the Native Lands. Sessional Paper No. 10 of 1958/59

1964   Kenya Population Census, 1962 (4 vols.) Economic and Statistics Division Ministry of Finance and Economic Planning

Legislative Council Debates
District Files in Kenya National Archives

BOOKS

Adelphoi, *His Kingdom in Kenya*, London, 1953

Almond, G. A. and Coleman, J. S., *The Politics of Developing Areas*, Princeton, 1960

Altrincham, Lord, *Kenya's Opportunity*, London, 1955

Aaronovitch, S. and K., *Crisis in Kenya*, London, 1947

Banton, Michael, *Race Relations*, London, 1967

Barnes, Leonard, *Soviet Light on the Colonies*, London, 1944

Barnett, Donald L. and Karari Njama, *Mau Mau From Within*, London, 1966

Bartlett, Vernon, *Struggle for Africa*, London, 1953

Bennett, George, *Kenya: A Political History: The Colonial Period*, London, 1963

Bennett, George and Rosberg, Carl G., Jr., *The Kenyatta Election: Kenya 1960-61*, London, 1961

Blixen, Karen, *Out of Africa*, London, 1937

Blundell, Sir Michael, *So Rough a Wind*, London, 1964

Cameron, Sir Donald, *My Tanganyika Service and Some Nigeria*, London, 1939

Cagnolo, Fr. C., *The Akikuyu*, Nyeri, 1933

Carothers, Dr. J. C., *The Psychology of Mau Mau*, Govt. Printer, Nairobi, 1954

Carson, J. B., *Sun, Sand and Safari: Some Leaves from a Kenya Notebook*, London, 1957

Carter, Gwendolen, M. and Brown, William O. (editors): *Transition in Africa: Studies in Colonial Adaptation*, Boston University Press, 1958

Churchill, W. S., *My African Journey*, London, 1908

Cohen, Sir Andrew, *British Policy in Changing Africa*, London, 1959

Corfield, F. D., *Historical Survey of the Origins and Growth of Mau Mau*, Cmd. 1030, H.M.S.O., 1960

Cranworth, Lord, *A Colony in the Making*, London 1912 (Revised as *Profit and Sport in British East Africa*, London, 1919)

Delf, George, *Jomo Kenyatta, Towards Truth about 'The Light of Kenya'*, London, 1959

Diamond, Stanley and Burke, Fred. G. (editors) *Transformation of East Africa: Studies in Political Anthropology*, New York, 1966

Dilley, Marjorie Ruth, *British Policy in Kenya Colony*, New York, 1937

Dinesen, Isak, *Shadows on the Grass*, London, 1960

Eliot, Sir Charles, *The East Africa Protectorate*, London, 1905

Evans, Peter, *Law and Disorder*, London, 1956

Farson, Negley, *Last Chance in Africa*, London, 1949

Fey, Venn, *Cloud Over Kenya*, London, 1964

First, Ruth, *The Barrel of a Gun*, London, 1970

Foran, W. Robert, *The Kenya Police 1887–1960*, London, 1962

Foster, Paul, *White to Move*, London, 1961

Gann, L. H. and Duignan, P., *White Settlers in Tropical Africa*, London, 1962

Gatheru, R. Mugo, *Child of Two Worlds*, London, 1964

Gertzel, Cherry, Maure Goldschmid, Donald Rothchild (editors), *Government and Politics in Kenya*, Nairobi, 1969

Ghai, Dharam P., *Portrait of a Minority: Asians in East Africa*, Nairobi, 1965

Ghai, Yash R. and McAuslan, J. P. W. B., *Public Law and Political Change in Kenya*, Nairobi, 1969

Gicaru, Muga, *Land of Sunshine: Scenes of Life in Kenya before Mau Mau*, London, 1958

Goldsworthy, David, *Colonial Issues in British Politics*, Oxford, 1971

Goldthorpe, J. E., *Outlines of East African Society*, Kampala, 1958

Greaves, L. B., *Carey Francis of Kenya*, London, 1969

Gregory, Robert S., *Sidney Webb and East Africa*, University of California Press, Berkeley, 1962

Gussman, Boris, *Out In the Midday Sun*, London, 1962

Hancock, W. K., *Survey of British Commonwealth Affairs*, Vols. 1 and 2, London, 1937

——*Argument of Empire*, London, 1943

Hailey, Lord, *An African Survey*, London, 1938, Revised edition, 1957

Harlow, Vincent and Chilver, E. M. (editors), *History of East Africa*, Vol. II Oxford, 1965

Hennings, R. O., *African Morning*, London, 1951

Hill, M. F., *The Dual Policy in Kenya*, Nakuru, 1944

——*Permanent Way. The Story of the Kenya and Uganda Railway*, Nairobi, 1949

Hillaby, John, *Journey to the Jade Sea*, London, 1964

Hinden, Rita, *Empire and After*, A Study of British Imperial Attitudes, London

Hobley, C. W., *Bantu Beliefs and Magic*, London, 1922

Hobson, J. A., *Imperialism, A Study*, London, 1902, Revised Edition, 1938

Books 275

Hollingsworth, L. W., *The Asians in East Africa*, London, 1960
Hunter, Guy, *The New Societies of Tropical Africa*, London, 1962
Hunter, J. A. and Mannix, D., *African Bush Adventures*, London, 1954
Huntingford, G. W. B., *The Nandi of Kenya*, London, 1953
Huxley, Elspeth, *The Flame Trees of Thika: Memories of an African Childhood*, London, 1959
———*A New Earth: An Experiment in Colonialism*, London, 1960
———*Settlers of Kenya*, London, 1948
———*The Sorcerer's Apprentice: A Journey Through East Africa* London, 1948
———*A Thing to Love*, London, 1953
———*White Man's Country: Lord Delamere and the Making of Kenya*, London, 1935
Huxley, Elspeth and Perham, Margery: *Race and Politics in Kenya*, London, 1944. Revised Edition, 1956
Ingham, Kenneth, *A History of East Africa*, London, 1962
Itote, Waruhiu, *Mau Mau General*, Nairobi, 1967
Jones, N. S. Carey, *The Anatomy of Uhuru: An Essay on Kenya's Independence*, Manchester University Press, 1966
Kariuki, J. M., *Mau Mau Detainee*, London, 1963
Kenyatta, Jomo, *Facing Mount Kenya*, London, 1938
Leakey, L. S. B., *Defeating Mau Mau*, London, 1954
———*Kenya Contrasts and Problems*, London, 1936
———*Mau Mau and the Kikuyu*, London, 1952
Lee, J. M., *Colonial Development and Good Government*, Oxford, 1967
Leigh, Ione, *In the Shadow of Mau Mau*, London, 1954
Lewin, Julius, *The Struggle for Racial Equality*, London, 1967
Leys, Norman, *The Colour Bar in East Africa*, London, 1941
———*A Last Chance in Africa*, London, 1931
Lipscombe, J. F., *We Built a Country*, London, 1956
———*White Africans*, London, 1955
Lyttelton, Oliver, Viscount Chandos, *The Memoirs of Lord Chandos*, London, 1962
Mair, L. P., *Native Policies in Africa*
McDougall, Jan, *African Turmoil*, London, 1954
McPhee, A. Marshall, *Kenya*, London, 1968
Majdalany, Fred, *State of Emergency: The Full Story of Mau Mau*, London, 1962

Mangat, N. S., *A History of the Asians in East Africa, c.1886–1945*, Oxford, 1970

Mason, Philip, *An Essay on Racial Tension*, London, 1954

Mboya, Tom, *Freedom and After*, London, 1962

Meinertzhagen, Colonel R., *African Diary 1902–1906*, Edinburgh, 1957

Meister, Albert, *East Africa, The Past in Chains, the Future in Pawn*, trans. Phyllis Nauts Ott., New York 1968 from the French: *L'Afrique Peut-elle Partir*, 1966

Mitchell, Sir Philip, *African Afterthoughts*, London, 1954

Morgan, W. T. W., *Nairobi City and Region*, Nairobi, 1967

Morgan, W. T. W. and Shaffer N. M., *Population of Kenya*, Nairobi, 1966

Morris, Colin, *A Humanist in Africa: Letters to Colin Morris from Kenneth Kaunda*, London, 1966

Ngugi, James, *Weep Not Child*, London, 1964

Ogot, B. A. (editor), *Politics and Nationalism in Colonial Kenya*, *Hadith 4*, Nairobi, 1972

Ogot, B. A. and Welbourn, F. B., *A Place to Feel at Home: A Study of Two Independent Churches in Kenya*, London, 1966

Oldham, J. H., *White and Black in Africa*, London, 1930

————*Christianity and the Race Problem*, London, 1925

————*New Hope in Africa*, London, 1955

Oliver, Roland, *The Missionary Factor in East Africa*, London, 1952

Ominde, S. H., *Land and Population Movements in Kenya*, London, 1958

Padmore, George, *Africa: Britain's Third Empire*, London, 1949

————*How Britain Rules Africa*, London, 1936

Perham, Margery, *Colonial Sequence*, 1930–1949, London, 1967

————*Colonial Sequence*, 1949–1969, London, 1970

Perham, Margery and Huxley, Elspeth, *Race and Politics in Kenya*, London, 1944. Revised edition, 1956

Peristiany, J. G., *The Social Institutions of the Kipsigis*, London, 1939

Plamenatz, John, *On Alien Rule and Self-Government*, London, 1960

Ponsonby, Col. Sir Charles, *Ponsonby Remembers*, Oxford, 1965

Rawcliffe, D. H., *The Struggle for Kenya*, London, 1954

Reynold, Reginald, *Beware of Africans*, London, 1955

Robinson, Kenneth, *The Dilemmas of Trusteeship*, London, 1965

Robinson, Kenneth and Madden, Frederick, *Essays in Imperial Government*, Presented to Margery Perham, Oxford, 1963

Rosberg, Carl, G. Jr. and Bennett, George, *The Kenyatta Election: Kenya 1960–1961*, London, 1961

Rosberg, Carl, G. Jr. and Nottingham, John, *The Myth of 'Mau Mau,'* New York, 1966

Ross, W. McGregor, *Kenya From Within*, London, 1927

Sachs, Emil Solomon, *Rebel's Daughters*, London, 1957

Seligman, C. G., *The Races of Africa*, London, 1930

Shaffer, N. Manfred and Morgan, W. T. W., *Population of Kenya*, Nairobi, 1966

Slater, Montagu, *The Trial of Jomo Kenyatta*, London, 1955

Smuts, General J. C., *Africa and Some World Problems*, Oxford, 1930

Sorrenson, M. P. K., *Land Reform in the Kikuyu Country*, London, 1967

——*Origins of European Settlement in Kenya*, London, 1968

Southall, Aidan, editor, *Social Change in Modern Africa*, London, 1961

Taylor, J. V., *Christianity and Politics in Africa*, London, 1957

Thuku, Harry, *An Autobiography*, Nairobi, 1970

Van Der Post, Laurens, *The Dark Eye in Africa*, London, 1955

Wagner, Gunter, *The Bantu of North Kavirondo*, London, 1949

Welbourn, F. B., *East African Rebels: A Study of Some Independent Churches*, London, 1961

Welbourn, F. B. and Ogot, B. A., *A Place to feel at Home: A Study of Two Independent Churches in Kenya*, London, 1966

Were, Gideon, A., *A History of the Abaluyia of Western Kenya*, Nairobi, 1967

Wood, Susan, *A Fly in Amber*, London, 1964

——*Kenya: The Tensions of Progress*, London, 1960

Whittall, Errol, *Dimbilili. The Story of a Kenya Farm*, London, 1956

BOOKLETS AND PAMPHLETS

Askwith, T. G., *Community Development*, mimeo, July, 1952
———*Some Observations on the Growth of Unrest in Kenya*, mimeo, October, 1952
———*The Problems of Youth*, June, 1952
Carey, Bishop Walter, *Crisis in Kenya*, London, 1953
Carlsbach, Julius, *The Position of Women in Kenya*, mimeo, U.N. Economic and Social Council, 1963
Committee for Racial Co-operation in Kenya, *Kenya 1960*, London, 1960
Education, Ministry of, *Education in Kenya Schools*, mimeo, 1960
———*Memorandum on Education in Kenya*, Princeton Conference, 1960
Electors' Union; *An Outline of Policy*, Nairobi, 1946
———*The Kenya Plan*, Nairobi, 1949
European Elected Members Organization. *A Statement of Policy*, Nairobi, 1953
Evans, G. K., *Public Opinion on Colonial Affairs*, A Survey made in May and June, 1948 for the Colonial Office, mimeo
Fabian Colonial Bureau, *White Man's Country?* London, 1944
———*Opportunity in Kenya*, London, 1953
Frost, Richard, A., *The British Council in East Africa*, Two Broadcast Talks, Nairobi, 1948
Goldthorpe, J. E., *An African Elite*, Makerere College Students, 1922–1960, Nairobi, 1965
Goodhart, Philip, *In the Shadow of the Spear*, London, 1962
Hyslop, Graham, *Music in Education*, Nairobi, 1964
Kenyatta, Jomo, *Kenya: The Land of Conflict*, Manchester, 1945
Mason, Philip, *Race Relations in East Africa* (The Burge Memorial Lecture of 31st March, 1960), S.C.M. Press, London, 1960
Mboya, Tom, *Kenya Faces the Future* (Africa Today Pamphlets 3), American Committee on Africa, New York, 1959
———*The Kenya Question: An African Answer*, London, 1956
Mitchell, Sir Philip, *Speech to the Empire Parliamentary Association*, London, 1945
Monday Club, *A Clear and Solemn Duty*, London, 1962
Movement for a Democracy of Content; *Kenya Under the Iron Heel*, London, January, 1953
Nazareth, J. M., *Presidential Address to the East African Indian Congress, 1950*, Nairobi, 1950
Parker, Mary, *How Kenya is Governed*, East African Literature Bureau

Bureau, 1958

Political and Social Aspects of the Development of Municipal Government in Kenya with Special Reference to Nairobi, mimeo, A study for the Colonial Office, 1950

Parliamentary Delegation, *Report of the Parliamentary Delegation, January-February, 1957* (Rt. Hon. Sir Thomas Dugdale, chairman) Commonwealth Parliamentary Association, 1957

Potts, Margaret, J., *St. Julian's: An Experiment in Two Continents*, S.C.M. Press Ltd., London, 1968.

Tyson, George, *The African Housing Problem*, (A Memorandum submitted to the Nairobi Chamber of Commerce), Nairobi, 1953

Articles

Alport, C. J. M., 'Kenya's Answer to the Mau Mau Challenge', *African Affairs*, *53*, 212, July, 1954

Banton, Michael, 'Sociology and Race Relations', *Race*, *1*, 1, November, 1959

Barrett, David, B., 'Two Hundred Church Movements in East Africa', Conference Paper, *Makerere Institute of Social Research*, January, 1967

Bennett, George, 'The Development of Political Organizations in Kenya', *Political Studies*, *V*, 2, 1957

———'Kenyatta and the Kikuyu', *International Affairs*, 37, 4 October, 1961

———'Revolutionary Kenya: The Fifties, A Review', *Race*, 8, 4 April, 1967

Bewes, Canon, T. C. F., 'Kikuyu Religion Old and New', *African Affairs*, *52*, 207, April, 1953

Bharati, A., 'Race Relations in East Africa', *Maxwell Graduate School of Citizenship and Public Affairs, Syracuse University*, Occasional Paper No. 12, 1964

Blundell, Michael, 'The Present Situation in Kenya', *African Affairs*, *54*, 215, April, 1955

———'Making A Nation In Kenya', *African Affairs*, 58, 232, July, 1959

Bovill, E. W., 'East Africa Today', *African Affairs*, *50*, 200, July, 1951

Bunche, Ralph, J., 'The Land Equation in Kenya', *Journal of Negro History*, January, 1939

Coleman, James, S., 'Nationalism in Tropical Africa', *The American Political Science Review*, 28

Fane, Rebecca, '*Nationalism in Kenya*', African Affairs, 55, 211, October, 1956

Frost, Richard, 'Nairobi', *The Geographical Magazine*, November, 1950

Goldsworthy, David, 'Parliamentary Questions on Colonial Affairs', *Parliamentary Affairs*, *23*, 2, Spring 1970

Hill, M. F., 'The White Settler's Role in Kenya', *Foreign Affairs*, *38*, 4, July, 1959

Homan, F. W., 'Consolidation, Enclosure and Registration of Title in Kenya', *Journal of Local Administration Owners*, *1*, 1

Jahadhmy, Ali Ahmed, 'A Note on Arab Schooling and the Arab Role in East Africa', *African Affairs*, 51, 203, April, 1952

Jones, A. Creech, 'Africa and the British Political Parties: Labour and the Colonies', *African Affairs*, 44, 176, July, 1945

Kieran, J. A., 'Some Roman Catholic Missionary Attitudes to Africans in Nineteenth Century East Africa', *Race*, *10*, 3, January, 1964

Kuper, Leo, 'The Heightening of Racial Tension', *Race*, *11*, 1, November 1960

Leakey, L. S. B., 'Some Aspects of the Black and White Problem in Kenya', *Bulletin of John Rylands Library*, *15*, 2, July, 1931

Lonsdale, J. M., 'European Attitudes and African Pressures: Missions and Government in Kenya between the wars'. *Race*, *10*, 2, October, 1968

Mboya, Tom, 'The Future of Kenya', *African Affairs*, *62*, 250, January, 1964

———'The Party System and Democracy in Africa, *Foreign Affairs*, *41*, 4, July, 1963

Mitchell, Sir Philip, 'Press Conference on Mau Mau', *Africa Today*, Ed. C. Grove Haines (Conference, August, 1954)

———'Africa and the West in Historical Perspective', *Africa Today*, Ed. C. Grove Haines (Conference, August, 1954)

Mohiddin, Ahmed, 'An African Approach to Democracy', *East Africa Journal*, 7, 2, February, 1970

———'Sessional Paper No. 10 Revisited', *East Africa Journal*, 6, 3, March, 1960

Ominde, S. H., 'Population Movements to the Main Urban Areas of Kenya', *Cahiers d'Etudes Africaines*, 5, 4e

Padmore, George, 'French and British Colonial Policies', *Pan Africa*, July, 1947

Pan Africa, Report of 'Memorandum submitted to the Colonial Office by James S. Gichuru and W. W. W. Awori', January, 1947

———'Post War Problems in Kenya', May, 1947

———Text of Eliud Mathu's 'Speech at Mwakinyungu', June, 1947

———'Education in Kenya Colony', August, 1947

Parker, Mary, 'Race Relations and Political Development in Kenya', *African Affairs*, 50, 198, January, 1951

Perham, Margery, 'The British Problem in Africa', *Foreign Affairs*, 29, 4, July, 1951

———'White minorities in Africa', *Foreign Affairs*, 37, 4, July, 1959

Ponsonby, Colonel, C. E., 'Africa and the British Political Parties: A Conservative View', *African Affairs*, 44, 176, July, 1945

Pratt, Cranford, 'Multi-Racialism and Local Government in Tanganyika', *Race*, *11*, 1, November, 1960

Rennell, Lord, 'Africa and the British Political Parties: A Liberal View Point', *African Affairs*, *44*, 176, July, 1945

Rothchild, Donald, 'Kenya's Minorities and the African Crisis over Citizenship', *Race*, *9*, 4, April, 1968

Shannon, Mary, 'Rehabilitating the Kikuyu', *African Affairs*, *54*, 215, April, 1955

———'Rebuilding the Social Life of the Kikuyu', *African Affairs*, *56*, 225, October, 1957

Swynnerton, J. R. M., 'Kenya's Agricultural Planning', *African Affairs*, *56*, 224, July, 1957

Tanner, R. E. S., 'European Leadership in Small Communities in Tanganyika prior to Independence', *Race*, *7*, 3, January, 1966

Trowell, H. C., 'Medical Examination of 500 African Railway Workers', *East African Medical Journal*, *25*, 6, June, 1948

Welbourn, F. B., 'Comment on Corfield', *Race*, *2*, 2, May, 1961

Whittlesey, Derwent, 'Kenya, The Land and Mau Mau', *Foreign Affairs*, *32*, 1, October, 1953

Were, G. S., 'Dini Ya Msambwa: A Re-Assessment', *Makerere Institute of Social Research*, Conference Papers, January, 1967

Principal Newspaper Sources

The East African Standard, Nairobi

The Kenya Weekly News, Nakuru

East Africa and Rhodesia, London

Comment and New Comment, Nairobi

Private papers

Blundell, Sir Michael, in Rhodes House, Oxford (restricted)

Cooke, S. V., 2 confidential files in private possession

Frost, Richard, A., in private possession at Appleton, Oxfordshire

Havelock, Sir Wilfred, in the National Archives, Nairobi, (restricted)

Hughes, Richard, in private possession in Nairobi

Miller, Lt. Commander, J. P. B., in Rhodes House, Oxford (restricted)

Mitchell, Sir Philip, Diaries, in Rhodes House, Oxford (restricted)

Raw, Mrs. Joyce, in private possession in Nairobi

St. Julian's Community, files and Miss Clarke's Diary, in private possession at St. Julian's, Limuru

Tyson, George, A., in private possession in Nairobi

Ward, Kendall, M.B.E. in the Kenya National Archives (restricted)

Young, Colonel Sir Arthur, in private possession in London

Interviews

Amalemba, Musa, businessman, formerly Member of Legislative Council.

Askwith, T. G., formerly Commissioner for Community Development.

Awori, W. W. W., formerly Member of Legislative Council and Acting President of Kenya African Union.

Baraza, Jonathan, Senior Chief of the Bukusu.

Barmalel, T. arap, Member of Parliament, formerly Police Inspector.

Beecher, Most Rev. Dr. L. J., formerly Archbishop of East Africa (Anglican).

Block, J., businessman, land owner, hotel proprietor.

Blundell, Sir Michael, formerly Member of Legislative Council and Minister of Agriculture.

Brunner, E., hotel manager.

Buchanan-Allen, D. R., farmer and journalist.

Colchester, T. C., formerly Civil Servant.

Cooke, S. V., formerly Member of Legislative Council.

Erskine, Sir Derek, businessman, formerly Member of Legislative Council.

Erskine, Lady, wife of Sir Derek.

Fedha, N., Chief Archivist.

Fletcher, P., formerly Headmaster of Prince of Wales School

Gaitskell, L. F., farmer.

Gathecha, D., Public Relations Officer, Shell Company.

Gatu, Rev. J., General Secretary, Presbyterian Church of East Africa.

Gethegi, Dedan, formerly Welfare Officer, Nairobi Municipality.

Gregory, Dr. J. R., former Mayor of Nairobi.

Havelock, Sir Wilfred, former Member of Legislative Council and Minister of Health and Local Government.

Howard, Roy, farmer.

Hughes, Mrs. D. E., architect and leading figure in social work, former Member of Legislative Council.

Hughes, H. R., Architect, formerly President, Kenya branch of Capricorn Africa Society.

Malinda, T. N., businessman, former Member of Parliament.

Memia, Solomon, Kikuyu politician.

Merritt, C. V., farmer.

Miller, Lt. Commander, J. P. B., formerly Civil Servant.

Muchura, J. B., businessman, formerly Civil Servant.

Muketha, G., businessman.
Muliro, Masinde, Cabinet Minister.
Mwenesi, M., formerly Civil Servant.
Nihill, Sir Barclay, formerly Chief Justice of Kenya.
Nottingham, J. C., publisher, formerly Civil Servant.
Nyagah, J., Cabinet Minister.
Odongo, D. H., businessman.
Okola, P., Chief Superintendent of Police.
Okungu, Rev. P., priest in Nyanza.
Olang', Most Rev. F., Archbishop of Kenya (Anglican).
Otiende, J. D., formerly Cabinet Minister.
Otunga, Most Rev. M., Archbishop of Kenya (Roman Catholic).
Owen, Rev. W., formerly Principal of Limuru Divinity School.
Oyugi, J. H., Director of Shell Company of East Africa.
Raw, Mrs. J., formerly Chief Hansard Editor.
Riddoch, J. L., businessman.
Sprott, Major F. H., farmer.
Stott, Miss J., formerly Headmistress, Kenya High School.
Stovold, Ven. K. E., Archdeacon of Nairobi, formerly Archdeacon
    of Nyanza.
Thuo, J., formerly on staff of *Baraza*.
Tyson, G. A., businessman, former Mayor of Nairobi.
Vasey, Sir E. A., businessman, formerly Member of Legislative
    Council and Minister of Finance.
Ward, Kendall, formerly Executive Officer, Electors' Union.
Wilson, D. Macdowall, formerly editor of *Baraza*.
Weaver, A., businessman.
Whyatt, Sir John, formerly Attorney General of Kenya.
Wyndham, Sir R., formerly Member of East African Court of
    Appeal.
Young, Sir Arthur, formerly Commissioner of Police.

INDEX

African contact with Europeans was limited, 96–97
African elite, emerging after Second World War, 37–38
African ethnic groups. 4–5
African frustration, 212–213
African integrity, lack of at times, 39–40
African interests, paramountcy of, 16–18
African Members of Legislative Council, on courtesy, 105
African National Congress in South Africa, 125
African overcrowding, 27:47–49
African political nationalism, 250–252
African poverty, 49–50
African suspicion, 50–51
African urban wages were inadequate for subsistence, 98
Afrikaners settle in Kenya, 12
Aga Khan tells Ismailis to identify themselves with Kenya, 36
Agriculture, African, 48–49
Agriculture, European, size of farms, 23; census in 1954, 22; number of farms, 23; value of farms, 49
Alexander, R. S., 195
Alliance High School, 131, 191
Amalemba, Musa, Specially Elected Member, 252; and New Kenya Group, 254; Shares platform with Blundell, 244
American animosity, 252–253
American ignorance of situation, 261
Anderson, General, 104
Anglican Church, 174–178
Arabs, 4
Argwings-Kodhek, C.M.G., returns from England, 211; speaks at inter-racial lunch, 222; connection with Capricorn Africa Society, 249; political exaggeration, 252
Arthur, Dr. J. W., 17
Asians, economic contribution and technical skills, 28–29; African jealousy of, 29–30; financial help to African politicians, 31; fail to be regarded as champions of African interests, 31; composition of community, 32–34; immigration, 34–35; dilemma facing Asians, 35–36; political discontent, 52
Askwith, T.G., 82, 155
Automobile Association becomes inter-racial, 77

Awori, W. W. W., suffers discrimination in hotel, 120; accepted at New Stanley restaurant, 121; meets Blundell at lunch, 210; Acting President of Kenya African Union, 211; official neglect of, 211

Baring, Sir Evelyn: and African Civil Service Association, 169; on arrogance and suspicion, 215
Barker, S.J., 164
Barmalel, Tamason arap, 58
Barton, Raymond, 188
Beecher, Most Rev. Dr. L. J., represents African Interests in Legislative Council, 31; warning of Kikuyu discontent disregarded, 133; amalgamates two racial church councils, 175; unable to see Secretary of State, 212; on growth of European liberalism, 216–217
Beecher Committee on Education, 124
Belyon, George arap, 76
Bi-Partisan Agreement at Westminster, 83–85
Blundell, Michael; on composition of European community, 24–25; on European ignorance of situation, 93; elected European Leader, 204; policy of in 1952, 204–206; faces die-hard opposition, 206–207; meets African leaders at lunch, 210; supported by young Europeans, 216–220; against racial press reporting, 222; wants establishment of Kenya citizenship, 223–234; supports policy of Royal Commission on Land, 243–244; on slowness of official policy, 258; position after Lancaster House Conference, 261–262
Boit, Paul arap, 257
Boit, Sila arap, 257
Bovill, E. W., 255
Boy Scout Movement, 194
Boyes, J., 12
Briggs, Group Captain, L. R., 220, 244
British American Tobacco Company, 256
British Council: starts work in East Africa, 71; uses agricultural interests and music to bring races together, 74–75; concerned with housing, 186; gives inter-racial lunch party, 210; convenes inter-racial conference on Rural

Published by Rex Collings Ltd., 69 Marylebone High Street, London, England
and Transafrica Book Distributors, Kenwood House, Kimathi Street,
P.O. Box 49421, Nairobi, Kenya.